Bookweirder

Bookweirder

Paul Glennon

DOUBLEDAY CANADA

Library and Archives Canada Cataloguing in Publication

Glennon, Paul, 1968–
Bookweirder / Paul Glennon.

ISBN 978-0-385-66548-3

 I. Title.

PS8563.L46B67 2010   jC813'.6   C2010-902518-0

This book is a work of fiction. Names, characters, places and incidents are products of the author's imagination or are used fictitiously. Any resemblance to actual events or locales or persons, living or dead, is entirely coincidental.

Book design: Jennifer Lum
Printed and bound in the USA

Published in Canada by Doubleday Canada,
a division of Random House of Canada Limited

Visit Random House of Canada Limited's website: www.randomhouse.ca

10 9 8 7 6 5 4 3 2 1

For Kate

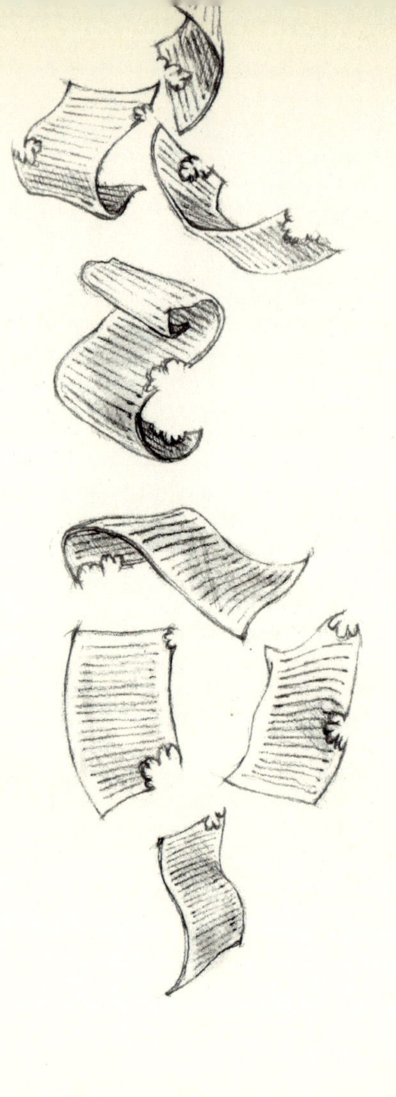

Contents

Bookweirder

Prologue

It could have been a forest back home. There was nothing differ-ent about the trees or the flowers or the animal paths worn into the mud. He recognized several prints: bank voles, red squirrels, foxes. Only the sounds of the forest were foreign. It wasn't just a different dialect. Malcolm couldn't make out a single word.

For three days now he had been wandering these woods. The abbot had told him that Norman would be nearby, but Malcolm had seen no sign of him—and Norman was hard to miss. He was more and more sure that the abbot had made a mistake. There was some-thing wrong with this forest.

His few meetings with the forest dwellers reinforced this feeling that this was entirely the wrong forest. They seemed so shocked to see him—terrified, even. They scurried away down their holes or up their trees the moment they saw him. It wasn't just the voles and the mice. It was the larger animals, too. The badger Malcolm had met along the path yesterday morning had no reason to fear him. Malcolm had just opened his mouth to say hello, but the big thing went berserk. He bared his teeth, let out that horrible warning growl that badgers have when cornered and backed away down the trail. Malcolm had called after it, telling the poor brute that he meant no harm. He'd even taken a few steps after him, but

Malcolm was too smart to chase an angry badger on his home turf.

"Mad creature, like the rest of them," Malcolm had mumbled to himself as he watched the badger disappear.

So when Malcolm spotted the hare in the clearing as he prepared to make his camp for the third night, he was more cautious. His family had always gotten along with the hares. There was hardly a smarter animal in the woods. Surely this fellow would be more reasonable than the terrified mice and the befuddled old badger. Only, like the mice and the badger and every other creature he'd spied in this strange forest, the hare wore no clothes. Was this forest inhabited entirely by primitive tribes that spoke strange languages and did not have the decency to cover themselves up?

"'Scuse me," Malcolm said finally. He spoke in his calmest voice, not wanting to startle the hare. "My name is Malcolm of Lochwarren. I'm a stranger here in these lands, and I seek the home of Norman Strong Arm."

The hare just froze on its hind legs and stared glassily at Malcolm as if it had never heard a stoat speak before.

"There's no need to fear. Look, I'll put down my weapons." Malcolm slipped the bow and quiver from his shoulders and laid them down on the ground. He held his paws out wide and tried to smile without showing a fang. "Could you spare a stranger some directions?"

The hare didn't move. It just stood there, its muscles tense, ready to bolt. What did you have to do to make a creature trust you in this place?

"You've got to be kiddin' me." The voice was too big to have come from the hare and was from entirely the wrong direction.

Malcolm turned towards the voice. There, at the opposite side of the clearing, stood a man. He was much, much bigger than Norman, but unmistakably a man. You could not miss one, their skin so pale and their fur so patchy. This one's head was as bare as a newborn squirrel's.

Malcolm glanced back towards the hare, but the creature had fled. Never mind, Malcolm thought, surely this man-creature would be more useful. He introduced himself again.

"Good even', good sir. I am Malcolm. I have come from the highlands in search of my friend, one of your kind. We call him Strong Arm, but he is Norman of the family Jespers and Vilnius."

"I've freakin' lost my mind now," the big man mumbled. He ran one of his gigantic paws across his bald head. "Freakin' talkin' weasels." He shook his head back and forth in disbelief.

"I've no desire to trouble you, sir," Malcolm continued in a calm voice. Clearly this was a simple peasant, perhaps some village idiot. "Are the Jespers-Vilniuses known to you? Is their castle nearby?"

"Castle?" the big brute repeated. "Can't believe I'm giving directions to a talkin' weasel, but yea, there's some sorta big castle thing over near Kestleton."

"Excellent news. Excellent." This was Malcolm's first bit of luck since he'd arrived. He picked up his bow and arrow and stepped lightly towards the hulking man. "Can you tell me how to get there? In what direction ought I to go?"

A glint appeared in the big man's eye, as if he had just realized or understood something.

"Sure, sure." The brute spoke more softly now. "I can take you there myself."

Malcolm put the man's change in tone down to the mention of the Jespers-Vilniuses. They must be an important family in these parts. The big lout likely expected a reward for guiding their lost visitor.

It was too far for them to reach before nightfall. Malcolm, who had spent enough nights in this weird forest, was all for pushing on, but the big man insisted they camp for the night. As Malcolm followed him through the woods, he saw why. The man's night vision was terrible. He stumbled over every root and struck every low-hanging branch with his battering-ram-like forehead. Malcolm was glad that he wasn't riding on his shoulder, as he would have with his friend Norman. He would have had to duck for every branch. Instead the stoat bounced from tree to tree, easily keeping up with the man's slow, stumbling progress through the woods.

The camp was just a single green tent and a strung-up tarpaulin, but it still made Malcolm dizzy to look at. The tent was about as large as the chapel back at Lochwarren. The tarpaulin could have covered half the town square of Edgeweir.

The vegetable soup that he was offered was watery and burnt, but it was the only warm food he'd had in days, and Malcolm didn't want to complain. He sat on a crate across from the big peasant's cot under the green canvas of the tent and tried to learn more about this forest, but the man was no help.

"I'm from the city," the big creature said, explaining his ignorance. Malcolm imagined some gigantic version of Cuaderno or one of the other Great Cites of Undergrowth.

After soup, the man poured himself a cup of some clear liquid from a blue bottle and took a swig before offering some to Malcolm. The drink was powerful. Malcolm could tell that from just sniffing it, but it would have been churlish to refuse the man's hospitality now. The first sip made his eyes water. It was much stronger than any ale served in the taverns of Edgeweir. The big man saw it and chuckled to himself as he took another swig. Malcolm nodded politely and took another gulp of the fiery liquid. It was even worse than the grog that the river pirates favoured, but he smiled politely and drank.

Malcolm had once been knocked unconscious by a raven's battle torpedo, but his head had never hurt as much as it did when he woke up the next morning. He didn't remember saying his goodnights or being offered a bed. By the feel of his back and the hard surface beneath him, he'd fallen asleep right there on the crate. Perhaps it hadn't been so smart to drink the peasant's firewater on a nearly empty stomach. The stoat groaned as he drew himself up to his feet. He head throbbed and he needed a drink of water. He squinted into the morning light and cursed at what he saw.

He was a fool. How could he have let himself be tricked like this? It was embarrassing. The big man was a peasant, a dumb, stumbling oaf. Malcolm leaned himself against the bars of his cage. They were strong all right. It would take more than a few nights to chew his way out of this. He cast around the cage to see what he could use to get himself out of here. It was empty except for a cup, mercifully full of water. Out on the crate beside the sleeping peasant were his hunting bow and quiver of arrows.

The blankets on the cot moved now, like a rock formation slowly shaking and coming to life. The giant man turned and opened his eyes, staring greedily at Malcolm.

"Gotcha," he growled, smiling wide to bare a mouth full of ugly, blunt teeth. "You think I'm going to let a talkin' weasel walk away just like that? You could be my ticket outta here."

The Folly

Norman had imagined that this summer in England would be a great adventure. He had expected fortresses and Roman ruins. Norman's England was the England of knights and castles, battles and conspiracies. That's what you got for reading books. The real England was altogether different, more like one long museum trip. He had stopped getting his hopes up every time the family piled into the tiny car and set out on one of their excursions—one more church, one more cemetery, or worse, like today, one more stately home.

At least this one was close. The drive had been less than an hour. Norman stood on the balcony of the hall's second storey looking out at the grey sky and the rain. His mother, torn reluctantly from gilt-framed paintings and the ornate furniture of the roped-off room behind them, stood at Norman's side and pointed out what could be seen from this high vantage point on the hill.

"We're actually not far from our house. That over there is Summerside." Meg Jespers-Vilnius pointed to a smudge of brown in the green countryside. "The Shrubberies is just behind that bit of dark woods there. If you could walk it in a straight line, you'd probably be home in twenty minutes."

"I wish." Norman dropped his chin to rest on the stone balustrade and stared out sullenly at the gathering clouds. The Shrubberies was their home for the summer. The English were weird about many things, like naming their houses.

"Don't be like that," his mother admonished. "Try to find something that captures your imagination. It's not every summer you spend in England."

Norman might have had a smartass answer for that, too, but his eyes had dropped to the back lawn and settled on a pile of grey stones and moss.

"Is that. . . ?" he began breathlessly. His voice trailed off, unwilling to finish the question.

"Yes, you remember—it's called a folly," Meg replied, gratified that something had caught the boy's imagination. "Some sort of half-ruined chapel or something. You remember the tour guide at the other place told us that they built them like that, fake ruins. It's like a garden decoration, an eighteenth-century aristocrat's version of a garden gnome."

This wasn't the first folly Norman had seen on their summer tour. In Cheshire he'd seen a pyramid the size of a garden shed. In Derbyshire there'd been a miniature Greek temple and fake castle ruin. But this one was different. This one Norman had seen before.

"We'll get a closer look when we do the garden tour," his mother promised, and she returned to the dark room inside.

Norman was never going to wait that long. While his mother and father studied the paintings and the furniture intently, he slipped back down the stairs and scraped through the low hedge onto the lawn.

From the lawn, the folly was even more real. It brought everything back, everything he wanted to remember and could not believe was true. He had seen this ruined church before. He had been inside it. He had ducked through the arched doorway. He had steadied himself on these rough, worn columns. He had even rested his head on the soft moss carpet that covered the cracked slate floor. Or at least, he had dreamed it. But if it was here now, didn't that mean it wasn't a dream after all?

He didn't recall crossing the wet lawn or passing any fence. He didn't recall opening any gate that said "Off Limits to Visitors." He just found himself inside the church, dry and out of the rain. It was like being back in Undergrowth again, back in the ruined church at Tintern outside the village of Edgeweir, a place inhabited by badgers, foxes, hares and stoats. Here in the folly it all felt true again. In Undergrowth he had fallen asleep under the arches of this ruined church. That strange fox abbot had sheltered him here.

Norman lay down on the moss inside the folly and stared up at the rafters. The church at Tintern Abbey had been built by foxes, but they had never completed it. A war with some other animal kingdom had stopped the construction. Its roof had half caved in. Norman stared up at the clouds that moved across the hole now. One hand reached out to touch the curtain of dark green ivy that covered the wall, while the other felt the thick carpet of moss that covered the flagstone floor. A tingle went up his spine as he touched it. This was exactly how it had felt last time.

But that was just a story. Undergrowth was a place in books. In real life foxes didn't build churches. Norman had been obsessed with the Undergrowth series, especially that book about Malcolm— *The Brothers of Lochwarren*. He'd lived and died by the fortunes of the stoat princes of Undergrowth. It had once seemed so real to him, as real as this.

Norman used to imagine that he lived in Undergrowth, and that his best friend was Malcolm, a young stoat prince. Together they had fought and defeated an evil wolf empire to restore the stoats' highland kingdom. That was when he was a kid, almost a year ago. When he was younger he used to confuse fantasy with reality. He'd imagined a magical force called the bookweird that could put you inside a book you loved. For the longest time, Norman would "remember" having been there. He didn't think about it as much anymore. Norman had run out of Undergrowth books to read, and the bookweird seemed more and more impossible. He was pretty much convinced he'd imagined it all.

Inside the folly again, it all rushed back to him. How could it not be real if he remembered it so vividly? How could his friend Malcolm have been imaginary? You can forget a lot of things that happen to you, or start to believe that you just imagined them, but you can't forget a really true friendship, and Norman would always remember his brave friend Malcolm.

As he lay there on the grass, he could imagine the feel of Malcolm sleeping next to him. He was a tiny creature. He'd often slept in the crook of Norman's arm, especially when they'd first met and the little stoat was recovering from his battle wounds. The stoat's slender rib cage would rise and fall with each breath. Sometimes he'd smack his chops and lick his little white fangs while he slept, as if he was eating some dreamed-of delicacy. Norman had saved the tiny creature's life, and had sworn to protect him. It made it all the more amazing when you saw him fit and well, fearlessly brandishing his needle-like sword in the face of an enormous wolf.

Norman's thoughts continued to drift to those days. He was struggling to stay in the dream, to keep himself imagining the little stoat there in the crook of his arm, but once you start trying, you're already falling out of the dream.

It would have been easier if he'd been alone. The other voices were distracting him.

"No, Ambrose, it is not safe," one stern voice was saying.

"But, Brother Timothy, since the days of the pilgrimage we have celebrated St. Peter's Eve here at the abbey."

"It isn't safe anymore, not with all the two-footers about these days."

"Not at night. The two-footers stay away at night. Please, Brother Timothy, the whole warren is looking forward to it."

Another, more familiar voice disrupted this strange conversation.

"Have you any idea how long we've been looking for you?" It was his dad's voice.

Norman was speechless. He really had no idea how long he'd lain there on the moss. It didn't seem that long. Maybe he had fallen asleep. He stared at the two silhouettes framed by the arched back doorway of the church. They looked for all the world like rabbits, but they wore hooded cloaks. One leaned on a crooked stick, but both were perfectly still.

"Norman, get up. You're not supposed to be in there." His father's voice called him again from the other direction.

Norman turned and met his father's eye. His father sighed and shook his head wearily. Norman tried to look contrite and started to rise to his feet. When he glanced back towards the doorway the rabbit silhouettes had vanished.

"You can't just disappear like that. You have to tell us where you're going," his father lectured, exasperated, as they trod back towards the main house. "We had the staff looking through the hedge maze for nearly an hour. You're lucky that your mother remembered your thing for follies."

The lecture continued in the car on the way home. Norman hardly heard a word of it. Even his little sister, Dora, in the back seat next to him, was ignorable. He turned away from her smug face and leaned his head against the car window and watched the woods wind by. There could be talking animals in these woods, he thought. This could just as easily be Undergrowth. Out there beyond the hedgerows and the stone fences, who knew what was hiding? A ridge of gloomy clouds moved across the sky, casting dark shadows on the green hills, making the dark woods even darker. *Who am I kidding?* he asked himself. *I'm just a stupid kid who imagines stupid things.* It is hard to want something and know that what you want is impossible.

The rented car rolled slowly onto the gravel driveway in front of the Shrubberies. Norman didn't think of it as home yet. It was still like living in someone else's house. It *was* somebody else's house. It had been his grandparents' house. Uncle Kit, his mom's brother, lived there normally, but he was away. It was the first of many disappointments of the summer. Norman had been looking forward to meeting his uncle Kit. He sounded cool. When Norman was ten, Uncle Kit had sent him a wavy dagger called a kris. He'd had it for only a few minutes before his mom had confiscated it. She'd let him keep the blowgun that Uncle Kit had sent last year, but she'd taken away the darts.

Norman's mom didn't have anything good to say about her brother. When Norman asked about him, she usually just rolled her eyes or sighed. The two had grown up here in this house. It was Kit's now, but Norman's mom still called it home.

As soon as the car came to a stop Dora leapt out and scrambled across the gravel driveway to the thick-planked door of their temporary home. She waited impatiently for the door to be opened, then dashed upstairs to her room. She'd be going to her new friend Penny's for the afternoon, Norman guessed. Back home, the prospect of having his sister out of the way would have cheered him up, but somehow today it bugged him.

It annoyed Norman even more when he was forced to stay downstairs and help make lunch. Just because he had no one to hang out with shouldn't mean that he got extra chores. Setting the table and slicing cheese for sandwiches might have been the equivalent to ten years' hard labour.

Dora clattered down the stairs in her new riding pants and borrowed riding boots. "Can we go right now, Mom?" she asked breathlessly.

Meg shook her head, but not angrily. "Lunch first."

Dora plonked herself down at the dining table and waited to be served.

"We're heading into town this afternoon, Norman. Would you like to come?" his mother asked as she handed him a plate of sandwiches.

Norman grabbed a sandwich for himself before placing the plate on the table, just a little beyond Dora's reach. She grimaced at him but didn't give him the satisfaction of complaining. She stood up to slide the plate back towards her and ignored him.

"What are you doing in town?" Norman asked warily. There wasn't much to choose from—another day hanging out doing nothing at the house or a trip into town with his mother. He knew by now that going into town was no great adventure.

"I have some contracts to send back home," his mother replied. "Then there are a few things we should pick up."

"Can we get a PSP?" Norman asked half-heartedly.

His mother's bemused smile was answer enough.

"There's nothing to do," Norman complained. "Do you think we could get my computer couriered here?"

His father, Edward, was putting the finishing touches on a pot of coffee. There was no coffee machine in the summer house, and the coffee had to be made by hand in a stove-top coffee maker. It seemed to be a lot of work to make a drink, but Norman had seen Edward Vilnius go without coffee and he wasn't going to argue with the effort.

"If we are doing that, Meg," Edward asked, "can we also get our espresso machine sent over?"

Meg Jespers-Vilnius rolled her eyes. "Are you all out of books again?" she asked Norman.

"I'm rereading *The Manacle of Munster*," he answered as he piled clotted cream and jam onto a scone.

"Have you looked through the library here?"

"There's nothing good."

His mother smirked. It was true, though. Norman had looked. The novels were all pretty lame.

"Is Dora going with you?" he asked. It could be the deciding factor between car boredom and house boredom.

"She's going to Penny's for the afternoon."

Just as Norman had predicted. Dora had made a friend on the first afternoon they'd been here—a friend with a stable of ponies, too. Dora was in heaven. She and Penny rode almost every day. Norman didn't want to admit it, but he sometimes wished his little sister were around more. He might have been able to convince her to go exploring or play some games. That's how bored he was.

"Penny says that I was born to ride Dandy," Dora bragged. "He's very naughty with other girls, but he's *brilliant* with me." Recently Dora had begun to use these British words and phrases that she'd picked up from her friend Penny. Everything was now "brilliant" and "super." If Norman had been paying attention, he would have taken time to make fun of Dora's fake British accent, but he was busy with his own thoughts.

"Dad, is there a particular reason that animals can't talk?" He was thinking about the rabbits he'd imagined seeing back in the folly, and in a sideways way about Undergrowth.

Edward Vilnius nearly spat out a mouthful of coffee, but he managed to stifle the laugh. "Is this a commentary on your sister or the horse?"

"Uh!" Dora cried shrilly, exaggeratedly offended. Her father winked at her.

Norman pressed on. "I mean, is there a physical reason they can't talk—like their mouths can't make the sounds?"

"Almost all animals communicate in some sort of language," Norman's mother pointed out. "Whales have huge repertoires of songs, for example."

"No," Norman elaborated, "I mean, could they speak a human language, like English?"

"Well, parrots can be taught to mimic human language. Is that what you mean?" his father asked.

"I guess so." Norman didn't know why he'd bothered asking. It wasn't like he could explain it.

"Is there a particular animal you are thinking of? Are you thinking of having a conversation with this horse, Dandy, to ask him what the trick is to getting along with your sister?" his mother asked.

"What about a rabbit?"

"That's an interesting one—talking rabbits," his father mused, putting his coffee down and pulling up a chair. "Lots of talking rabbits in literature, you know—*Alice in Wonderland*, *Watership Down*, those horrible Beatrix Potter books. I wonder what that's all about." Edward pondered this for a while. "Might be worth a paper on the subject: "Talking Rabbits in English Literature." You think the department would like that, Meg?"

Meg Jespers-Vilnius had made a career out of motivational speaking, but even she couldn't quite sound convincing when she replied, "I think that's a brilliant topic for a paper. You'll be the star of the English Department."

Edward Vilnius smiled like a man who was used to being mocked.

"Right, are you coming, Norman?" Meg asked.

Norman contorted his face as if this was a difficult question. "Can I use your laptop when you're gone?"

"Yes," she agreed patiently, "just be careful with it."

Norman, in the Library, with a Book

That was something, then . . . but it wasn't like having his own computer. There was no Internet, and his mother's laptop had none of his games. He was stuck playing Minesweeper and Hearts. It killed a few hours, though. He played in "the library," the room where his mother worked. His father had "the study." The Shrubberies wasn't like their house back home. It had dozens of small rooms, each with its own specific name and purpose. There was a real dining room rather than just a space off the kitchen, and there was something called a "morning room," as well as a "drawing room." Like most British things it all sounded a little ridiculous. When they had arrived at the house at the beginning of the summer, Norman and Dora had seized on the room names as if they were playing Clue, and now the game had extended to any British word they thought was funny—"Colonel Mustard in the drawing room with the clotted cream!" or "Miss Scarlet in the lift with a lorry!"

Of all the rooms, the library was Norman's favourite. After a few frustrating games of Minesweeper, he closed the laptop and surveyed the bookshelves one more time. How could it not have a single book worth reading? Three of the room's four walls were covered in books. It was just like a real library, with huge floor-to-ceiling shelves and a little ladder that slid on wheels across the face.

Everything about it promised adventure and excitement. A long, carved wooden tube leaned in one corner. Norman's dad said it was called a didgeridoo, but Norman thought he might be making that up. In the middle of one shelf was a brass statue of some crazy six-armed dancing goddess. There were statues and strange carvings in every nook and cranny, but his favourite thing in the room was a painting of a fox hunt. There were dozens of hunters riding around in the woods, falling off their horses into ponds and hedges. The dogs all looked lost or bored. Back at the stables a fox was stealing sausages from a picnic hamper. It wasn't just a library full of books. It was like a library out of a book. *There has to be*, Norman thought, *at least one decent book in here.*

The ladder was tempting, but he'd found out weeks ago that the higher shelves held the most boring books—old science books, histories, whole shelves of Latin and Greek. Norman lay on his side on the carpet and surveyed the lowest shelf. It made sense that kids' books would be down there, didn't it? He ran his finger across the spines of an *Encyclopaedia Britannica*. He had resorted to this before, and it was a decent last resort. This encyclopaedia was ancient and full of articles on places and people that no longer existed—Finnveden and Pengwern, Wallachia and Tamburlaine. Beside the encyclopaedia was something called *The Illustrated History of the Imperial Wars*, which contained pictures and stories of wars in places called Boer and Crimea. Norman often imagined that the encyclopaedia and the history were partially made up. The next shelf had a series of books called the Harvard Classics, which was about as boring as it sounded. Norman pulled a volume out and leafed through it. Sophocles—boring; Plutarch—boration; Seneca—boremungus.

He was about to slide the volume back when he noticed through the gap left in the series that there was another row of books behind. He removed more Harvard Classics to get access. It revealed a row of thin hardcovers, their red dust covers torn and faded. He reached in to remove two—*Terror of the Intrepid Trio* and *The Clue of the Coughing Dragon: An Intrepid Trio Mystery*.

"Hmmm," Norman muttered. He was afraid of getting his

hopes up, but he stripped the Harvard Classics shelf bare, and sure enough there was a whole shelf of them. *Intrepid into the Night, The Intrepid Three at Sea, The Scourge of Malbranche: An Intrepid Trio Mystery*. Okay, this was worth trying.

Norman wasn't so finicky as to need to read a series in order. He knew that it didn't really matter. He just grabbed the title that jumped out at him and descended to the kitchen to finish off the scones. He couldn't have explained why he picked *Intrepid Amongst the Gypsies*. He didn't reflect on it. All he cared about was reading something that he hadn't read before.

Edward Vilnius was in the kitchen when he arrived. Norman's father had had the same idea about the scones and was making coffee again to go with them.

"Hullo, Spiny, how goes it?" Edward asked. Since they had been in England, Edward had taken to using a rather comical British accent around the house. Unlike Dora, he knew he was doing it and thought he was rather funny. Norman wondered whether he used it with the other professors at the university, and whether they thought he was crazy or just insulting.

"Found a book," Norman managed through a mouthful of scone.

"Huzzah!" Edward cheered ironically, raising his scone in a toast. It was his new favourite word, apparently a British way of saying "Yay."

"Huzzah," Norman repeated, but less enthusiastically. "You ever heard of this?" He held up *Intrepid Amongst the Gypsies* for his father to see.

"Nope," he said. "It's probably one of your mother's old books."

Norman opened the front cover to see if she'd written her name in it. There was a name, but it was not his mother's. Written very exaggeratedly, in cobalt blue ink, as if somebody was trying out a new pen or just very proud of his handwriting, was the following inscription:

Property of Christopher T. Jespers

"Ah, your mysterious uncle," Edward intoned.

"Why don't we ever see Uncle Kit?" Norman asked. "I thought he'd be here."

"Off travelling the world, I expect. Your mother probably wouldn't have agreed to stay here at the Shrubberies if your uncle weren't away."

Norman had no idea what Uncle Kit did for a job. He imagined him as some sort of international explorer, crossing a desert on camelback or hacking his way through some jungle to uncover a hidden Aztec temple.

Norman paused before asking a question he'd never before dared to. "Why don't they talk anymore? What happened?"

Edward Vilnius paused for a moment and considered the question. "I don't know, really. Probably started as a little thing and snowballed. It doesn't sound like they ever got along." He took a last bite of his scone and wiped the crumbs from the goatee he had decided to grow this summer. "Better be nice to your sister," he warned, rising from the table. "She might decide never to see you when she grows up."

Norman opened his mouth but left the obvious reply unspoken. He loaded a plate with scones and carried them and the book up to the small room that served as his bedroom and lay down on the bed, propping himself up on his elbows to read.

Intrepid Amongst the Gypsies

Intrepid Amongst the Gypsies didn't exactly grab Norman right away—it was slow to start and full of old-fashioned British slang, but after a while he started to get into it. The Intrepid Three were three kids. George Kelmsworth was tall, dark-haired, with something called an "aristocratic nose." He was only fifteen, but somehow he lived alone in a hunting lodge at the edge of Kelmsworth estate. The estate's main house, Kelmsworth Hall, was George's family home, but it had been commandeered and was going to be turned into a First World War army hospital. The other two Intrepids were Pippa Cook, a red-headed girl George's age, and her younger brother, Gordon. Their mother worked for the new administrator, Mr. Hepplewaithe, making arrangements to convert the hall into a hospital, but that did not stop the Cooks from befriending George.

The three kids seemed to be able go wherever they liked and do whatever they wanted. Their parents hardly appeared in the book at all. Pippa and Gordon's father was with the army in France. George's own father, Lord Kelmsworth, was being held in prison for a crime he did not commit. Lord Kelmsworth had worked for the Admiralty before the Great War and was being held responsible for the disappearance of some important papers.

As far as Norman could tell, George had been trying to prove his father's innocence since the beginning of the series. Since there were at least twenty books, it didn't look as though Lord Kelmsworth was coming home any time soon.

At the opening of *Intrepid Amongst the Gypsies* the Cook children snuck out after dark to meet George at the ancient stone lodge. Cloaked with moss, the lodge blended into the dark woods behind it, but the thick leaded glass of its windows flickered orange from the light of the wood fire that burned inside. George strode back and forth in front of the great stone hearth, waving his hands as he'd seen his father do when practising a speech. Pippa sat quietly, her brow furrowed. She had a serious look to her in her school uniform with her hair tied back in a tidy braid. Gordon fidgeted in his seat. He was shorter than his sister with more obvious freckles and excitable features beneath a head of unruly ginger hair.

The Intrepids were faced with two problems. Two nights ago there had been a break-in at the hall. One of the back doors had been forced and the larder raided. The intruder had taken a ham, a wheel of cheese and several carving knives. The burglary had stalled their latest plan to exonerate George's father.

The Intrepids had planned to take the train to London to search the offices of the Kelmsworth family lawyers. George was certain that the family solicitor had something to do with the plot against his father. Pippa wasn't convinced but was too loyal to disagree very loudly. Young Gordon believed everything his idol told him and was ready for an adventure at any time.

The three of them had concocted an elaborate plan to distract the lawyers by releasing some sort of animal in the office. Once they had driven the lawyers out, the Intrepids would ransack the files for proof that the lawyer was working against them. George had wanted to use a snake, preferably an Armenian mountain viper or a king cobra, to execute this plan. Gordon was all for getting a trained monkey. But Pippa prevailed, and they decided that mice would be just as distracting and easier to get hold of.

The break-in had put this scheme on hold. George had led

them on several expeditions around the grounds. The previous night they had come across a Gypsy encampment at the edge of the estate—just a few tents in the clearing on the other side of the ravine, dim triangular shapes lit by the yellow light of two lanterns in the trees. When they'd returned the next day in daylight, the camp was gone, but George was now convinced that the Gypsies were behind the break-in.

George paced before the fire, watched anxiously by the Cook children. "Now that Hepplewaithe has dismissed most of the servants, the hall is poorly guarded."

There had been more than a dozen full-time staff at the hall. Now there were only the Cooks, Administrator Hepplewaithe, a single housekeeper and a part-time cook.

"In the old days, the groundskeeper would have made his rounds at dusk, checking that the doors and casements were locked. When there was trouble, he used to bring in extra men from the village. If Father were here, we'd have five or six men scouring the grounds."

"Don't let it bother you, George," Pippa soothed. She spoke softly and thoughtfully. Her eyes followed George as he paced back and forth. "You've better things to do than watch for kitchen theft. We've our trip to London to plan. That's the important thing— proving your father is innocent."

George didn't seem to hear her. He swept a dark forelock out of his eyes. "The thieves must have been scared off before they found anything truly valuable," he concluded. "I expect they'll try again another night. I'm not having the silverware and family portraits stolen on my watch."

Pippa tried to convince him that he was judging the Gypsies too harshly.

"They are travelling people. They live in their wagons. What do you suppose they would do with your family portraits?" she asked sensibly.

"Sell them, of course," George insisted. "My father always said that they would not be out of place in a museum. There are collectors all over the country who would pay handsomely to get their hands on them."

Gordon chuckled. "I have to walk past the portraits of some of your ancestors to have my bath. I'd pay a good penny to have them taken away."

George shot Gordon a stern look and the younger boy instantly dropped the smile from his face.

"How can you be sure it's the Gypsies?" Pippa asked.

"It has to be the Gypsies," Gordon cried. "Who else could it be? George is right. We have to stay here and defend the hall."

Gordon's bravado brought a frown to George's face. Gordon was only repeating the argument George had made to Hepplewaithe earlier that day, but it sounded ridiculous. He thought for a long moment as he gathered his ideas. "The Gypsies wouldn't dare come near the house in broad daylight. We're safe to go to London for the day still. We just have to be back for the night to keep watch."

"Were you planning on sleeping at all during this?" Pippa asked.

Now that a plan was forming, George was less easily offended. "I won't have to stay awake all night. I'll sleep at the top of the Rook on the south lawn. It has a perfect view of the house, and if there's any break-in, I'll be sure to see it."

"You can't sleep in the folly," Pippa protested. "You'll catch your death."

"Nonsense," George replied. "I've plenty of blankets and a waterproof, if required. I'll keep watch for a few nights to make sure our intruder isn't coming back. We can take the train to London in a few days."

Gordon offered to join George on his vigil in the folly, but both George and his sister overruled him.

Pippa glanced from Gordon to George wearily. "This whole thing is folly, if you ask me."

George ignored her objection. "You'll be more use to us up here at the house, old bean," he told Gordon. "Keep an ear open for anything strange, yes?"

Gordon snapped to attention and saluted sharply in the manner his father had shown him when he'd sailed off for France.

The sound of a car on the gravel outside made Norman put the book down. That would be his mom and Dora returning, so there would be hope of dinner soon.

Norman closed his eyes. He couldn't decide if it was weird that George had a folly, too. A month ago he hadn't even heard of them. Now they were appearing everywhere.

That morning in the ruined abbey folly he had been able to imagine himself inside a book. Could he do it again? Could he make the bookweird work? It had started the first time when he'd eaten part of a book. It had been difficult to break the habit of nibbling the corners of his pages, but he had forced himself to stop— partly out of fear of it happening again, partly out of fear of it *not* happening. He wanted to hang on to the possibility of going back there someday.

Norman inhaled deeply and tried to visualize it. He told himself he was in the great hall of Lochwarren. All the stoats were asleep, but the castle would soon be roused by the bells of the nearby chapel of St. Sleekyn. Young Malcolm would come bounding down the stairs and order breakfast. Once again, Norman could almost taste the lingonberry pie.

A voice called from below, "Norman, we've brought pizza!"

That wasn't a stoat's voice or a hare's. It was his mother's.

It was a mixed blessing. Pizza was, as Norman's mother frequently declared, God's gift to boys. Back home, Norman could have eaten a whole pizza by himself if they'd let him. But the English managed to mess it up. He couldn't say why, but their pizzas tasted funny—something about the sauce, maybe. Since he had recently decided to be a vegetarian, though, it was about the only thing that he could eat and enjoy in this country. Everything else, even the chips, was usually beef-flavoured.

Norman brought *Intrepid Amongst the Gypsies* down with him. He could easily eat pizza and read at the same time. It would save him having to listen to Dora's pony stories. Everyone else was already in the dining room when he arrived. It always felt weird eating pizza right out of the box on that big wooden table, but Norman had gradually gotten over the sense that he should always be eating something on a plate and with the right-sized fork in this ornate room. He slid his hand inside the pizza box, marked with a "V" on the top, and was opening his book and his mouth simultaneously when his mom spoke.

"I see you've found a book," she said cheerfully. "What have you got?"

Norman bit down on the wedge of pizza before replying.

"It's called *Intrepid Amongst the Gypsies*. There's a whole series of them up there in the library."

Meg Jespers-Vilnius rolled her eyes as she listened. "Perhaps you could be slightly less barbaric and finish chewing before you speak."

Norman nodded but took another bite.

"I remember those. I had the whole series," she continued.

Norman lifted a pizza slice to his mouth. "Actually, these are Uncle Kit's," he said and took another bite.

"No, they aren't," Meg replied sharply. Norman was briefly stunned by her tone. Meg Jespers-Vilnius was almost annoyingly positive about everything. It was practically impossible to make her angry or provoke an argument.

"It's true. He wrote his name in the front." Norman held the book up for her to see.

"That may be so, but those Intrepids books were my books. He just wrote his name in them to be spiteful."

Norman wasn't sure what to say to that. A few times now, when they'd mentioned Uncle Kit, she'd lost her cool.

"What's the book about?" Edward Vilnius asked.

"It's about these three kids," Norman said. "One of them is some sort of junior earl or something. He lives in a cottage by himself. The other two live at some old house that's been turned into a hospital. I guess they solve mysteries or something. Have you read it?"

Edward thought about this for a while, wrinkling his forehead and chewing slowly. "Nope," he said finally.

"You've never read anything good," Meg chided. "I bet you only read Shakespeare and Dickens when you were a kid."

Edward stroked his new goatee solemnly. "And we loved it," he declared in his horrible fake English accent. "Kids these days are spoiled with their Computerboxes and their automagic video platters."

"I remember loving those books," Meg recalled wistfully, ignoring her husband's comedy act. She put aside her annoyance with her brother. "The oldest boy is George—do I remember that right? His father has been put in prison for a crime he did not commit," she continued enthusiastically. "And the children seem to be able to go anywhere and do anything without any parental supervision."

Norman took another slice of pizza. "Sounds perfect to me."

"I'd love to read those again," Meg said. "Where did you say you found them?"

"In the library, behind the Harvard Classics. There's a whole series."

The Rook and the Poacher

Norman almost didn't mind going to bed that night. For once he had a book to read. It might not have won him over from the start, but he was starting to get into it. He slid *Intrepid Amongst the Gypsies* from where he'd left it in the stack of books on his windowsill and, pulling the fleecy orange blanket over his knees, found the place where he had left off.

George had been about to spend the night in the folly. The Kelmsworth Folly was not a ruin, like Norman's abbey, but a miniature round tower called the Rook because it looked exactly like the castle in a chess set. George brought his torch (which Norman finally realized was just a flashlight, not a long pole dipped in oil) and a waterproof groundsheet, along with his blankets.

George carried his provisions up the spiral staircase to the top of the Rook. His dog, Nelson, padded silently up the stairs behind him. Drawing from his pocket the giant ring of keys that gave him access to every door on the estate, he identified the key that opened the folly's door and used it once more on the trap door that opened to the tower roof. The border collie leapt ahead of him onto the roof.

It was a perfect vantage point from which to keep watch on the hall. It was a clear night, and a waxing moon illuminated the sombre grey stone of the hall against the dark backdrop of Kelmsworth Wood. The hall was ancient, built originally by George's ancestors on land granted to them by King Henry VIII. It had burned down twice and was partially destroyed by cannon fire once, so the present structure was a combination of styles and periods. The thick, castle-like walls of the original house were bridged with decorated segments carved with gargoyles and family shields. The newest windows were rounded and diamond-paned. The oldest were tall, narrow and arched. Behind those of the third floor, pale lights winked on and off. This was where Hepplewaithe and the Cooks stayed, the only part of the house still occupied. The other rooms were gradually being emptied to make way for hospital beds.

The imposing columns of the great hall's front entrance were out of sight, but no intruder would approach from the open lawn in front. No, it was the sides and the rear of the house that were vulnerable, and George had them covered. George lay on the cold stone roof of the Rook for several hours without seeing anything between the crenellations. Occasionally he took out the brass naval telescope presented to his great-uncle Toby by his crew on the HMS *Britomart* and scanned the edge of the forest, but the forest was as still as the hall. George took some satisfaction from knowing that he was doing his ancestors proud, guarding the family seat.

But even George, who had long trained himself to go with very little sleep, was feeling drowsy. It was well past midnight when he finally drifted off. Nelson, at his side, rested his chin on his paw and stood watch over his master.

The sky beyond Kelmsworth Wood had started to turn pink when Nelson's low growl woke George. The dog was too clever to give himself away by barking. George patted the collie on the head and rummaged for his telescope. Raising it to his eye he trained it on the house, scanning for and focusing on the doors and windows one by one.

"I don't see a thing, old boy," he whispered to the dog. "Where is it?"

George followed the stare of the dog's penetrating brown eyes. There, at the edge of the wood, was movement. In the dim, pre-dawn light it was difficult to see detail, but there definitely was someone out there, a tall figure moving furtively along the copse away from the hall. In his hand he held something large and boxy. How could he have entered the house and taken something without Nelson seeing?

"Come on, then," George told the dog, rising and patting the border collie's narrow head. "Let's get a closer look."

There were enough obstacles on the lawn of Kelmsworth Hall to conceal George and Nelson as they snuck closer. Dog and boy ducked and followed the low stone wall as far as the arboretum, where George took his next sighting with the brass telescope. The man was definitely a stranger. George would have recognized Henry the gardener from his silhouette alone. This man was tall but walked stooped over, as if trying to conceal himself—or due to the burden of the load he carried. George still couldn't decide what it was that he had in his arms. The stranger wore no hat or uniform, so it wasn't one of Hepplewaithe's army liaisons, either.

George skirted the edge of the arboretum, dodging from tree to tree as he crept up on the intruder. Then he patted Nelson on the side and pointed silently to the wood. The collie set off briskly and noiselessly around the edge of arboretum to cut off the intruder.

At the greenhouses, George brought the telescope to his eyes again. He could see the man's features now. Swarthy and unshaven, he was a real ruffian. He wore a red kerchief around his neck, a rough, shapeless jumper and a long, unbuttoned coat, but no hat on his bald head. George guessed immediately that he was a Gypsy.

As George watched him, the Gypsy halted in his tracks. The intruder turned slowly and stared directly towards the greenhouse. George knew exactly what had happened. The sun now coming up behind the wood must have caught the lens of his telescope. He collapsed the spyglass and charged fearlessly towards the intruder. As soon as he started moving he heard Nelson's bark from close in. The dog would get there first, of course.

The intruder was motionless for a moment, surprised by the dog's bark perhaps, but he did not let his surprise last long. He peered around furtively a moment longer before dropping his load and dashing into the forest. Nelson burst into the forest after him while George made a beeline for the box. When he reached the box, he understood much better.

"Here, Nelson!" He whistled sharply, calling the dog back. Holding up the box trap that the Gypsy had left, he knew that it was not safe for Nelson to pursue.

"Poacher," he told the dog, who tilted his head questioningly. "It wouldn't have happened if Father were here. If Father were here, we'd still have a proper gamekeeper."

The Intrepids Go to London

For three nights George maintained his watch from the Rook, but the poacher did not return. The Intrepids scouted the ravine where they'd seen the Gypsy tents, but the camp had been evacuated. Perhaps they'd scared the intruder off. George felt confident enough to leave Kelmsworth for London to carry out his other mission.

They stepped down onto the platform at Paddington Station just before dinner. Behind them the bottle green engine let off a hiss of steam.

Gordon pulled his woven cap down over his unruly hair and marched down the platform. "Right, follow me to Dodgeworth's, then," he said.

George and Pippa followed more slowly.

"You sure you can find this place?" George asked, unused to following other people's directions. He glanced towards Pippa for corroboration.

"Of course. I've been there millions of times. Dad used to bring me when he needed something special. Pippa wouldn't go. She's too squeamish."

"That's not true at all. It's just that I don't like London."

They had stepped out of the station into what back home

would have been sunlight. Pippa wrinkled her nose at the scents and sounds of Praed Street. In front of them, a double-decker omnibus was disgorging its passengers, who hurried up the steps to the station or through the crowds onwards down the street. The air was grey with smoke and fog. It might only have been the idea of the smoke pouring from nearby factories and train yards that made Pippa's eyes water, but they watered all the same.

"Right, gang, after me." Gordon waved his encouragement as he trotted down the stone steps. Pippa and George followed.

"I have to tell you, old bean," George said as they clambered onto a red London bus and climbed the stairs to the second deck, "I'd feel an awful lot better if you knew the address. We'd get there more directly, I expect, if we used the *London Street Atlas*." He patted the pocket of his jacket.

"Don't need an address. I've an explorer's nose." Gordon tapped his nose with his finger. "Besides, Dad's brought me here a million times—every time the Zoological Society called him in. Dad was indispensable to the zoo, you know. If it was anything to do with the rare animals, it was him they'd have down to look after them. We always stopped at Dodgy's first to get supplies, especially if it was the Tassie Tiger. They fed it on rabbits usually, but Dad said it needed a platypus or a potoroo every once in a while to remind it of home."

"A potoroo?" George asked, skeptical but curious.

"It's a half-rat, half-kangaroo thing," George explained. "Dodgy's bound to have one."

George glanced at Pippa for some confirmation, but she was staring out the window, her thoughts elsewhere. London reminded her of her father.

Oblivious, Gordon warmed to his theme. "If you did want a king cobra or one of those Persian vipers you were looking for, Dodgeworth'd be the man to get it for you. Dad told me he had a two-headed kitten for sale once. I never saw that kitten, but I did see an Amazonian parrot. Dodgeworth claimed it knew two hundred different words and phrases." Gordon's emphasis on the words "two hundred" told them they were meant to be impressed.

"Did it say anything to you?" George asked, more amused than curious.

"It told him to mind his manners, that's all," Pippa replied in an even voice. So she had been listening. "There's the Zoological Society there. Oughtn't this Dodgeworth's place be nearby?"

Gordon looked out, squinting through the steamy omnibus window. "Right you are, Pips. Good spot. Let's be off."

Recognizing Regent's Park, George extracted his street atlas and located himself on the map. It wasn't that he didn't trust his young friend; it was just that he liked to know where he was at all times. They left the main thoroughfare and entered a neighbourhood of smaller winding streets. It was not a part of London that George knew well. As Gordon led them on confidently, deeper into the maze, George followed along as best he could in his street atlas. Ahead Gordon bobbed along cheerfully, re-telling long and exaggerated tales that his father had told him about Dodgeworth and his menagerie.

George and Pippa followed Gordon, if not his conversation. Pippa was alert, aware that they were heading into London's less salubrious neighbourhoods. Two things always gave it away: the hats and the smell. In the gardens and along the high streets it was all top hats and bonnets. As they passed through the business district, they waded through a sea of black bowler hats. Here, in the labyrinth of small streets, the bowler hats were brown with dust, and there were more flat caps and bare heads.

With the descent of hats there came a descent of smells. Pippa didn't especially like any of London's smells, but at least near the parks you'd get a whiff of clean air. As you got into the narrower streets, the smoke hung around, the yellow smoke of coal fires, and mingled were the pungent scents of the wares being manufactured or sold. Pippa's nose twitched as she picked up the scents of fish, new rope, old fruit . . . some very old fruit somewhere rotting. The city made Pippa nervous, and she couldn't help wondering again if George's plan was as well thought out as it should be. She kept her worries to herself, but once or twice gave George a question-ing glance. George was his usual confident self. Even as the fog descended and the streets narrowed, he strolled along with assurance, intent on his mission.

They passed several curious-looking bookshops that doubtless stocked the stranger books that George sought out. Here was a vendor of Oriental and African goods, its window full of twisted, spindly wood sculptures and long-faced masks. George made note of a manufacturer of fine scientific lenses and a crimson-and-gold sign advertising the outfitter to the Royal Geographical Society expeditions. He would have loved to spend the afternoon idling in these back lanes, but he had a job to do.

He was almost disappointed when Gordon pulled them up.

"Is this it?" Pippa asked dubiously.

Gordon bit the side of his lips and screwed up his eyes. He peered over one shoulder and then the other. George lifted his street atlas expectantly.

"We should have turned left back there."

When they finally did find Dodgeworth's it was only after three or four more wrong turns and a good deal of backtracking. In the yellow fog, the dingy storefront was easy to miss.

"Alexander Dodgeworth's Zoological Supplies and Exotic Menagerie," Gordon read the faded yellow letters on the dingy green sign triumphantly. The blackened windows gave no indication of what was inside. A smaller notice on the door read: "Ornithological, Herpetological, Marsupial and Exotic Mammal Supply Our Specialty."

George pushed the door open and all three children waited for their eyes to adjust to the darkness. When they did they were met by a long line of wooden cages that made a sort of corridor from the door to a tall counter at the back.

The three moved slowly towards the back of the store, craning their necks to peer into the dark cages. Most of the animals were asleep. In the dim light of the store, with the animals curled up like that, it was difficult to tell just what animals they were, so George and Pippa were obliged to believe Gordon as he pointed and whispered, "Arctic fox, red panda, wombat. That'll be a marmoset in there." As he said it the little monkey in the crate leapt to life,

33

sticking its face between the bars and shrieking, as if it had been lying in wait for them.

The Intrepids leapt backwards. Pippa let out a little shriek, then began to laugh as she saw the tiny monkey's grinning face.

"Actually, what you're looking at is a spider monkey, Master Cook."

Dodgeworth was a tall, thin man with a long, thin moustache that curled up towards the ends. The moustache mimicked the easy smile on his face as he emerged from the back of the shop, wiping the dust from his hands on his apron front.

He chatted with Gordon cheerfully, asking after his mother and whether they'd had any letters from his father in France. Pippa's face darkened at the mention of their father, and Dodgeworth noticed.

"I'm sure he's having a great adventure. Looking after them horses, he'll be nowhere near the fighting. He'll be back at Christmas with some tales to tell, no doubt."

Pippa smiled appreciatively at his reassurances.

"So you're after some mice, are you?" he asked, when they told him what they were looking for. "You haven't bought yourself a snake, have you?"

"We've rescued a kestrel. It has an injured wing," George explained, telling him the story they'd agreed to. "We're looking after it until it can fly again."

Dodgeworth listened intently, nodding all the while. "You'll be thinking of training it, then. Noble sport, that—falconry. The place for your falconer's paraphernalia is Peregrine's around the corner."

"Actually," George replied, "we're going to let it go." Nevertheless he took out a small notebook and pencil from his blazer pocket and made note of Peregrine's. It was the sort of information he liked to keep track of.

"I'll fetch you some juicy ones. As they're meant to be eaten, you won't be bothered about colour." He disappeared into the back of the store.

While George counted some silver and copper coins onto the counter, Gordon's eyes roamed over the cages of exotic birds and small monkeys. "Had any two-headed kittens lately, Mr. Dodgeworth?" the younger boy asked hopefully. "Miniature cows, perhaps, like from Lilliput?"

"Nothing nearly so interesting," Dodgeworth replied from the backroom. He emerged with a brown, perforated cardboard box that jiggled ever so slightly as he placed it on the counter. "Trade in your stranger fauna has fallen off since the war," he said with some regret. "Did have some dodgy geezer in here earlier trying to fob a talking stoat off on me, but it was a dud. The Yank who was flogging it didn't know a stoat from a weasel."

Pippa's eyes lit up. "Could it speak at all?" she asked.

"Not a word. The gent had dressed it up in some sort of Robin Hood costume, too—the whole kit and caboodle—but I wasn't having it. That stoat could no more speak a word of English than it could teach a course at Oxford."

The children laughed, and after some instruction on the care and feeding of falcons, Dodgeworth bade them goodbye. The lanky shopkeeper saw them to the door with their box of mice. As they crossed the threshold back into the foggy street, he offered them a good price for their kestrel if they thought twice about releasing it.

Norman could not stop reading here. This bit about the talking stoat bothered him. To the Intrepid Three it had just been a colourful story, something to laugh about, but it never could be to Norman. What if that really was a talking stoat? What if they really existed and somebody had caught one? It was a terrible thought. If animals could talk, they shouldn't be treated like that. They should be treated like human beings. Norman couldn't stop worrying about it. He couldn't help imagining Prince Malcolm in that cage, caught by some ignorant trapper who just wanted to make some money off him by selling him to a circus or a freak show.

He read on, hoping that the children would mention it, but they were too preoccupied with their raid on the lawyer's office.

George carried the box of mice and went over the instructions. He would go in by himself first and distract the solicitor. The Cooks would sneak in after him and find some likely place to set the mice loose.

Norman was hardly paying attention, just skimming this part, more and more disappointed that the talking stoat went unmentioned. It was driving him crazy. Why all these reminders of Undergrowth recently: that folly the other day that was an exact replica of Tintern in the Borders, that dream about talking rabbits, and now this mention of a talking stoat in *Intrepid Amongst the Gypsies*? It was all starting to get to him. His fingers itched as he turned the page. It would be so easy to rip off a corner. His mouth grew moist at the thought of chewing the paper. That was how it had started before, wasn't it? But this was his mother's book. She would freak if she found out.

Norman read as far as the lawyer's office.

36

The Intrepids emerged from the narrow streets of cloth caps and horse carts to the broad boulevards of omnibuses and bowler hats. The crowds were now dotted with the white wigs and black robes of the barristers shuffling between their offices and the courts. The three children climbed the steps of a white stone building. They paused for only a moment, exchanging silent, questioning glances to confirm that they were ready. George handed the cardboard box of mice to Gordon. The younger boy nodded gravely as he took it. Pippa bit her lip and scanned the street around them nervously.

George gave her a reassuring smile and pushed the huge brass door open. Alone he ducked into the marbled lobby beyond. The Cooks waited nervously outside. A moment later George's head re-emerged.

"Come on," he whispered. "It's as we hoped. Todd's in there alone."

George held the giant brass door open for Pippa and Gordon to follow. Gordon held up the quivering box of mice, indicating that he was ready for his mission. George gave the younger boy a silent, friendly slap on the shoulder, put a finger to his lips and headed up the wide staircase to the second floor. Below, the Cooks waited for his signal.

The office at the top of the stairs was nearly empty. Wide and tall, with marble tile on the floor and stone columns supporting its decorated ceiling, the office spoke of wealth and power. A dozen imposing oak desks were spread evenly across the floor. Only one was occupied. Its occupant looked up as George entered.

"Ah, young Master Kelmsworth. What a surprise."

The smug grin on Mr. Todd's face made him look anything but surprised. His mutton-chop sideburns merely twitched in amusement.

"You ought to have rung. What brings you to the city?" The lawyer twisted a fountain pen gingerly at the end of his long fingers, as if afraid the ink might stain his pristine white cuffs. He was elegantly dressed in a dark grey suit and a high white collar that obscured his neck completely.

George was not intimidated. He stretched himself to his full height and pushed out his chest. "I've come about the gamekeeper," he began haughtily, taking the tone he expected to take with employees who were not doing their job correctly. "The grounds at Kelmsworth are not being looked after properly. I came across a poacher myself the other day. We absolutely must have a proper gamekeeper back on the estate."

Mr. Todd frowned and did his best to ignore the scuffling sounds of Pippa and Gordon Cook sneaking up the stairs. "Well, I'm afraid there's not much we can do on that account at this point. While we put together the appeal, the grounds are under the jurisdiction of Administrator Hepplewaithe. We'll sort it all out in the end, of course. You know that. But I'm afraid that in the meantime, it is out of our hands."

The lawyer put down his pen and held out his hands. He suppressed a small smirk as, out of the corner of his eye, he spied Pippa and Gordon ducking beneath a nearby desk.

"But I nearly caught the poacher myself," George protested. "He was on the lawn. He likely also broke into the kitchen several nights ago. Administrator Hepplewaithe is incompetent."

Todd's superior tone elevated once more. "That may well be, but you, my boy"—he pointed at George with the end of his pen—"should not be stalking the woods looking for poachers."

Pippa's high-pitched scream interrupted them.

A dozen small white mice burst from beneath the desk where Gordon had set them free. They looked tiny and insignificant on the floor of the vast office. Their white coats blended with the marble tile, camouflaging them perfectly. They all darted immediately under the legs of desks or towards the walls, where they began disappearing into cracks in the wainscotting. There was a sort of stunned silence as Todd and the three children stared at the floor. The lawyer made a show of craning his neck about looking for stragglers.

Pippa screamed again, but it was an unconvincing scream that trailed off to a whispering sort of high note and left her blushing with embarrassment. This was not the chaos that they had intended to provoke.

Mr. Todd remained where he was at his desk, his expression one of quiet amusement. The slim smile on his face widened ever so slightly as a large ginger cat padded out from behind one of the stone columns. A stunned white mouse dangled from the cat's satisfied maw. It dropped the poor creature on the floor and placed a massive ginger paw on its catch. The cat scanned the floor for more of the same, but the rest of the rodents had scattered and could not be seen.

"Oh, dear," said Mr. Todd, sounding rather bored. "I do hope that wasn't a special mouse. I doubt that Vilnius will be persuaded to give it up now." As if to make his point, the orange cat began licking his wide chops.

George, Pippa and Gordon stood and looked on in stunned silence. This was not how this was supposed to work at all.

Norman put the book down carefully on his windowsill and closed his eyes. What was he supposed to make of this? Vilnius was not a common name. In fact, Norman had never seen or heard his father's surname anywhere, and the last place he had ever expected to see it was as the name of a cat in a book called *Intrepid Amongst the Gypsies*.

A Morning Conversation

When the muted sunlight hit Norman's face, it came from the wrong direction. It woke him up but made it difficult to open his eyes. The sounds were wrong, too. There were birds outside his window, chirping madly at each other in some nearby tree. In the distance he heard the faint echo of a train whistle. There were no train tracks near his house. There was no tree near his window.

He sat bolt upright. He must be there. He must be in the book! It was the only possible explanation. And then he recognized the room, the cluttered windowsill and the orange blanket.

It was *not* the only possible explanation. He had forgotten he was in England. He was still not used to waking up in this bedroom. He pulled on his jeans and T-shirt, grabbed *Intrepid Amongst the Gypsies* and headed downstairs.

His father was the only one in the kitchen. As Norman appeared at the door, Edward Vilnius was fiddling with the little stove-top coffee maker again. He slammed it down on the countertop in frustration, water and coffee grounds splashing over him. Norman tried not to stare while Edward drummed his fingers heavily on the counter and regained his composure.

Norman guessed this was the wrong time to be asking questions, but he was not very good at suppressing his curiosity. He put his book down on the kitchen table, poured some cereal and watched as his father reassembled the coffee maker and lit the gas burner.

"Dad, Vilnius is a city in Russia, right?" He'd been told this before but hadn't paid much attention.

"Lithuania," Edward replied, not taking his eyes off the coffee maker.

"So our family must be from there, right?"

"My side, yes." The coffee maker was bubbling away now, and Edward Vilnius turned to face his son, his expression unreadable. Norman could not bring himself to ask any other questions. He'd never met his father's parents. They were never mentioned.

"There's a cat in this book called Vilnius," Norman continued. He held up the book.

"Is it an especially brilliant cat?" his father asked, a small smile breaking out, probably in anticipation of the coffee.

"Actually, it's quite evil."

"The two are often confused." His father took the first sip of his coffee and nodded with satisfaction.

Norman slurped the last of his cereal and was about to bolt back upstairs with his book when his father coughed and pointed to the empty bowl. Norman returned and placed his bowl in the sink.

"You're not staying in, are you?" his father asked. "How many sunny days do you get here?" The way he said it made it clear that Norman was supposed to stay out of the way while his father worked.

Norman glanced out the window. The pale sun that had been there only ten minutes ago was gone, and the sky was slate grey again, as usual.

"It's raining," he reported glumly.

His father turned to look. "What a country," he muttered, shaking his head in disbelief.

Norman tromped back upstairs to his room and flopped down on his bed. He eyed *Intrepid Amongst the Gypsies* suspiciously before picking it up again and thumbing through the pages.

It was so late last night when he'd finally put the book down that he wasn't sure he'd understood everything that was going on in the story. There was something wrong about that part in the lawyer's office. It didn't fit somehow. He flipped back to the start of the chapter and began to reread from the part where the Intrepids arrived in London. He wanted to make sure he'd actually read what he'd read.

He tapped his fingers rhythmically against the window as he read. The argument of the sparrows in the tree outside had settled down to a quiet conversation of chirps and whistles. Norman pulled the orange blanket back over him. It was perfectly cozy. Thinking he'd probably stayed up too late again last night, he placed the book face down on his chest. He closed his eyes for just a moment. He was only resting them.

41

In the Cage

It was much colder when he woke up and much darker. Had he really slept all day? Surely somebody would have come and got him. He reached for the book on his chest, but it must have fallen off in his sleep. He groped around for it drowsily under the covers, but found there were no covers. This wasn't even his bed. It was as if he'd fallen on the floor. His eyes opened slowly and he tried to put it all together. This wasn't even his bedroom.

Now that his eyes had adjusted to the light he could see that he was lying on a rough plank floor inside a storeroom of sorts. It was dark and dusty, and he was surrounded by crates and boxes.

It was the monkey that sealed it—the wild, toothy grin of the monkey in the crate next to him. It had happened. It had finally happened again. *He was in the book!* He had fallen asleep in his room at the Shrubberies and he had woken up in the book. The book-weird was *real.*

The monkey was poking Norman through the bars of its crate with a long, crooked stick. It was starting to hurt. Norman shifted out of the way. The little white-faced monkey went berserk. The game was on, he guessed, but Norman had no time for it. He had to think, had to get his bearings. He had to figure out what was happening, why he was here. He felt dizzy, almost giddy. His heart beat so hard inside his chest that he was sure it would give him away.

He had to figure out whether he had arrived before the Intrepids or after. He needed to decide how to introduce himself. Introducing yourself to characters in books was a tricky thing. Norman knew this from experience.

Norman did his best to ignore the shrieks and cackles of the grinning spider monkey. Another crate shielded him from the counter. He could not tell if Dodgeworth stood there or not, but if he moved just slightly to his left, he might be able to spy the counter through the bars of the spider monkey's crate.

The tinkling of the bell turned Norman's head. His heart leapt. That would be the Intrepids, he thought. They'd be coming in to buy those stupid mice. Heavy footsteps immediately told him he was wrong. It was not George, Gordon and Pippa. It was someone else. Norman ducked behind the crate and watched. Even the monkey went silent as the stranger entered. His loud, shuffling steps resounded on the wood floor. The stranger was big and scruffy. His hair was cropped so close that you could see his thick, tanned skull between the bristles. There was more hair on his chin than his head. He wore a long, green coat, dull with mud. Something about the dirty red kerchief tied around his neck was familiar. Where had Norman seen that before?

The voice of Dodgeworth was just as he'd imagined it. He'd heard this accent in the market stalls of London, but there was no friendly lilt to the storekeeper's question. "What can I do for you, sir?" Dodgeworth clearly liked the look of the stranger about as much as Norman and the monkey did.

"You're gonna wanna see this," the stranger declared abruptly. The accent was completely different. That's right, Dodgeworth had said that the stranger was an American, a Yank . . . the one trying to sell the talking stoat.

The stranger swung the cage he carried onto the counter and pulled the dirty canvas covering aside.

Norman stared, his mouth agape from the shout that had not come. His few minutes in the pet store had allowed him to come to grips with a few things. He had accepted the fact that he was in the book *Intrepid Amongst the Gypsies*. He had accepted that it was possible to be in a book. It was something he wanted to believe. He wanted Undergrowth to be real. But he didn't want to believe what he saw now. He didn't want to see anyone from Undergrowth here in Dodgeworth's—not here, not like this, and especially not this someone.

Ducking back behind the monkey crate Norman closed his eyes and took a deep breath through his nose, following his mother's advice for stressful situations, but when he looked again he felt no better prepared to deal with what he saw. The ruffian in the long, green coat was leaning on the counter now, talking to Dodgeworth in a low, threatening voice. The lanky pet store owner was not to be intimidated. He remained behind the counter, his arms folded in front of him, regarding the other man and the contents of the cage skeptically.

"I don't care if it can talk, dance and play cricket. I wouldn't pay halfpence for any animal in that condition," Dodgeworth countered, shaking his head dismissively. "It looks half dead already."

Norman felt a sharp pain in his stomach, as if somebody had punched him hard without him expecting it. The creature at the bottom of the cage had not stirred since it was dumped roughly on the counter. It had raised its head just slightly then and Norman had seen its face. It was a stoat, a sort of weasel, russet-coloured on top with a white underbelly. It had small, inquisitive eyes. They were sharp eyes, Norman knew, far sharper than his own. Under normal conditions, the little creature in the cage would easily have spied Norman in his hiding place amongst the crates. Tired or sick as he was, the stoat didn't even open its eyes.

It physically hurt Norman to see this stoat lying there so lifelessly, because this particular stoat was Malcolm, Norman's best friend in this or any universe.

He had to stop himself from screaming, from leaping out and clutching at Malcolm's cage. He wanted to yell out Malcolm's name, but he could not give himself away.

The bookweird was acting up. Norman had seen it before. When you broke into a book, some things broke out, and it was never good. But why Malcolm? Something was very wrong.

Malcolm's captor was now waving an angry fist at the still nonplussed Dodgeworth.

"Why don't you leave the poor beast with me?" Dodgeworth suggested. "I'll see what I can do to bring it back to good health, and we can talk about price then. It's no good to anyone dead."

The seller was having none of it.

"You'd like that, wouldn'tcha, little man! You think I'm stupid? If you want it now, then pay up. If not I'll find someone else who knows the value of a little freak weasel like this."

The man's American accent sounded out of place. Norman had assumed that British books had British villains.

Dodgeworth placed his palms calmly on the counter. "Good luck to you, then, but no one's going to throw good money after a dying animal." He peered into the cage. Malcolm appeared to stir ever so slightly. "It's not a weasel, just so you know," Dodgeworth added. "It's a stoat. The black tip on the tail is the giveaway. If you're not going to leave him with me, you'd best look after him a little better yourself."

The man in the green coat grunted and grabbed the cage viciously. He swung around so quickly Norman hardly had time to duck and hide. He sat there on the floor behind the monkey crates for a few seconds longer, his mind racing, until the ring of the bell and slam of the door spurred him to action.

Norman didn't stop for a second to see the look on Dodgeworth's face when he burst out from behind the crates. Nor did he turn to see the distorted face of the little monkey, whose frantic screams woke every sleeping creature in the shop. He hurtled through the door out onto the street, skidding to a stop on the wet cobblestones.

The man in the green coat was already at the corner. Norman dashed off after him, his sneakers squeaking on the slick cobbles as he dodged crates, delivery carts and slow-moving shoppers. The next street was even narrower and more crowded. Workers in grey coveralls poured out of a warehouse door into the lane. Ahead, Malcolm's captor bulldozed through the crowd. Norman's sneakers slipped on the smooth cobblestones as he chased, dodging this way and that around the sauntering workers.

Again and again Norman lost sight of his quarry in the fog. Each time he made out the red flash of the man's bandana he was farther away. If the man turned down any one of these side alleys, Norman would lose him for good. Norman ducked and weaved through gaps in the crowd. He was moving as fast as he could, but he was losing ground.

Soon Norman could no longer see the bald head and red bandana above the crowd. His only clue that he was still on the right track was the way the traffic parted up ahead to make way for the big man.

At each winding the turns grew tighter and the walls higher. The crowds thinned slowly as the factory workers peeled off down side streets or ducked into pubs along the road. The streets darkened as buildings grew taller and their upper storeys began to overhang the street, but Norman hardly noticed. He didn't notice the figures in the dark doorways peering out after him. He just kept running. He could not lose Malcolm.

Up ahead he could hear the hard *knock, knock* of the man's big boots on the cobblestones as he swaggered down an alley, but Norman was tiring. He could not make himself go faster. Ahead the big man turned again.

Norman raced to the mouth of one alley, his lungs burning. He turned the corner and stopped, unable to keep going. He buckled over, put his hands on his knees and gasped for air. Alone at the other end of the long alley, almost indistinct in the fog that surrounded him, was the man with the cage.

"Hey! Hey, you!" Norman shouted breathlessly.

His quarry either never heard him or ignored him. Norman was wasting his breath.

"That's my stoat!" he bellowed.

For a moment, the man with the cage stopped and turned just

his head to look back. There was a flurry of movement in the cage. Norman caught the flash of white fur on the stoat's chest as Malcolm leapt to his feet and clutched the bars. The stoat moved as quickly as his old self, his ears twitching as he sought the source of the shout. Norman opened his mouth again. "Malcolm!" he cried. The name echoed down the alley. But the big man had turned back again, rounding the corner and disappearing out of sight.

When Norman reached the end of the alley, his quarry had already disappeared. He eyed the doorways along the abandoned street. Had the bald man ducked inside one of these buildings? The doorways were dark and forbidding. The few windows on the street were shuttered or boarded over. Norman listened for voices, but the alley was eerily silent. As he stared and listened, a figure stirred on one of the doorsteps. A gaunt man, dressed in rags, unravelled himself from the knot of blankets that concealed him and shuffled slowly towards Norman.

"Did you see a man with a cage come down this street?" Norman asked, gasping for breath.

The thin, beggarly figure drew closer, his wrinkled mouth open in a sort of wordless croak. He held out a withered hand towards Norman, who backed away slowly.

"A bald man in a green coat, carrying an animal in a cage—which way did he go?" Norman asked, a timid squeak in his voice.

The silent figure beckoned with the curled fingers of his emaciated hand, but Norman could not bear to go nearer. He turned and fled. Fear fuelled his legs better than anger, but it did nothing for his sense of direction. He fled blindly through the web of mazy alleys, turning left and right without thinking, looking only for wider streets, a glimpse of sunlight breaking through a gap in the warehouses.

It might have been only a matter of minutes, but Norman felt as if he'd been running for hours. He ran as though he were running for his life, and Norman knew what it felt like to be running for your life. The fog, the smoke, the muttering voices in doorways drove him on and on until finally the streets grew wider and busier, and he gradually allowed himself to slow down. As his legs slowed, his thoughts slowed, too. He had no idea where he was. He began to look around at the painted wooden storefronts, the delivery men in their loose shirts and wool caps. There were no T-shirts or sneakers here, no bright colours, except for him in his jeans and his bright blue-and-yellow St. Louis Rams sweatshirt. People were starting to stare.

"Dodgeworth's? Dodgeworth's pet store. Can you tell me how to find Dodgeworth's pet store?" he asked each passerby. It was his only point of reference. If he went back there now, perhaps Dodgeworth could help him track the man in the green coat. But the few people who paid attention to his question merely stared and frowned before walking on.

Norman wandered onwards and repeated his question, ever more forlornly. Soon he was out into a wide boulevard. The sidewalks were filled with men in dark suits and round hats. Bowler hats—what had he read about them?—businessmen. Perhaps they would be more helpful.

"Excuse me," he called out. "Can someone tell me how to find Dodgeworth's?" The men in the bowler hats streamed by. They didn't even bother to stare at the strange boy in the bright blue sweatshirt. "Dodgeworth's?" he repeated defiantly. Norman was genuinely afraid now. Modern London had been scary enough. To be lost in this big city, in the past, in a book, was to be triply lost.

"Dodgeworth's?" a plummy little voice asked. "You're looking for Dodgeworth's? Rare animals and animal feed?" There was a little surprise and incredulity in the question.

A red-haired boy turned to him from the crowd. He was Norman's height, dressed in grey flannel shorts and a matching V-neck sweater. One side of his white collar was tucked in and the other was sticking out. Beside him a taller boy looked down bemusedly and shook a shank of dark brown hair out of his eyes. A red-haired girl hung back a little farther. She wore her school sweater, too, but her blouse and skirt were neatly tucked and ironed. Brother and sister had the same pale, freckled skin and red hair. The girl's was braided tidily, but little wisps of it curled in the humid London air. Norman had to stop himself from calling out their names.

"What do you want with Dodgeworth?" George asked, taking over from Gordon. "You'll not find any puppies or kittens there, you know. Dodgeworth's specializes in much more exotic animals." His voice was high and reedy but still conveyed an adult's confidence and authority.

Norman told the truth, as much of it as he could. He found this worked best in books. "I'm looking for my stoat, my pet stoat. Someone stole it from me. I followed the thief to Dodgeworth's."

"If you followed the villain there, then you ought to know very well where Dodgeworth's is," George pointed out.

"I wasn't paying attention," Norman explained. "I was just following the thief."

"Well, you've a lot to learn about the art of detection," George declared.

"I suppose so," Norman admitted. "The thief tried to sell my stoat to Dodgeworth, but Dodgeworth didn't want it, so I followed the thief again. I lost him in an alley."

"Well, London *is* a big city. I don't expect you see much like it in America," George conceded. "Unless of course you are from New York. You're not from New York, are you?"

"No," Norman replied emphatically. He had been to New York once, in another book, and had not enjoyed it.

Gordon reasserted his right to be part of the questioning. "We're actually going to Dodgy's right now. You should come along."

"That's right," George agreed. "And we'd best be off if we're to get everything done."

As they walked, the Cook children and George quizzed Norman on life in America. Norman kept it simple and hoped he didn't mention anything too modern. There were buses and trams on the London streets, but the few cars were very old-fashioned, with skinny, exposed tires and tall, square compartments, like buggy carriages. Norman didn't care enough about cars to guess the era, but he knew not to talk about computers and televisions. As for his reason for being in London, it was as close to the truth as possible— his father was a professor over here for the summer.

The Intrepids found this completely plausible. Only Pippa Cook appeared suspicious. Norman caught her pale blue eyes assessing his clothes critically: his nearly white sneakers, his blue jeans and his brightly coloured Rams sweatshirt. She made Norman realize how much he stood out in London's sea of grey wool. He wanted to shrink and hide, but he did his best to walk normally and smiled faintly every time he caught Pippa giving him the once-over.

Dodgeworth's was surprisingly easy to find once you knew where it was. Gordon was completely at home on the London streets, scurrying forward eagerly, proud to be at the head of the little group. George strode behind him, taking it all in, occasionally pausing to jot down little notes in his notebook. Pippa, quiet and wary, kept an eye on them all. In a few turns they were at Dodgeworth's door.

"Ah, young Master Cook," Dodgeworth greeted them, "and friends." His eyes flickered momentarily over Norman, surely recognizing him as the boy who had been hidden in his shop not an hour ago. The monkey certainly recognized him, too, pressing his manic face to the bars and gibbering as if making some rude joke. Norman edged away, doing his best to stand back behind the Cooks and out of sight.

"What can I do for you young people today?" Dodgeworth asked.

George explained that they needed mice, telling him the story they'd concocted about feeding a wounded hawk they'd found. Norman watched Dodgeworth's face as George spoke. The shopkeeper's thin lips stretched in a bemused smile, making his long moustache twitch. It was not that he didn't believe them. He just didn't seem to care if the story was true, as long as it was harmless.

When Dodgeworth disappeared into the back to fetch the box of mice, Pippa Cook turned her freckled face to Norman.

"Do you want us to ask Dodgy about your stoat?" she asked helpfully.

"No, thanks," Norman replied. "I'll do it."

Pippa's face scrunched into a frown. "That's horrible, someone stealing your pet. Have you reported it to the police?"

George interrupted Norman before he could answer. "A stoat is an unusual pet. Is it tame?"

The question made Norman smile despite himself. He would hardly have called Malcolm tame.

"I've known him . . . I mean, I've had him since he was a kit," Norman said. It was almost true. Norman had saved Malcolm's life when he was still very young. "He's good with me, but not so much with other people."

Dodgeworth returned with the box of mice.

"I'm sorry about earlier." Norman stepped forward as the storekeeper put the cardboard carton down on the counter. "Bursting out of here like that . . . hiding in here."

Unconcerned, Dodgeworth shrugged and smiled. "Did you catch our man with the stoat?" he asked.

"I lost him in an alley," Norman told him. "That's why I came back. George, Gordon and Pippa helped me find the place again."

"That stoat was stolen," George declared. "The ruffian who offered it to you is a thief. It belongs to Norman here." George had taken Norman at his word and was now prepared to champion him.

Dodgeworth nodded knowingly, as if he had guessed as much. "I'm afraid to say your little stoat was in a sorry state. It's not been well taken care of."

Norman bit his lower lip and clenched his fists.

"I was of half a mind to buy it just to save the poor creature, but I'm loath to give my money to villains of his kind. I'll tell you what, though, if he comes in again, I'll have it off him and we'll settle up after."

"Thank you," Norman began to say, but George interrupted him.

"What did this fellow look like?"

"He was a big specimen, strong. By the way he swung that cage around I'd say he's done some heavy lifting in his day. Looked like he'd been living rough for a while—unshaven, in need of a bath. Wore a long green hunting coat that looks like it's been doubling as a sleeping bag, filthy red neckerchief. Spoke like an American, but not like this one here." He indicated Norman. "A harder accent. I'd say New York, but I'm no expert."

George furrowed his brow as if deep in thought. "Red neckerchief and a green hunting coat, you say. What colour was this man's hair?"

"Grey and black over his chin, but there wasn't much of any colour on his head," Dodgeworth replied.

George nodded as if in possession of a great secret. "This sounds uncannily like the poacher who's been skulking around Kelmsworth Hall."

Norman hadn't thought of it before, but it made total sense. Malcolm had been dropped into the Intrepids back at George's home. Malcolm's captor and the Kelmsworth poacher were one and the same! Norman thought quickly. He had to go back with them to continue the chase. Malcolm needed him.

"Kelmsworth Hall?" Norman tried to sound surprised, as if he'd had no idea where George lived. "That's right near where I'm staying. It really could be the same man."

George and the Cooks stared at him for a moment. "Of course. Your father's a professor. He'll be over at the university," Pippa said thoughtfully. "That's not far from Kelmsworth Hall at all."

"I'll bet it really is the same villain!" Gordon declared with some vehemence.

Mr. Todd, Solicitor

orman was quickly invited to join the Intrepids' raid on the lawyer's office.

"Nice to have some reinforcements," Gordon enthused as they walked. He was by far the friendliest of the Intrepids. There was nothing wrong with the others, but George's mind was obviously elsewhere. And Pippa . . . it was hard to tell what she was thinking. Maybe she was just shy, but she looked at Norman so thoughtfully. She seemed to be the only one who thought he might look out of place.

"We're after the same villain," Gordon rambled. "You ought to come back to Kelmsworth with us. Shouldn't he, eh, George?"

George Kelmsworth grunted his agreement. "Yes, of course. You'll stay at the lodge with me."

It was all so easy. No one asked if he needed permission, but Norman felt he had to say something. "My dad's busy at the university on some secret project," he told them, hoping that would allow him to keep it vague. "I've spent most of the summer reading and exploring the countryside with Malcolm."

The Intrepids stared at him with the same blank face. "Who's Malcolm, then?" Gordon asked, as if he'd missed something.

"That's my stoat," Norman explained. It felt weird saying "my" stoat. He could imagine what Malcolm would have to say about that.

"Is it only tame with you?" Pippa asked. She spoke so infrequently that Norman was surprised to hear her voice. "Or would it let us look after it, too? If it's injured, I should think it would need some expert care."

Gordon snorted as if his sister had said something funny. "Pippa's gaga for animals of all sorts. She thinks she'll be a vet, like Dad. As if a girl could be a vet!"

Pippa just scowled and looked away, a glint of defiance in her pale blue eyes.

"I'm not so sure," George mused. "Father even says that women ought to be able to vote. I don't see why they shouldn't, do you?"

Norman rolled his eyes, imagining what his mom might say to Gordon.

"Girls can do whatever they want," he replied. "She could be a vet, or any kind of doctor."

"You must be joking," Gordon scoffed. "She's so squeamish. She's even worried about the mice getting hurt." He indicated the box that Pippa carried so carefully.

"She'll probably make a great vet, then," Norman concluded. It only made sense, but Pippa smiled at him as if it was the kindest thing he could have said.

Emboldened by the smile, he ventured another question. "Are you sure that this plan with the mice will work?" he asked tentatively. He knew very well it wouldn't—it was going to be a disaster—but thought that maybe he shouldn't meddle.

"Of course it'll work!" Gordon insisted, his pale, freckled face flushed, as if Norman had questioned the force of gravity or the might of the British navy. "Mice scurrying every which way underfoot, girls screaming." He looked meaningfully at his sister. "Those fussy geezers will scatter. While they're in a tizzy we'll have a look through that solicitor's desk for those papers."

"What if they have a cat?" Norman asked, as if it were just a remote possibility and not a certainty he'd read the night before.

"Why would a solicitor's office have cats?" Gordon scoffed.

"Maybe they've had mouse problems before," Norman offered. "Mice can't be all that uncommon in London."

Gordon's faith was not to be swayed, but Pippa had been listening thoughtfully. "Maybe it is a bit silly to expect grown men to lose their heads over a few mice." She looked to George for reassurance.

The dark-haired boy appeared unworried. "Well, it's the best plan we have at the moment," he declared, a trifle annoyed that anyone would dare to doubt him. "If it doesn't work we shall have to try something else. I'm utterly convinced that the key to exonerating my father is in that office."

Nevertheless, the Intrepids climbed the steps to the lawyer's office just a little less defiantly than they had when Norman had read this scene. George went ahead into the office while Norman and the Cooks remained outside on the landing, listening at the open door.

"Ah, young Master Kelmsworth. What a surprise. What brings you to the city?" Todd did not sound surprised at all. The lawyer sounded as if he had been expecting George.

"I've come about the gamekeeper," George announced, repeating the words that Norman had read just yesterday. "The grounds at Kelmsworth are not being looked after properly. I came across a poacher myself the other day. We absolutely must have a proper gamekeeper back on the estate."

Mr. Todd frowned as Norman and the Cooks snuck in through the open door. His eyes shifted to them for only a moment, but Norman was certain that he had seen them. Todd looked directly at Norman and smiled a smug little smile of recognition. Norman ducked behind a desk with Pippa. Neither she nor Gordon realized that Mr. Todd had seen them, and that this was no surprise at all.

"Well, I'm afraid there's not much we can do on that account at this point," Todd was telling George. "While we put together the appeal, the grounds are under the jurisdiction of Administrator Hepplewaithe. We'll sort it out in the end, of course. You know that. But I'm afraid that in the meantime, it is out of our hands."

"But I nearly caught the poacher myself. We think he's here in London now. We just missed him at Dodgeworth's . . ."

"You don't say? And what might Dodgeworth's be?"

Pippa's high-pitched scream interrupted them.

It happened just the way it had in the book. Pippa climbed onto a chair and continued to scream as twelve grey and white mice scurried from beneath the desk where Gordon had set them free. Norman stood and watched in silence. They made a pathetic sight, quickly disappearing into the wainscotting and under cabinets.

Mr. Todd stood up at his desk to observe their escape. "Shhhh," he scolded Pippa warily, whose screams had quickly become less shrill. She blushed, got down off the chair and looked meekly at her shoes.

Gordon, for one, was not giving up so easily. "Rats!" he bellowed. "Rats! We'll all get the plague!"

Mr. Todd turned to stare at Norman, rolling his eyes as if inviting Norman to share the joke. The lawyer tilted his head to indicate the large ginger cat crouched behind a nearby column. The cat sprang with a ferocity and velocity that belied its round belly and complacent smile. Beneath one ginger paw it held a single stunned white mouse.

"Oh, dear," said Mr. Todd. It was the exact bored, arrogant tone that Norman had expected when he'd read it. "I do hope that wasn't a special mouse. I doubt that Vilnius will be persuaded to give it up now."

Hearing his name spoken, or half of it at least, Norman looked up reflexively. There was something about this Todd character, something familiar. The lawyer's long face and sunken cheeks were framed by ridiculous sideburns that reached down to his chin. They made him look like some sort of felt puppet, but Norman was sure he knew the face under all that hair.

"You know, Master Kelmsworth," he was lecturing now, "I must ask you not to go chasing suspected poachers around the grounds of the estate, or here in London. It isn't safe at all." He was speaking to George, but his eyes were fixed on Norman all the while. *Perhaps it is my clothes*, Norman thought.

"If there was a poacher on the estate, what could he possibly take of any value? I doubt there is any real game on the estate, except for a few pheasants, perhaps the odd rabbit."

"That's not true," Gordon argued. His voice became shrill and indignant. "Kelmsworth estate is full of valuable game, not just rabbits. There are badgers and foxes and—"

"Foxes, you say? Well, that is an outrage." Mr. Todd winked at Norman. "I'm very much opposed to the fox hunt."

With that wink Norman recognized him. It was Fuchs. Norman knew him by many guises and names, but he would always be Fuchs, the mysterious librarian from his local library. Fuchs was the only person from the real world that he had ever met in a book. He had turned up as the fox abbot of Tintern in Undergrowth and had once saved Norman from a murder mystery. It was Fuchs who had explained the bookweird, as much as it could be explained. Norman stood there, his jaw hanging, trying to imagine what he should say. Nothing came to mind.

Mr. Todd smiled with satisfaction. Now that he was sure Norman recognized him, he turned away and spoke directly to George. They spoke for a few more minutes about the problems at the estate. Todd was sympathetic but unhelpful. George was quickly frustrated, and they were soon trudging down the steps again. Norman trailed behind the other three, deep in thought.

He stopped as they reached the door. "Just a minute," he said. "I have to ask your Mr. Todd something."

He ignored the inquisitive looks from the Intrepids and dashed back up the stairs before they could object.

"Why am I here?" Norman asked, placing his palms down on the massive oak desk.

Mr. Todd signed a paper with a flourish, then looked up. He placed his fingers together in front of his face and considered the question seriously for a moment, "It is a difficult question, one better suited to a priest or a philosopher than a lawyer."

Norman was used to this sort of obtuseness from Fuchs—or Todd, as he now called himself. "No. Why am I *here*, in this book?"

"Why are you ever here?" Todd replied distractedly. Even as he pulled the sleeves of his suit jacket over his white shirt cuffs, he looked just a bit animal-like. In Undergrowth he was the fox abbot of Tintern and chaplain to the stoat princes.

"But I didn't do it. I didn't eat any of this book," Norman pressed. "I haven't eaten a book since the last time."

Todd stroked his ridiculous mutton-chop sideburns in mock contemplation. "You haven't? Are you sure?"

Norman thought momentarily but nodded, convinced he hadn't so much as nibbled the corners of a page. He had cured himself of the habit that had unlocked the bookweird for him. He knew he couldn't risk it.

"Then someone else must have brought you here," Todd declared, as if that were the end of it.

Norman leaned over the edge of the desk and stared. "Did you do it?" he demanded.

"I doubt it," Todd replied, unperturbed.

As usual, the man's attitude was testing Norman's patience. "What do you mean you doubt it? Why don't you ever answer a question simply?"

"I am a lawyer, after all," he replied with a smile.

"And a fox and . . . and sometimes a librarian." Norman sputtered. He took a deep breath and changed his tack. "I saw Malcolm here. Did you know he was here? Did you bring him?" He watched for a flicker in Todd's eyes, a twitch in his sideburns, but the lawyer was inscrutable.

"Perhaps the young king brought himself here. He was becoming something of a bookworm."

The lawyer and former fox abbot didn't seem at all surprised to hear that Malcolm was here in London.

"You're saying *he* ate some of the Intrepids book?" Norman asked, incredulous. "How would an Intrepids book get there in *his* book? That makes no sense at all."

"I'm not suggesting anything of the sort," Todd protested, "but if, as you say, the stoat is here, then it can only be the bookweird at work. There are ways into the bookweird other than that nasty little consumption *ingresso* of yours."

Norman ignored the comment about his *ingresso*. The man he knew as Fuchs had told him there were other ways to get into books, but as usual he hadn't explained them.

"But he's been caught and injured, probably by the same poacher George was telling you about." Norman pounded his fist on the desk. On television this was the sort of thing that got a lawyer's attention. Todd did look a little shocked, or at least offended, as he reordered the papers that Norman had disturbed.

"Then you'd better stick with George," he replied. "If I remember my Intrepids books correctly, he rarely stays out of trouble, but he usually stumbles onto a solution."

Norman just stared at him. As usual, he felt that there was a lot he wasn't saying. As if to illustrate the point, the lawyer now opened a drawer in his desk and removed a small leather change purse.

"You'll be needing this," he said, sliding it across the desk towards Norman. When the boy looked up questioningly, the lawyer finished his sentence with a small smile: "For train fare."

Flashlights

At midnight Norman was sipping warm tea from a Thermos cup while he lay behind the fortifications of the Kelmsworth Folly and surveyed the forest edge through the lens of George's brass telescope. It didn't seem at all strange to be sitting there next to a dozing George Kelmsworth and the dog, Nelson. It felt strangely normal, and that was possibly more disturbing. Not believing in the bookweird had been difficult for Norman. It had made him anxious. His experiences in Undergrowth and in the horse book *Fortune's Foal* had been so real, it had been a struggle to convince himself that they were dreams. So though this morning when he'd woken up the last place he'd have expected to be by evening was at the top of the Kelmsworth Folly on the watch for poachers, there was really no place he'd rather have been.

If Malcolm was in trouble, then Norman needed to be here right now. Malcolm was no ordinary talking medieval stoat prince. Malcolm was Norman's friend. In Undergrowth, Norman had saved Malcolm from a raven ambush. He had carried him in a sling across his chest for days as the little stoat recovered. It sent a rush of protectiveness through him as he recalled the warmth of the animal's body and the beating of his tiny heart against his own. Norman had never felt that connected to any human person. Their experience in the forest had bound them together. They had fought together and fled for their lives together.

When wolf assassins pursued them, it was Malcolm who got them through it. The stoat prince had always been sure that they would make it out of the wolf lands, and that if it came to a fight, his arrows would settle the matter. He was smarter and funnier and better company than any human friend Norman had ever had, and if he was lying now on the floor of a cage injured or sick, Norman had something to say about it.

They had been watching for hours now, but each time he felt the slightest drowsiness during his watch he needed only to conjure up that image of Malcolm and he snapped to full vigilance.

George Kelmsworth had made them soup and they'd dozed by the fire in his little cottage while waiting for nightfall. Pippa and Gordon had returned to the house "for tea," as they called dinner, but the Cooks were taking turns on watch from the house itself. They used a flashlight to blink a signal every half hour from their bedroom window on the third floor. Three short flashes meant that all was clear. Two long ones would mean that the poacher had been spotted and the chase was on.

Norman wasn't at all sure that he and the Intrepids could bring down the poacher. If the poacher was the same man he'd seen in Dodgeworth's, it might take more than a few plucky kids, but Norman was willing to try, for Malcolm's sake. George assured him that capturing villains was something they did all the time, and that what they lacked in brawn they made up for in guile. In the previous days George had laid a series of tripwires and snares along the paths leading to and from Kelmsworth Hall. All they needed to do was chase the poacher towards one of these traps and he'd be theirs.

"What if he doesn't run away from us?" Norman had asked.

George had replied quickly, as if he'd already thought of this. "Then we'll have to make sure that he chases us."

It was all so simple to George. The plan didn't sound crazy at all to him. Norman just hoped that it would come off better than the mouse fiasco at Todd's office.

George was stirring beside him now. He had been sleeping soundly, since Norman had committed to the first watch. Now he rolled from his side to his back and was almost instantly awake and chipper.

"Well done, Norman," he said breezily as he glanced at his watch. "Old Gordon would have been sound asleep by now. Have you spotted anything?"

"Nothing so far," Norman replied, checking his own watch as a reflex, "and Gordon's been on time with his signals from the house."

"Nah, that'll be Pippa with the signals," George said, rising from his sleeping bag to a crouched position. "She's a brick."

Norman guessed that being a brick was a good thing. He handed George the Thermos of tea.

George took the Thermos from his hand. "I say," he enthused, "that's a cracking watch you have there." Norman hadn't thought of it when he'd pressed the button to illuminate the digits. "I suppose it's an American thing. Brilliant, all the same. I'll have to have one sent over."

Norman smiled, not wanting to burst his bubble.

"I'll take over now," George declared, placing the empty Thermos aside. "I'll wake you in a few hours."

Norman still had not removed the telescope from his eye. He did not want to miss anything.

George didn't insist. "I should like to go to America when all this business here is done with," the older boy continued. Something about his tone at this moment was less convincing than before. The confidence and maturity for a moment became bluster. George was just a kid, too. And Norman realized that "this business here" wasn't just the poacher or even the legal issues about the house. This was happening only because his father was in prison. Norman wanted to say something, but he had no idea what.

A movement at the edge of the forest stopped that thought dead. "George," he whispered hoarsely, "there's something there." He handed the telescope over and pointed towards the treeline.

George raised the telescope to his eye and trained it on the spot

Norman had indicated. He was silent and still for a moment, adjusting the scope for a better look before announcing, "That's our man, all right. Send the signal."

Within moments they were in motion. Norman and George hurried down the Rook's spiral staircase and sprinted across the lawn in the shadow of a low stone wall. The border collie, Nelson, bounded silently ahead of them. Summoned by Norman's signal, Pippa and Gordon were letting themselves out the kitchen door. Norman and George caught up to Nelson at the forest's edge.

George drew the spyglass from his coat and confirmed that their quarry had not moved from his spot at the end of the forest path. "He's setting a trap," George told Norman as they watched and waited for the Cooks to come into view. "But he's falling into ours," he added dramatically.

He handed the telescope to Norman and crouched down to set up the flashlight on the ground, fixing it on an angle behind the wall so that when they flicked it on, the light would just clear the top of the stones.

Through the telescope Norman watched the progress of the poacher. From the dark silhouette he looked like the man from London, but it was impossible to know for sure. Pivoting to the side Norman trained the telescope on the two smaller figures of the Cooks creeping along the path.

"Okay," Norman murmured, "Gordon and Pippa are behind him now on the main path."

George waited, crouched down on the ground, and stared grimly into the dark like an action hero.

"George," Norman whispered more loudly.

George raised his head sharply and flicked on his flashlight. Its beam shone upwards on an angle over the stone wall. In unison George and Norman leapt onto the wall and shouted in the deepest voices they could muster:

"You there, stop!"

Nelson backed them up with a frenzy of barking.

The poacher turned and stared towards them. With the flashlight lighting them up from behind, he could not see their faces. He
could not tell that they were only kids. Standing on the wall, and
with the light elongating their shadows, they appeared much taller
than they were.

The poacher froze for a moment, staring back at his pursuers.
It was him, all right—the man from Dodgeworth's. Norman gritted
his teeth. This was the man who had Malcolm. The poacher seemed
to regain his senses, turned and ducked clumsily into the woods.

Norman and George gave chase. They could hear the big man
crashing heavily along the path up ahead. Nelson made sure that
their pursuit was noisy. They wanted the intruder to know they
were after him. The plan depended on driving him towards their
trap. Norman hoped that Pippa and Gordon had been quick
enough to get in position ahead of them on the trail.

Up ahead there was a fork in the trail. They needed the poacher
to take the right turn. Pippa and Gordon were supposed to make
sure of that.

"Nearly there," George said huskily, almost out of breath. "The
fork is at that big oak." They kept running. Where were Pippa and
Gordon? If they didn't spring their surprise soon, the poacher
might take the left fork and escape.

The beams of four flashlights suddenly snapped on up ahead to
the left. The silhouette of the poacher froze. Perhaps he was calcu-
lating his odds. Was he better to face the four new pursuers who
had cut him off, or the two with a dog behind him?

Norman aimed the beam of his flashlight directly at their
quarry's face. It was him, all right. The same bristly bald head, the
same mean, squinting eyes, the same ragged red bandana. The
poacher blinked back angrily into the light, then made his decision,
careening down the right fork.

The four children set off in combined pursuit. The trail narrowed, angling down the side of a ridge, forcing them to run in
single file. Soon they were all hurtling down the ridge as fast as they
could. Norman could hear the ragged breathing of Gordon Cook

behind him. Up ahead, George had stopped shouting encourage-ment, saving his breath for the chase. Norman could just keep up, but the Cooks were falling back quickly. It didn't matter to Norman. All he could think of was rescuing Malcolm. It probably didn't matter to George, either. George had never met a criminal that he could not take on single-handedly.

Ahead of them all, the big man smashed through the forest, his heavy boots crushing twigs and brush beneath him, his bulk whip-ping and snapping branches as he ran.

Suddenly there was a shout or a surprised grunt. He had fallen into the trap.

Norman and George skidded to a halt. Both boys lifted their flashlights to illuminate the huge old pine tree that spanned the path. The big poacher should have been up there. He should have been dangling by his foot from the thick rope they'd tied to the overhanging branch—but there was no overhanging branch.

They dipped their flashlights, swinging their beams across the forest. There in front of them, lying across the path, was the branch. Beside it lay the poacher, who looked as though he was just recovering his senses after a nasty fall. The branch had snapped under his weight.

"Stop there, you!" George commanded in his usual tone of offended authority.

The big thief pulled himself to a sitting position and began tugging at the rope around his ankle.

"I said stop. Stay where you are!" George repeated haughtily.

The man in the red bandana looked up. His eyes wild with anger, he spat out an insult that Norman had heard once or twice on the playground but never in a book. The poacher was nearly loose from the trap now—a few more tugs and he would be free.

George just cried, "Get him!" and dove at the captive poacher. Had he thought about it, Norman would have stayed back. But he acted instinctively. This was the man who had captured and tor-tured his friend.

Norman hurled himself at the thug, but the big man just shrugged off his tackle. Norman heard an "umph" that might have come from him or George as they both tumbled to the ground. The poacher resumed his efforts with the rope.

George struggled to his hands and knees and launched another attack, grasping the man's arm. Nelson barked and nipped at the big man's heels. Their efforts barely slowed the struggling giant.

Norman thought for half a second about how dangerous this was, then he grabbed the villain's other arm. The three struggled together for a few more moments in an uneven wrestling match.

The poacher was too strong and too mean for them. One vicious swing of his elbow caught George in the ribs. The boy hit the ground with a gasp. He lay there stunned for a moment, holding his chest.

A heavy boot caught Nelson in the hip. The dog yelped and skittered away sideways. Taking a position between his master and the poacher, the collie bared his teeth and let out a low growl, but kept his distance. Norman clung to the poacher's back, making futile grasps at his arms. He felt himself rising as the poacher undid the last of the knots and staggered to his feet.

With one furious twist the poacher shook Norman from his back, flinging him violently to the ground. Norman winced and peered fearfully up at the bald criminal who loomed over him.

"Stupid brat," he snarled. "You tryin' to get yourself killed?" His accent reminded Norman of the noisy New York police station in *The Magpie*.

Suddenly the look in the poacher's eyes changed. "Rams? That's a Rams jersey," he growled. He grabbed the shoulders of Norman's sweatshirt and shook him. "Where'd you get this?" Norman stared back uncomprehendingly as the bald man's anger swelled. "You tell me where you got that shirt, kid, or I'll knock your teeth out."

"My . . . my . . . my mom," Norman answered, confused and scared by the question. What did his shirt have to do with anything?

The poacher's eyes opened wide and stared manically.

The guy is crazy, on top of everything, Norman thought. *He's going to kill me because I'm wearing a Rams shirt.* Norman wasn't even much of a football fan.

"You're not from here," the thug growled, bringing his face in close. The smell of his sour breath brought Norman back to the last time he'd been cornered by an angry enemy. It was wolves that time, but this was just as terrifying.

"You're from the other place. The real place, the future, and you're taking me back with you," the poacher fumed.

Norman blinked and stared. What did he mean, the other place? A terrible thought began to occur to him.

The beam of a flashlight blinded Norman. "Put him down right now," George commanded.

The thug turned and sneered, but now four new beams of light shone down from the path. A whistle sounded, followed by a shrill "Halt! Police!"

It wasn't the police, it turned out. It was only Gordon and Pippa, each holding two flashlights, but in the dark and chaos of Kelmsworth Wood, the poacher was hardly to know this. He could deal with two crazy kids, their dog and their lame traps, but the prospect of four policemen weighing in was a little much. He dropped Norman unceremoniously to the ground.

Norman scrambled to the other side of the tree, lest the poacher change his mind. For a moment the bald man didn't move, unwilling to leave even now. He stared at Norman for a long time, his eyes wide with anger and frustration. He looked more like a rabid animal than a man.

The whistle sounded again. The bald man gave Norman one last wild look and went crashing into the forest.

They knew better than to chase him. Norman and the Intrepids were relieved to have escaped without serious injury.

"Are you sure you're all right, George?" Pippa asked for the third or thirteenth time, handing over the mugs of cocoa she'd prepared back at the lodge.

George furrowed his eyebrows but didn't answer the question. Since they'd left the forest he'd been lost in thought, as if struggling with an impenetrable riddle.

"Strange," he mused to himself as he sipped his cocoa. "That ought to have worked." He was genuinely perplexed that he had not been able to capture a criminal more than twice his size. He was so used to his schemes working, the failure was unaccountable. "I can't explain it. First London, and now this."

Norman shifted uncomfortably in his chair. He had an idea why neither scheme had worked.

"Just a run of bad luck," Gordon opined cheerfully. "We'll have him out in the next over." He sat back and licked the cocoa moustache from his upper lip.

Norman wasn't so sure. George was used to coming up against a different kind of villain. The world of the Intrepids didn't include opponents who were too smart or too tough for George. That wasn't how it worked. But Mr. Todd didn't play by these rules because Mr. Todd was Fuchs. Fuchs wasn't from the world of the Intrepids. Fuchs didn't care that their mouse distraction was supposed to work. The poacher didn't care either, and Norman had a terrible suspicion that the reason was the same. Neither of them belonged in the pages of the Intrepids.

"You ought to give me your jumper," Pippa said, obviously trying to change the subject. "I'll have it mended. George, you'll lend him one of yours, won't you?"

George mumbled a distracted agreement.

When Norman pulled his sweatshirt over his head, he noticed how badly it was ripped. The violence of the poacher's grip came back to him and made him shiver.

"By the way, Norman, what's Rams?" Gordon asked blithely. "What's that all about, then? Is it your school PE kit?"

It took a while for Gordon to explain that PE was what Norman knew as Phys. Ed., and in the end it was easiest for Norman to agree that yes, it was his gym uniform.

Gordon grinned, content with his perspicacity, and drained his mug. "So what do you think of our poacher, then, now you've heard him? Is old Dodgeworth right? Is he from New York?"

Norman nodded, and lifted his cup to his lips to avoid saying more. He had been to New York only once, and he had not enjoyed it. When the bookweird had started to go wrong before, he'd been transported into *The Magpie*, a crime novel that his mother had been reading. The detectives in *The Magpie*, Rorschach and Darwin, had been on the trail of a killer when Norman had turned up at the alleyway crime scene. He'd spent two hours in a dingy interrogation room before Fuchs had saved him.

Norman had no idea how the bookweird worked, how you got from one book to another. It had all started for him when he'd accidentally eaten a page of *The Brothers of Lochwarren* and fallen into the world of Undergrowth. Fuchs had called this his *ingresso*. Eating book pages had side effects. It was contagious. It caused things to move from book to book.

When Norman escaped Undergrowth something else escaped with him. The wolves that hunted him in Undergrowth pursued him into Dora's horse book, *Fortune's Foal*, killing a horse and nearly wrecking the book completely. It was as if his *ingresso* created doorways between books. When he fell into that New York alleyway in *The Magpie,* he accidentally brought a horse with him. He'd never thought of what might have been displaced from *The Magpie* when he escaped . . . until now.

"What is it, Norman?" Pippa asked. Norman had looked up suddenly from his cup as the idea hit him.

His mind immediately leapt to the worst of all possibilities— the killer. A killer who could elude the wily Rorschach and Darwin for more than four hundred pages could easily wreak havoc in the world of the Intrepids.

He bit his lip and pretended to sip his cocoa again. He would have to tell Todd. As Fuchs, he had intervened before to get Norman out of a book. He'd been there in the interrogation room with Rorschach and Darwin, and had given him the page to eat himself out of *The Magpie*. Fuchs knew how dangerous that world was. If he knew the killer was loose here with the Intrepids, he'd do some-thing to stop it. Wouldn't he?

"When are you going back to London?" Norman asked George.

"Not until we've got this sorted out here," George replied. "It's obvious that this poacher is something to be reckoned with."

"Couldn't Fu— I mean, Todd help?" Norman asked.

"Mr. Todd doesn't seem to be able to help anybody," Pippa replied a little bitterly. "He's been working on Lord Kelmsworth's appeal for ages now, and we haven't seen any progress at all. I think George ought to talk to his MP."

George scowled but did not disagree. "It's more vital than ever that we stay here. That poacher is a villain of the first water. It's obvious that your pet stoat is in serious danger."

Norman didn't need to be told. If the poacher was the Magpie, then killing a small forest animal would be the least of his crimes.

"What we need to do is rescue your stoat," George declared, putting his mug down emphatically. "We'll get him out of harm's way and prove that old baldy is a thief. Then we can get the con-stabulary involved."

The Cooks nodded their red heads solemnly in agreement, and Norman wasn't about to argue. He'd have liked nothing better than to rescue Malcolm and get out of there. He wished that he shared the Intrepids' confidence. He smiled weakly and agreed—yes, of course—doing everything he could to pretend that this was a wise plan certain to succeed.

When the Cooks had returned to the main house and George had retired to his room, Norman tossed and fretted on the couch. Things were bad. In fact, they couldn't be much worse. It was almost a year since Norman had woken up in the public library after his last trip inside the pages of a book. He had thought that it was all over, that he had stopped falling into books and that their characters had stopped falling out of them and into the pages of other books. If the poacher was a character from *The Magpie*, he had been in the Intrepids books for months. And if he was the Magpie himself, then there was no telling what damage he'd already done. A murderer from one book was likely to remain a murderer in another.

Norman tapped his foot rhythmically on the floor beside the sofa. He couldn't sleep like this. He hadn't been this afraid since the last time. It wasn't just Malcolm he was worried about anymore. He was afraid for his own life. It was enough to make him fantasize about going home now, getting out of this book right away. He didn't do it—couldn't really do it—but he wanted to. Even the thought of abandoning Malcolm made him feel guilty.

Since he wasn't sleeping anyway, Norman rose and tiptoed quietly to the desk where George had sat all evening. Methodically and quietly he tore a page from the notebook where George had scribbled his observations. Tonight was not the time to learn how to use a fountain pen. He ferreted through the drawers until he found a suitable pencil. Then he sat down and began to write a story.

"That summer, Norman and his parents and sister moved to the house of his mother's family in England," he began. "The house belonged to Norman's uncle Kit, his mother's brother. Uncle Kit was away and let them stay at the house while he was gone."

Feeling the need to be as specific as possible, Norman wrote the full address, the postal code and the date of their arrival. He did not stop writing until he had described the house and his family completely. He did his best to remember details of the house—the crack in the sand-coloured masonry above the back kitchen door; the one wall that was covered with glossy, dark green ivy; the five matching and one mismatched chairs in the dining room; the way that the big oak door of his bedroom caught on the jamb and honked to the entire house that he was leaving his room.

He described his family: Dora as kindly as he could with her nine years of accumulated experience annoying him; his distracted professor father, obsessed with coffee and books; his unnaturally cheerful mother, whose habit and job of motivational coaching was infuriating and yet made him strangely proud. It comforted Norman to write these things. He had to think about his reality in order to describe it. He was not used to thinking about his family. He was used to living with them.

It must have taken him more than an hour to fill the page. He made it as vivid and as accurate as he could. Once he was done, he read it over to himself to make sure that it felt right. His eyes grew hot and itchy as he read the description. He wasn't at all sure that *ingresso* still worked, but there was not much more he could do. He folded the paper in four and tucked it in his back pocket and lay down on the couch again. Perhaps the evening's exertions had just caught up to him, but he finally felt tired enough to sleep. It was easier to sleep, too, with the thought that he had an escape plan in his back pocket.

The Raid

They crept towards the poacher's encampment, through the thickest part of Kelmsworth Wood, where slim new alder filled the ground between the gnarled old beech trees. They took the long way around so they could approach from upwind. Norman had been pretty sure that the poacher wasn't about to smell their approach, but George had insisted on carrying out this raid like "Red Indians." He'd also insisted on saying "Red Indians," no matter how many times Norman had tried to correct him with "Native Americans."

George wasn't used to being corrected. The expressions on the Cook children's faces told the story. Pippa gave Norman a perplexed, curious look, wrinkling her nose and forehead as if watching something unexpected and very peculiar. Hero-worshipping Gordon's reaction was a comic double take, as if he could not imagine that anyone could be so stupid as to question the wisdom of the incomparable George Kelmsworth.

Gordon had taken the "Red Indian" part of the plan so seriously that he had wanted them to wear war paint and feathers in headbands. George had vetoed the idea, not because it was crazy but because they did not have time to find feathers and war paint.

They had spent the last two days scouting the poacher. From the Rook they had seen him skulking around the lodge, peering in the windows and checking the latches. Norman shivered as he watched, thankful that he was hidden in the tower rather than lying on the couch in the lodge. A pane of glass wasn't going to stop a criminal mastermind from *The Magpie*'s New York.

In the daylight, they followed the trail of snapped branches and trodden plants to this small clearing in the woods. In the middle of the clearing was a wide, blackened circle of grass made by the poacher's campfire. A faded green canvas tent was backed up against an escarpment.

"Red Indians wouldn't do that. They always make a very small, tidy fire to avoid detection," Gordon told them knowingly. Norman rolled his eyes.

The four children lay on top of the escarpment looking down at the clearing. The poacher was nowhere in sight. Earlier they had watched him go off on his rounds to check his traps, but they were still wary. There was nothing to say that he hadn't protected his camp with booby traps.

George finally made a move. "Right," he commanded. "Gordon, you stay here and keep watch from above." The younger boy's head snapped in a dutiful military nod. "Norman, you check the tent. I expect that's where your weasel will be. Pippa and I will guard the front of the camp and gather whatever evidence we can."

George slipped over the edge of the escarpment, sending a shower of loose gravel down the cliff. He landed confidently at the bottom, brushed the dust from his shirt and waited to give the others a hand down. Norman scrambled down last, eager to get this done. George was waiting for him when he landed. There was that look in his eye again. Norman had seen it a few times now, a look of quiet surprise at meeting someone who didn't need his help. It was as if he knew something weird was going on, something that Norman understood but that George could only sense. Then they both remembered that this was a raid.

Norman rushed towards the tent and grabbed the rough canvas flap to open it, but something made him pause there. What if they were wrong? What if the poacher had snuck back unseen and was sleeping on the other side of this flimsy canvas barrier?

The image of his friend Malcolm lying sick or hurt in the cage flashed through his mind and energized his body. His fingers worked at the knots on the tent flap. He wanted to call out. He wanted to whisper, "Malcolm, are you in there?" but George had ordered complete silence. Norman yanked the last knot apart and pushed through the canvas flap into the dark space behind.

"Took your time about it, Strong Arm! I've nearly gnawed through this cage on my own while you dawdled."

Norman's eyes adjusted to the dark and focused on the small cage at the far end of the tent. It was the same old Malcolm grinning there. Without his clothes, the white fur of his belly stood out in the dim light of the cave. He looked like any ordinary woodland animal, but Norman would have recognized him anywhere. How can you forget a friend?

"I thought you were dying," he said, relieved to see the tiny russet-brown creature standing defiantly in his cage, apparently unharmed.

"Good job I wasn't, with the time it takes you to organize a rescue. What? Have you been seeing the sights?" It was the same old Malcolm, cheerful and quick-witted, even in a crisis.

"Just tell me where the key is," Norman said.

"I don't happen to have the key on me," Malcolm replied. "But give this bar a good tug and I bet it'll come loose."

Norman grasped the bar tightly and yanked on it. It came away suddenly with a light snap at the bottom where Malcolm had bitten tidily around the edge.

"Nicely done, Norman Strong Arm. I'll knight you for that," Malcolm declared as he leapt free. "But for the Maker's sake could you fetch me my clothes? I'm as naked as a kit in the nest here." He pointed to the corner of the tent, where a small nylon gym bag lay. The words "Vito's Gym, Brooklyn" were written in white along its side.

Unzipping it, Norman found a hooded sweatshirt and some gym shoes. Reaching in deeper he uncovered a pile of loose cards and a metal dog tag at the bottom of the bag. The dog tag said

"Bernie Wentz," but the credit cards and ID cards were all in other names. There was a shiny gold card with a hologram for somebody called Martin Philips, a hospital ID belonging to Dr. Newhouse, a driver's licence for Chen Xiu. None of the pictures looked anything like the man he'd fought with the other night. *Stolen*, Norman thought to himself.

"Hurry up, man," Malcolm urged. "I'm a king now. I can't walk out of here like this."

Norman moved a pair of gym socks out of his way and uncovered Malcolm's fine hunting hose and jerkin. He tossed them to the ever-cheerful stoat.

"Ta very much," Malcolm thanked him, smiling as he jumped spryly into his clothes. "There ought to be a sword in there, too, and my best hunting bow."

Norman rooted around and discovered the scabbard, bow and quiver of arrows. Grasping the weapons in one hand, he beckoned his old friend onto his shoulder with the other. "Anything else you'd like, Your Highness? Shall I fetch your pipe and summon your minstrels?" he asked. He couldn't have described his relief to see Malcolm well and in his usual cheerful humour.

The stoat leapt nimbly from the top of the cage to that familiar spot beside his giant friend's ear. Boy and stoat ducked and turned towards the front of the tent, ready to make good their escape.

Framed in the triangle of light made by the open flap was a human figure. Norman blinked into the sudden rush of sunlight. It was Pippa. She stood there, silent, frozen in a look of utter amazement, her mouth actually gaping open as she stared at the tiny figure of Malcolm on Norman's shoulder.

"It's lovely," Pippa gushed, repeating it for the umpteenth time since they'd returned to Kelmsworth Lodge with the rescued Malcolm. The King of the Stoats himself was preoccupied with the tin of biscuits that had been laid out for him.

"Does it work on steam?" Gordon asked, with the serious frown of a schoolboy trying to solve a riddle.

"Of course I don't work on steam," Malcolm scoffed, spitting out shortbread crumbs as he did so. "Do you?"

Gordon blinked but had no reply.

"Can I talk to it?" Pippa asked, her voice still awash with wonder. "Will it talk to me?"

Gordon continued to try to fathom the mystery of how the little animal was made to move and speak. "It'll be magnets, then. Has it got magnets in it?"

Malcolm took a bite of another biscuit, not dignifying Gordon's question with an answer. "These Jaffa Cakes," he said, cheeks full of the stuff, "are fantastic, almost as good as my baker's lingonberry pies."

"Can I hold him, do you think?" Pippa pressed her hands together as she asked.

Between the Cooks' questions and Malcolm's enthusiastic appreciation for English biscuitry, it was impossible to have any serious discussion of what had happened and why Malcolm was here. Only George was silent. He sat frowning on the couch some distance off, sipping tea methodically and looking uncomfortable.

George regarded Malcolm warily out of the corner of his eye. Each time the little animal spoke, the young master of Kelmsworth cringed ever so slightly. Gordon might be fascinated with Malcolm and Pippa besotted, but George was distrustful. *Deep down he knows,* Norman thought. *He knows that this is his story, and that a talking stoat spoils it.*

Norman had hoped to keep Malcolm's powers of speech secret. His plan had been to rescue Malcolm and disappear out of this story as quickly as possible. Pippa's entry into the tent had made that impossible. He'd had no time to explain, and there was no stopping the stoat king from talking now.

Norman did his best to make up a story that wasn't too out of place in the world of the Intrepids. "He's not mechanical. He doesn't have magnets or clockwork inside. He's a real animal." Norman caught the stoat's eye with a look he hoped conveyed the idea that he should play along. "He came with me from America. I found him in the forest when he was very young. He'd fallen out of his nest and needed to be taken care of. The Native Americans have lots of stories about talking animals. I wouldn't have believed it if I hadn't seen it myself." Norman spoke very quickly, lest Malcolm intervene and contradict him, but the stoat king just kept chewing his biscuits.

"He must be worth a mint." Gordon whistled appreciatively.

Norman snapped round to glare at the red-headed boy. "Except he's not for sale," he scolded. "He's like a person. You can't sell a person."

George interrupted Gordon's mumbled apology. "No, but our poacher would," he intoned, rising from the couch. "Now I see why he went to Dodgeworth. If you were planning to sell a talking weasel, that's definitely where you'd go."

Malcolm, who was raising a jam-filled biscuit to his mouth at this time, paused to correct him. "While my family is related to the broader race of weasels, we prefer the term 'stoat.'" He sounded very regal as he did so.

George, who was nothing if not polite, apologized and made a little mental note to himself.

Gordon carried on blithely. "You really ought to have let Dodgeworth buy you, you know. He would have looked after you."

Malcolm sniffed. "I'd already made the mistake of trusting one human. Your Dodgeworth didn't look any different. I saw all those creatures in your Dodgeworth's prison."

Pippa broke the awkward silence with a little common sense:. "We ought to report this to the constabulary as soon as possible."

"No!" Norman blurted, more hastily than he'd wanted to. "We can't do that. If news gets out about Malcolm everyone will want to see him. It'll be a circus," he protested. "We have to keep it secret."

George stroked his chin pensively. "Yes, I suppose that's true. Every sideshow and travelling circus in England would be after him."

"Will you take him back to America, then?" Pippa asked, a little hopelessly.

"As soon as I can," Norman replied.

"Well, as much as it saddens me to say it," George said, "I think you ought to do so as quickly as possible. You've seen what that ruffian poacher can do. I don't think we can protect you here."

"What about that castle I saw on the way here?" Malcolm asked, brushing biscuit crumbs from his whiskers. "It looked as sturdy as any in the highlands. I daresay we could defend that keep for months with the five of us alone. Can anyone else here shoot a bow?"

Pippa brightened. "I'm actually quite good. I took the girls' archery ribbon at St. Edward's games day."

Norman shot Malcolm a recriminating look.

"We're probably safe enough in the lodge during the day. The poacher wouldn't dare show his face here in the daylight. Nelson's out there to give the alarm." Unsettled by the talking stoat, the dog had been banished outdoors. "But perhaps we should spend our nights in the Rook." The prospect of a medieval siege appealed momentarily to George Kelmsworth.

"I don't think we need to," Norman protested. "At least, not yet. I'll take Malcolm home with me tomorrow."

Everyone but Norman seemed disappointed that they weren't going to take up arms and defend Malcolm from the battlements of the Kelmsworth Folly.

That evening the Cooks returned reluctantly to the main house. Both would have loved to stay and fawn over Malcolm, and the stoat king would have been happy to soak it all up. But Norman was relieved to see them go. Once Malcolm got talking, there would have been no stopping him. It wouldn't have been long before he let slip that he was the King of the Stoats, or regaled them with stories of Norman and his escapes from the wolves of Undergrowth. No, the less contact Malcolm had with the Intrepids the better. Their book was already changed irrevocably by the introduction of a vicious American criminal and a talking stoat. It didn't need to know about a whole medieval kingdom of woodland creatures.

When George had retired to his room for the night, Norman and Malcolm were finally able to talk properly. Norman made his bed on the couch, pulling the blankets up around him. Malcolm curled up comfortably on the pillow beside him.

Norman turned his head and regarded the little stoat. It was hard to think of him as the king of anywhere. To Norman, he was still just his friend, the person he'd shared his most exciting adventure with, and the friend he'd so missed for nearly a year now. He could no longer contain his curiosity.

"What happened? How did you get here?" he asked across the pillow.

Malcolm propped himself up on his elbow. "I came looking for you."

"For me? How? Why?" Norman asked.

"I need that map my father gave you," Malcolm said, more urgently. "Do you have it with you?"

Norman recalled the ancient map that Malcolm's father, Duncan, had given him after the Battle of Scalded Rock. It was supposed to have helped him get to safety and to find Lochwarren, but it had never been much use.

"I don't have it. It's not here. I don't live here."

Malcolm didn't notice the quiver of doubt in Norman's voice. The answer was simple to him. "Well, let's go to your house tomorrow, then."

Norman didn't know how to explain that it wasn't just not *here* in George's cottage. It wasn't *here* in this book. It wasn't even *there* back in real life. He'd lost it months before they'd come to England. He would have to deal with that later. First he needed to determine exactly what his old friend understood. Did Malcolm even know he was in another book?

"How did you get here?" he asked, keeping the "here" deliberately ambiguous.

Malcolm propped himself up further, anxious to tell the story. "The Abbot of Tintern helped me."

"Fuchs?" Norman whispered the question.

Malcolm cocked his head, perplexed at the reaction. "You remember the abbot. He presided over my investiture at St. Sleekyn. He is teaching me about the bookweird."

Norman's thoughts rushed off in a dozen different directions.

Why would Fuchs teach Malcolm about the bookweird? Why would you even mention the word to a character in a book? More practically, though, why hadn't he said anything when they'd met in London? What game was he playing here?

All he said was "So the abbot knows you're here?"

"Yes," Malcolm repeated. "He brought me here."

"He brought you exactly here?" Norman asked cryptically.

Malcolm's little stoat brow furrowed as if trying to discern what was meant by "exactly here." "Well, to the woods near this house. The abbot said you'd be near. I asked the first person I met . . . turned out to be that treacherous villain with the neckerchief."

Norman tried to put it all together. Why hadn't Fuchs brought Malcolm directly to the real world? Why had he brought him to the Intrepid book? Could characters in books not come into reality? Maybe Fuchs had arranged this meeting here. Maybe it was Fuchs who had brought Norman. It was just like Fuchs to make a complicated plan and not tell him.

"You said that the Abbot of Tintern was teaching you about the bookweird. What did he tell you?"

"Well, I don't pretend to understand it. I'm no adept, like you. I don't have a whole *ingresso* named after me," Malcolm teased. "But he told me St. Augustine's basic concept: 'The World is a book, and those who do not travel read only a page.'"

Norman nodded slowly, as if this were common knowledge. He didn't want to admit that he knew less about the bookweird than it appeared. "So what *ingresso* did you use?"

"The scriptorium *ingresso*, of course," Malcolm replied matter-of-factly. "I'm only a beginner, so I've stuck to the rudiments. My paw was aching before I'd even copied the passage out a dozen times."

Norman had seen the scriptorium at St. Sleekyn in Undergrowth; it was a large, open room filled with lecterns where animal monks copied out books by hand. The scriptorium *ingresso* must have involved copying out the book over and over.

"And the Abbot of Tintern gave you *this* story to copy?" Norman asked, careful not to name it.

"Just the one page. It described the woods around George's palace here. Abbot said it would be easier if it was something I knew and could imagine for myself. He said there were things here I could not even imagine, and I'd never be able to ingress into a place I couldn't imagine. I've seen a few of these marvels already. Your city called London, those roaring wagons, double-decker . . ." He seemed about to drift off into some reverie of awe, but pulled himself back to practicalities. "Is your house far from here? I can't wait to meet your parents, and Dora. Is she as magnificent as the giantess Pippa?"

Norman gave his head a shake, not so much to disagree as to shake off an irrelevant comment. Not even a stoat could consider his sister magnificent. She was, in fact, the most annoying human in the world. "But, Malcolm, I don't live here in this book. I come from somewhere else. I come from the real world."

Malcolm chuckled. "'The real world.' I still can't get my head around that joke."

Norman blinked and jutted his head forward, waiting for Malcolm to explain.

"Until I arrived here I thought my world was the only real world. Now I can see that it is just one book in the Maker's universal library. I'm glad to see that even an adept like you still calls his home book 'the real world.'"

"No, I . . ." Norman started to explain that while all the other worlds were books, his was real. But it seemed unfair and a little cruel.

Malcolm lay back on the pillow and yawned. "When can we go?" he asked sleepily. "Will you show me your *ingresso*?"

Norman was grappling with this idea of a universal library where every world was a book—a library in which *his* world was a book, and he himself and his family were only fictional characters. It made him dizzy and a little sick to his stomach.

"We'll go in the morning," he concluded after a long pause. It was the safest thing to do. He needed to get Malcolm away from the poacher as quickly as possible. "Wait here," he told him. He tossed the covers back from the bed and fetched his shoes from the mat beside the door. He slid them on and pulled the folded sheet of paper from the pocket of his jeans.

"Your book?" Malcolm asked, his eyes widening in anticipation.

"Part of it," Norman replied, looking at the page he had written two nights before. He wasn't at all sure whether this would work. There was a lot he didn't understand about the bookweird. The bookweird was a tricky subject. After the first *ingresso*, it had become very unpredictable, and he'd begun to fall into books he'd never even tasted. A sort of corruption had overtaken all the books in Norman's house and he'd had an *ingresso* into all of them. The corruption had stopped only when he'd "fixed" Malcolm's book, *The Brothers of Lochwarren*.

Norman had been able to escape one book by eating another. Fuchs had once rescued him from *The Magpie* by giving him a typed page that described the very scene they were participating in, right down to Norman's own thoughts. Norman had tried this current trick once before, writing his own story. It had worked to get him out of *Fortune's Foal,* but nothing in the bookweird was predictable. He was by no means sure that it would work again.

Norman looked at his own ragged handwriting on the paper in front of him. He considered the proportions for a moment before ripping the page along two of its folds and handing Malcolm about an eighth of the page.

"Do you think you can handle that?" he asked the stoat.

"Depends what you want me to do with it—burn it or make a paper hat out of it?" Malcolm replied. He stood up on the pillow and took the piece of paper in his little paw.

"I want you to eat it," Norman told him.

Malcolm held the page up in front of his face. "My old mum once told me that if I didn't want an upset stomach, I shouldn't eat anything bigger than my head." The paper was in fact several times bigger than a stoat's head.

Norman frowned, took the paper back and ripped a corner off it.

"This better?" he asked.

Malcolm took it skeptically.

"You'll probably still have an upset stomach," Norman warned as he took a bite of his own.

Malcolm took an experimental nibble and read the fragments of sentence left on the page as he chewed.

"'. . . bottom shelf of the library had a row of red encyclopaedias with embossed gold spines . . . big brown leather armchair with a missing button . . . Dad's new coffee maker . . .' It all sounds very exotic."

Norman couldn't tell if he was serious. "Just finish it," he told him.

It was taking longer than either of them expected, but neither of them minded the wait. They might be exhausted, but they had waited months to talk to each other. They lay on the couch and caught up. Norman told him about how he was living in England for the summer. How he had given up the bookweird and had almost stopped believing in it. Malcolm told him about his first year of kingship. How it wasn't as exciting as he'd thought, how it was mostly about settling disputes and fixing roads. That was how Malcolm finally explained why he wanted Norman's Undergrowth map.

"Guillaume Long Tail turned up at Lochwarren last winter with a few knights and even more lawyers. He has something called the Skerry Parchment. He says it proves his right to the throne."

"But that's absurd! Your father's will . . . the chronicle of the Mustelids . . . the gifts in the chapel. I was there. I heard it read out," Norman protested. "Everyone agrees that you should be king, even Cuilean."

"Uncle Cuilean has been with me the whole time, but even he can't refute the Skerry Parchment, and he's a stickler for the law. Guillaume is a long-tailed weasel. They are our cousins from the south. We never heard anything from them during the long wars with the wolves. We always thought that they were fighting their own wars. It seems they just didn't care. The Skerry Parchment was written during the time of the Great Mustelid Empire. It gave the mountains to the stoats and the far plains to the long-tailed weasels, but it also says that if any king, stoat or long-tail, abdicated his throne, the other could claim it."

"So?" said Norman, not following the argument.

"Guillaume Long Tail says that we abdicated."

"Your grandfather didn't abdicate," Norman scoffed. "He was killed at Tista Kirk."

"And Uncle Cuilean and my father ran away." Malcolm repeated the arguments of the weasels with contempt. The stoat idolized his father.

"Escaped," Norman corrected. "They came back, didn't they? You conquered all their lands back."

"The weasel lawyers claim that when my father left, he gave up the throne."

"Stupid lawyers." Norman was thinking of Fuchs—as Todd. "So how does the map help?"

"The map my dad gave you is actually our treaty map. It was signed by all the Mustelid kings almost a century ago. The stoats saved the empire. We saved the long-tails' hides at St. Sauveur and we broke the Siege of Pulawy when the Ermine Kingdom was about to fall to the Corsac foxes. As a reward, the other kings recognized the Stoat Kingdom in perpetuity. No other weasel, ermine or any other Mustelid king could dispute it."

"Oh," Norman said. He heard his own loud chewing. "I didn't realize the map was so valuable."

"Dad wouldn't have ever thought that he'd need it," the stoat said.

This was typical of Malcolm's father, Duncan—brave and generous, but careless of the consequences.

"Still, he took a risk when he gave it to me."

"The old battler probably never gave it a second thought." The little creature choked up a little as he recalled his father. That was the real reason he was here: out of duty to his father, to keep the kingdom his father had died to regain.

The boy and the stoat finished their meal of fine English notepaper in silence.

"What do we do now?" asked Malcolm, lying back on the pillow and rubbing his furry belly.

"We sleep," Norman replied.

"Excellent." Malcolm sighed through a yawn. "I've a talent for that."

But neither boy nor stoat was able to sleep right away. Norman could not help worrying about the map. He really had no idea where it was. It might have been thrown in the garbage months ago. He would have to deal with that when he got back . . . if he got back. He was far from sure that this would work at all. According to Fuchs, Norman was the only one ever to sneak himself into a book by eating it. People must eat pieces of paper all the time. There had to be something more to it.

"Malcolm," he murmured drowsily, a thought occurring to him as he finally began to give in to sleep, "how did you learn that the map was a treaty map? Whose idea was it to come and get it?"

Malcolm replied wearily, "The abbot's, of course."

Norman was confused. "Why did the abbot help you? What does he want?" Fuchs didn't seem to care much what happened in books.

But Malcolm didn't answer. The only sign that the stoat had heard him was a long "*Hmmmmm*," indistinguishable from a snore.

Home Away from Home

The wet grass and the chill of the early-morning air finally became too much to sleep through. He had dreamed of home—his *real* home, his own bedroom and bed. In his dream he'd fallen asleep reading, and he was eager to wake up and pick up where he'd left off. It had been a book about a boy in a library, a giant library where the boy worked as a sort of librarian and guardian of books.

Norman struggled not only to wake himself, but to wake himself in the bedroom of that dream. The sound of the sparrows and the scratch of the grass on his cheeks wasn't helping. He woke up on the lawn. He sat up and rubbed the sleep and dew from his eyes.

A few blinks assured him where he was. Here was the arched back door of the English house. Here was the clothesline that they used here instead of a dryer—a pair of his jeans hung next to Dora's new riding pants. Usually the bookweird dropped him off where he'd last been—that should have been his bedroom—but once you've fallen into a book, very little is really "usual." The description he'd written and eaten back at George's described both the outside of the house and the inside. Perhaps it depended on the part of the page you ate. It was then he realized that he was alone, and that he shouldn't be alone.

"Malcolm," he called out in an urgent whisper. There was no response. "Malcolm, are you here?" he called out again.

The only sound was a quarrel of sparrows darting in and out of the wall of ivy under the eaves. There was movement now, too, in the house. Flowered curtains were moving in an upstairs window. Norman leapt to his feet and dashed across the lawn to the back door. Would it be locked? His mother was always nagging him to lock it when he came in. He jiggled the handle and put his faith in his own forgetfulness.

"What were you doing outside?" Dora asked as he ducked through the doorway. She was sitting at the kitchen table, dressed to go riding, a cereal spoon suspended between bowl and mouth.

"Feeding the wild ponies," he replied curtly, heading directly to the stairs.

Dora would know he was teasing—there couldn't really be wild ponies in the backyard—but she'd have to check. She'd never forgive herself if she missed them. She opened the door and stared out at the empty back garden. By the time she had thought of something to annoy him back, Norman had dashed up the stairs.

He was far too intent on getting to his bedroom. If Malcolm wasn't in the yard, surely he'd be there. Norman closed the door behind him and whispered again, "Malcolm, are you here? Come out. It's not funny." He opened the wardrobe and rummaged through the pile of clothing he'd left there—it was exactly the sort of place that a stoat would like to sleep but he was nowhere to be found.

Norman was about to close the wardrobe when he caught his reflection in the mirrored door. He was still wearing the sweater that George had given him. It wouldn't do to be caught wearing that. He hastily pulled it off over his head and stuffed it in the wardrobe before resuming his search.

It was the same in the drawing room and the dining room—no Malcolm. The library was his last, best hope. It was the room he'd described best. Its walls of books and corners stuffed with exotic bric-a-brac had stuck in his mind. He'd described it completely, from the square-panelled ceiling and the ladder that slid across the shelves to the uneven parquet floor protected by a worn red Persian carpet. It just made sense that Malcolm would be here. Norman could imagine the stoat gazing up wide-eyed at the walls of books. It would seem magnificent to him. There were more books here than in all the Kingdom of the Stoats. Norman could imagine him scrambling up the ladder to gaze at it all, or burrowing in the lower shelves, perhaps opening the crazy old encyclopaedia or the other Intrepids books.

He could imagine these things, but he couldn't make them true. There was a silence so empty when he opened the door to the library that he didn't even bother calling out Malcolm's name. Norman had to face reality. Malcolm had not made it through the *ingresso*.

Where would he be now? Could the bookweird have sent him back to Undergrowth, or was he still at Kelmsworth with the Intrepids? Only the book would tell.

It should have been on the bedside table where he'd left it. If not there, then beside the bed, or under it. Norman's skinny arms swept the dust bunnies under the bed—socks, old bits of paper, but no *Intrepid Amongst the Gypsies*. He had been here before. This had happened last time the bookweird had started acting up. There were other places to look, other people to ask, but deep down Norman knew the book was gone. He didn't know where it was gone. Who knew where books went when you messed them up with the bookweird? Some damaged book section of that crazy universal library Malcolm dreamed of? Norman just knew it was gone.

Over breakfast, Norman pondered his options as he spooned cereal mechanically into his mouth. He could try to get back to Kelmsworth through one of the other Intrepids books. If he went into a book later in the series, Malcolm might still be there. He could bring a copy of *The Brothers of Lochwarren* to Kelmsworth and the stoat could get back into his own world using that. But it might be too late. The criminal from *The Magpie* could have recaptured Malcolm by then, or worse. It would be better to arrive earlier.

Maybe he could get there before Malcolm was even captured. He had never tried that. He had never thought of going further back into the story.

"Norman, are you listening?" He realized that his mother had been talking to him.

"Yes," he replied reflexively. "I mean, no. I wasn't listening."

She was standing there in running gear sipping from a small bottle of water.

"I'm going in to Summerside again today after my run. Do you want to come with me?"

Norman mumbled, "No, thanks," distractedly.

"I know that look," his mother said with a smile. "Lost in a book."

Norman stared back at her, not sure if he had heard her properly.

"How are you liking it?" she continued. "How do the Intrepids stack up against your usual wizard-and-warrior fare?"

"It's okay," Norman replied noncommittally.

"It's *Intrepid Amongst the Gypsies* you are reading, right? That's the one where they finally find out that George's father has been framed—with the raid on the lawyer's office, isn't it? Or is it the one where they are camping and rescue the pit pony?"

"It's the one with the lawyer's office," Norman replied, suddenly interested. In his mother's version of the book the raid had worked. "With the mice," he continued, hoping his mother would tell him some more about the original raid. Why had it worked before? What had he done to wreck it?

His mother nearly spat out her mouthful of water, and her face was wrinkled with laughter. "It's silly when you think about it— grown men running away from something so harmless. I guess that's the beauty of books, making the unbelievable believable. They've built up Montague through the whole series as such a jittery, ineffective old bureaucrat, so you can completely believe that he'd run screaming from a box of mice."

"Montague?" Norman asked, confused.

"Yes, Montague. Wasn't that his name? The first lawyer, before he's replaced with Michaelmas, the one who finally exonerates Lord Kelmsworth. Funny how you remember these things."

"It's not Todd?" Norman asked, his voice squeaking a bit.

"Who?"

"The lawyer," Norman repeated nervously. "Are you sure his name's not Todd?"

"I don't think so. I don't know why I remember it. It's amazing, really. It's been twenty years, but I'm sure it's Montague. Tiny, wizened old man, face full of white whiskers. Here, hand over the book. I'll find it for you."

Norman opened his arms to show his empty hands and the empty counter beneath them. "It's upstairs in my room."

"Run up and bring it down while I stretch," she told him.

Norman looked down at his empty cereal bowl, hoping to find an excuse there. His mother was now pushing on the counter, stretching out her calf muscle.

"Go on," she whispered across the countertop. "Go fetch it." It was a whisper, but even a whisper from Meg Jespers-Vilnius could be commanding.

Norman made another half-hearted search of his room. He knew it wasn't on the bedside table. The drawer was stuffed with old knick-knacks, postage stamps, cloth crests, postcards, tiny screws and springs, but no book. The window ledge and dresser top were likewise cluttered but bookless. Nor was it under the pillow, or buried in his unmade bedcovers.

He was sitting on the edge of his bed, his head in his hands, when his mother finally called up, "Never mind. I'll look at it later." The back door slammed shut.

Norman kept his head in his hands. He didn't need his mom to show him. He knew she was right. He knew in his gut that the book was screwed up. That stunt in the lawyer's office was supposed to work. It had been written on George Kelmsworth's face, in the shock and utter disbelief that it had failed. George Kelmsworth's schemes weren't allowed to fail. But how could it be Norman's fault? Norman hadn't changed anything in the scene. The only thing that had changed was the lawyer. It wasn't this Montague character that his mother remembered. How had she described him? A nervous old paper-pusher with white whiskers? That wasn't Fuchs, or Todd, or whatever he was calling himself in this book. It was Fuchs who had screwed up the book this time. For once, it wasn't Norman's fault.

"You've lost it."

Norman looked up, surprised, to see his father peering in through the half-open door. "You've lost it, haven't you?" Edward Vilnius repeated.

Norman's silence was answer enough.

Edward rubbed his forehead, his lips curled in a grimacing smile. "I don't know how you do it. For a kid who loves books so much, you sure lose a lot of them."

"Uh-huh," Norman agreed sulkily. There was no use explaining that it wasn't his fault, that there were powerful forces working against him.

"I'll talk to your mother," his father said finally. Something in his voice said that he sympathized. Edward Vilnius had lost a few books in his time. "In the meantime, find that book. It's not just a book to your mother. You saw that. It means a lot to her."

He closed the door behind him.

All-New Intrepids!

"This is terrible," his mother declared, looking up from the counter where she was reading. "How could they have let this happen?"

Norman expected her to recount some disaster or scandal from the newspaper—a human rights violation in Burma or a new famine in Eritrea. The only reason Norman knew that Burma and Eritrea existed was because of his mother. If not for her editorializing, those places would have been as fantastical to him as Penwyr and the Ambrosian Republic. His friends back at school gave him funny looks when these little bits of knowledge slipped out, and he sometimes wished that his mom would let him share their ignorance.

Meg Jespers-Vilnius cast around to see if anyone felt her outrage. Neither Norman nor his father had said anything, but both watched her expectantly.

"They've completely changed it," she complained. She held up the book she was reading—not a newspaper at all, but a glossy paperback. Norman's eyes lit up as he read the title: *Intrepid Amongst the Gypsies*.

"You found a new copy!" he exclaimed with a gulp.

"Yes," she replied, her voice taking on that dry, dramatic tone that wasn't supposed to be lecturing but was. "Until you figure out where you put the original. I'm still very disappointed that you lost it."

Norman ducked his head contritely.

"I wanted you to be able to finish the story. It's one of my favourites from my own childhood, and I wanted to share that with you. Unfortunately …" Here she paused and sucked air through her teeth. "Unfortunately, the good people at."—she turned the book around to read the publisher's name from the spine—"the good people at Willow Publishing have different ideas."

She pushed the paperback across the kitchen counter to Norman. He immediately saw what was wrong. He didn't need to read a word. The cover told him everything.

"They've changed it completely," Meg repeated. "There are additional characters. The plot is completely different. There aren't even any Gypsies in it anymore. How stupid is that?"

The cover held all of Norman's attention. The new edition had a glossy illustration of the Intrepids standing shoulder to shoulder, with the Cook children either side of George Kelmsworth, who stood just a little farther forward. George was the same but different, his dark brown hair a little longer and shaggier than when Norman had met him. He posed like a rock star in front of the Rook, glaring out from the picture, his arms crossed defiantly across his chest. Gordon, beside him, was wearing his school uniform and wielding a cricket bat menacingly. They'd made Pippa look prettier. She gazed affectionately towards George. It was impossible to tell whether her eyes rested on George or the furry creature on his shoulder.

Meg was still waiting for someone to share her outrage. "Are they allowed to do this?"

Edward, sitting at the kitchen table with a stack of papers, shrugged, bemused. "To do what?" he asked, apparently enjoying her agitation. Meg Jespers-Vilnius's constant calm and cheerfulness could get irritating.

"To change the book like this." Her voice rose as she flourished the paperback. "To reissue the book fifty years later with so many changes."

Norman's throat was dry. He couldn't take his eyes off the cover. "Maybe they're making a movie," he croaked. "Sometimes they change the book when they make a movie." He halted to gulp some moisture into his constricted throat. "You know, to match the movie." He looked nervously from his mother to his father, hoping someone would agree that this must be exactly what was going on.

"It's called a tie-in," his mother explained, "and the movie studio's name would be all over it—'Now a major motion picture starring' blah, blah, blah."

"Do you notice that they never advertise *minor* motion pictures?" Edward asked playfully. One sour glance from Meg was enough for him to straighten his face.

"It still wouldn't justify changing the book like this. There's a talking weasel in it now, with a very poor Scottish accent. How do they get away with it, Edward? Shouldn't copyright law stop them?"

Norman realized he had never seen his mother quite so upset. Why should she care? To her it was only a book.

"Copyright law protects the copyright owner, not the reader," Edward replied. He was using his professor's voice now. "Whoever owns the copyright can do what they like. They can send your Intrepids to space. They could enlist in the CIA. They could have magical powers." He spouted a few more ideas, amused by his own suggestions, but it wasn't helping. He wasn't used to being the reasonable parent. It was usually Meg who had to talk him out of some outrage or manic funk, not the other way around.

Meg tapped her fingers on the counter forcefully. "On principle, though, this seems wrong," she declared. "There's a bond between readers and the story. This breaks the bond. It's like a contract has been broken."

It was not how Norman would have said it, but he felt it too. It wasn't right. It was wrong to change someone's whole life by changing his story.

"You know, this idea of textual purity is a relatively new one," Edward continued, in full lecture mode now. Both Meg and Norman regarded him suspiciously, but he could not stop. "This idea that

there is only one version of the story, and that it is the property of
the author, doesn't occur until books start to be published in large
quantities. Before that, stories were a sort of a shared inheritance.
They changed and evolved with the generations. King Arthur starts
as a minor historical chieftain. He's fictionalized in some Breton
troubadour songs, then somehow gets tangled up with the Grail
legend. Mark Twain sends a Connecticut Yankee back in time to
King Arthur's court. Monty Python has Arthur and his Knights of
the Round Table fetching shrubberies and clapping coconuts to
make the sounds of horses' hoofs."

Norman's mother didn't answer. His father's literary lectures
never helped. In fact, Norman had never seen her look so sad. She
put the book down on the counter and busied herself with the rest
of the contents of the bag. Her lips were folded tight and her eyes
focused elsewhere. Norman and his father didn't need to be told to
drop it.

As casually as he could, Norman pulled the paperback across
the counter towards him and flipped the pages. He expected his
own name to leap out from the book. That would be the culmina-
tion of the disaster.

Edward Vilnius was now helping unpack the shopping, trying
to cajole his wife back to good humour. Norman slipped off to his
room with the new version of *Intrepid Amongst the Gypsies*.

There was no time to read the whole thing again. He skimmed the
first part before dinner. It was much the same. The Intrepids were
troubled by the appearance of the poacher. They tracked him
unsuccessfully from the Rook. There was no mention of Norman.
It was always like that when Norman had been inside a book. His
presence was felt, the changes he'd made remained, but he disappeared or blurred into the background. The fiasco in the lawyer's
office went on as he'd witnessed it. Mr. Todd watched the mice
scatter harmlessly once more. Norman knew that wasn't his fault
now, at least not directly. The plan had failed because Fuchs, now
Todd, had replaced old Montague as the lawyer.

Norman had a funny feeling that Fuchs was in this book because of him. Maybe Fuchs knew about the poacher—Fuchs had entered *Intrepid Amongst the Gypsies* to fix what Norman had broken. Or was it his own mistake he was fixing? Fuchs was hard to figure. He'd helped Norman out before, but he was never obvious about it. He knew a lot more about the bookweird than Norman, and he liked it that way. Norman needed to talk to him.

Norman was exceptionally quiet at dinner. He wanted to apologize to his mom for losing the book, but he had no idea what his father had told her. At least she was back to her usual self now, cheerful and optimistic.

"I wouldn't read that new version if I were you," she advised.

Norman just looked at her.

"Wait until your dad manages to get the original back."

Norman peered quizzically at his father. Edward stared back meaningfully, as if sending a message telepathically, but Norman wasn't receiving it.

"It's not the first time he's done this, you know," Meg continued. "He once mailed his tax return to *The Journal of Fantastical Literature*. We might never have known if I hadn't checked the tax envelopes and found his paper on the tradition of the unicorn in European poetry. So dropping your book off at the university library book return is par for the course."

When Norman glanced again at his father, Edward passed a hand over his chin as if rubbing his goatee, but the fact that his fingers covered his lips conveyed the message that telepathy hadn't.

"Your mother's right. I'd leave the new version alone for now," Edward agreed, changing the topic. "A reinterpretation is all well and good, but you want to know the original first."

"How are you liking the Intrepids, anyway?" Meg asked. "The *real* Intrepids. You never answered me."

"It's okay," Norman replied cautiously. "I hadn't really gotten into it yet."

"You should actually read them in order, the way your uncle and I did. The story about his father being in jail will make more sense."

"Speaking of originality," Edward added, a fork suspended between plate and mouth, "I'm pretty sure that plot about the father being in jail was stolen from *The Railway Children*."

Meg Jespers-Vilnius gave him a warning look, hard but playful. Edward smirked, as if this was exactly the reaction that he wanted.

"Oh, I forgot, I shouldn't say anything against the Intrepids," he told Norman. "George Kelmsworth was your mother's first love, you know."

Meg just rolled her eyes. She was not easily teased. "Jealousy doesn't become you, Edward," she replied. "Besides, how can you compete with a dashing, dark-haired English lord who single-handedly saves his family from ruin?"

Norman's face wrinkled in distaste. He knew what it felt like to admire someone in a book to the point of obsession. But he had *met* George Kelmsworth.

Edward put his palms together in mock contrition. "You're right. I wouldn't even know how to single-handedly save my family from ruin."

Meg smiled. "Well, you and your son can start by washing the dishes."

It was bedtime before Norman got back to the paperback version of *Intrepid Amongst the Gypsies*. Even skimming, it took time to catch up to where he had left the story. George and the Cook children returned to Kelmsworth Hall from London and renewed their pursuit of the poacher. Their well-planned trap in the forest was sprung again, and George was soundly beaten again by a criminal who was way out of his league. It almost made Norman angrier to read it than to experience it.

In the new version it was Pippa who suggested they find the poacher's encampment and free the animals. Norman was sure that had been his idea. He had to skip back to figure out how they knew that the intruder was capturing animals, not just killing them. Sure enough, the scene at Dodgeworth's was different than he remembered. The monkeys were in a frantic state when the Intrepids arrived. Dodgeworth put it down to the previous client, who had come in claiming to have a talking weasel. The children recognized the poacher from his description. Norman's changes to the book remained, even if he was missing.

The raid on the poacher's camp went just as he'd experienced it, except without him. The poacher was away checking his traps, and the Intrepids managed to get in and get out without detection. In this version Malcolm lay silent in the cage while George rescued him. He must have been dying to get out of that cage, but he kept his mouth shut and continued to feign injury.

It wasn't until they were back in the cottage that Malcolm revealed himself. The stoat king waited for George to open the cage and for Pippa Cook to lift him gently out onto a cushion. She might have missed the wink he gave her as she let him down, but she couldn't ignore Malcolm's dramatic return to life. She leapt back in surprise as the stoat rose to two feet on the cushion and waved his arm in a flourish as he bowed.

"I thank you, Lady Pippa," he purred in his most regal tone.

This was about where Norman had left off, and where he had to jump in. If he could get back into the book here, he could limit the damage. His mother's reaction to the revised version of the Intrepids had made Norman even more sensitive to the changes he was making. He was wrecking things for thousands of readers. He had to do whatever he could to restore it. That meant dealing with the poacher. But first it meant getting Malcolm out of there. Guilt gripped him as he thought of the stoat king. He had meant to bring Malcolm with him. If Norman's *ingresso* didn't work for Malcolm, he'd need help . . . Fuchs's help.

Norman dug out George's sweater from the wardrobe, where he had stuffed it. He could always explain losing clothes. He did that all the time. Explaining where extra clothes came from was harder. He pulled the sweater on over his head, laced up his shoes, then took a deep breath. Here he went again, back into the grips of the bookweird. Taking the book deliberately in his hand he tugged the page free of its glued spine. He did it slowly, delaying it, not sure if he was ready, but the page came away in his hand suddenly, coming unglued along with a dozen pages either side of it. Norman cursed. Dad always said they didn't make books like they used to. He stuffed one page under his pillow and did his best to put the other pages back in order.

The door to his room opened, and a voice called out, "Have you brushed your—"

His mother saw him there, sitting on the side of the bed, fully dressed, a handful of pages of his new book in his hand. She stood there silently stunned for a moment. "Norman, what on earth are you doing?"

Norman's mouth opened, but no words came out. His mother stepped into the room. "Did you just rip those pages out of the book?"

He opened his mouth to deny it, but his mother stopped him with a raised finger. He wasn't a very good liar.

"Why would you do that?" Shocked more than outraged, she snatched the pages from his hand. Frown wrinkles crept across her forehead as she read. "It's the first time the weasel talks in the book." She gave him a deep, searching look, her eyes softening. "Is this because of me?" she asked. "Is it because I was upset today?"

Norman shrugged. What could he say? Meg put the pages down on his bedside table and sat down next to him on the bed. "It's just a book, Norman," she consoled him, putting her arm around his shoulder. "It's not your fault." It only made Norman feel even guiltier. It really *was* his fault.

Her hand squeezed his shoulder reassuringly. She started to say something but stopped, feeling the coarse grey wool at his collar between her fingers.

"Where did this sweater come from?" she asked.

"Ummm . . ." Norman stalled. "The closet, I guess."

His mother regarded him closely, one eyebrow raised ever so slightly. She took her arm from around him and picked up the book again. She stared at it for a moment, then stood up. Taking a step back from the bed, her eyes flicked from Norman to the cover.

"It's the same sweater that George is wearing."

Norman stared up at her, but he could think of no reply.

"It's his school sweater, his St. James school sweater," his mother continued, her voice rising and quickening. She leaned in closer and reached around the back of his neck, curling the sweater back to see the label. Norman had no idea what was written on it, but his mother inspected it for a very long time. Norman grew increasingly uncomfortable, sitting there with her looming over him. When she stepped back her face was contracted into a deep frown. He had never seen her look so conflicted. His mother always knew what to do and what to say, but now she stood there in front of him, her arms crossed, her weight on a back foot. Her lips pursed and her face tightened as if to conceal the argument she was conducting with herself.

"Norman," she said finally. Her voice was even and measured, warning him to be careful what he answered. "I'm going to ask you a question and I need you to tell me the truth. It's very important. Can you do that?"

All Norman could do was nod mutely.

"I need to know . . ." She paused now, as if reconsidering her question. "Is that George Kelmsworth's sweater?"

Norman blinked, not sure that she had actually asked this.

"Norman?" she pressed, her voice rising.

He could not believe that she was even asking this. She had just guessed his deepest secret. How could she even imagine it to be possible? He hardly believed it himself. It took too much effort to get his head around it. He had no mental capacity left to concoct a plausible lie. He merely nodded and gulped.

His mother winced, as if physically hurt by this answer.

"Did George give you that sweater?" she pressed. Her blue-grey eyes bore into him like daggers.

"Yes," Norman croaked dryly.

Meg stepped back, uncrossed her arms and covered her mouth with her hand as if suppressing a reaction. Norman was trying to make sense of it all. Why would she ask him about the sweater? Why would anyone even think that a character from a book had given him a sweater?

His mother interrupted his thoughts abruptly. "Norman," she said, a thought just occurring to her, "you had a map. Back home, in your room, I found a map on old parchment—a map of imaginary places."

Norman leapt up. "My map of Undergrowth!" he blurted out.

"This came from the same place?" she asked, her voice a low murmur.

Norman's cautiousness was overcome by his eagerness to get the map. "Not the same place. From Undergrowth. King Duncan gave me that."

"It's all the same place," she assured him. Shaking her head a little sadly, she glanced at the paperback in her hand and sighed.

Norman could hardly believe he was having this conversation. His mom was talking to him as if the bookweird was real, as if she knew that it was possible to slide into a book. And she knew about the map.

"Mom, I need that map back," Norman pleaded. "My friend Malcolm, he needs it back. Do you still have it? Did you keep it?"

His mother didn't answer the question. "Norman, what you are doing is very dangerous. You can't know how dangerous it is."

"But, Mom, it's not dangerous where I go. I have friends. It's safe." Norman was lying, but it didn't feel like lying. Maybe it wasn't completely safe, but if he stayed to the right books . . .

That unusual steeliness returned to Meg's voice. "Norman, I'm telling you," she admonished him, "you don't know how dangerous it is."

Her tone was ominous enough for Norman to wonder what she meant, but he didn't let it stop him.

"Do you have the map?" he entreated, desperate to know.

She stared back at him, as if determined to say as little as possible. "It's somewhere safe."

"Where?" he blurted. "Is it back home? Can we get someone to send it to us?"

"Norman, you can't have that map," she declared very firmly.

"But I need it," Norman implored. "If I don't take it back, people could die."

Meg Jespers-Vilnius was unmoved by his pleas. "People die in books all the time. It's not real life. If something happens to *you* there, that's different."

Norman didn't have to be told. He could still imagine himself in the vice-like grip of the bald-headed poacher.

"Mom," he asked, "how do you know?"

She looked away for a moment but didn't answer his question. "I'm going to ask you to promise something. I don't expect you to understand it yet, but it is for your own safety." She paused to make sure she had his attention. "I want you to promise not to go back there."

"Mom, I have to."

Her eyes stayed fixed on him. She whispered through her gritted teeth, "I want you to promise, Norman."

Norman opened his mouth to argue again, but he knew there was no point. Whatever his mother thought she knew, she wasn't going to change her mind about it.

"Are you sure the map is safe?" he asked resignedly. "Just tell me where it is, please," he begged. "I promise I won't mess with the bookweird anymore. If I knew for sure you'd put it some-where safe . . ."

Meg's eyes darkened and became more grey than blue. Norman was sure that she had started just a little bit when he'd said the word "bookweird."

"The map is safe," she replied in a measured, deliberate tone. She wasn't fooled at all.

"How can I know, though?" Norman persisted.

She smiled a little now, the thin, wily smile that curled her lip. Norman didn't like the look of that smile. It was the smile she smiled when she had an especially terrible lesson to teach him, like the time he had made Dora cry on her eighth birthday and she had made him stick around through the birthday party, serving juice and entertaining Dora's bratty friends.

"You don't need to know."

"But it's not mine," Norman protested. "I promised to look after it."

"Trust me, your purloined map is safely hidden away." She smiled a thin, tired smile. "Now, do you promise, or do I have to take all your books away from you?"

"Purloined?" Norman asked, not sure what the word meant.

"Never mind," she replied quickly. She seemed flustered for a moment. "Trust me, it's safe."

Norman was utterly defeated. He didn't even know what to ask or argue about anymore. "But, Mom, how do you know? Does everybody know about the bookweird?"

Meg seemed to flinch again when he said the word. She stared at him suspiciously for just a second before shaking her head slightly from side to side. "Do you promise?" she pressed, her voice firm and incontrovertible.

Norman's shoulders slumped. He sighed and nodded.

"You promise?" she repeated, tapping the book with her fingers for emphasis.

"I promise," he echoed weakly.

His mother looked down at him for a long moment. She seemed to want to say something, but once more she was, unusually, lost for words.

When Meg spoke again, the anger seemed truly gone from her voice. "It really is for the best, Norman. The game you're playing is very dangerous," she insisted. "Trust me, I know . . ." Her mouth opened, as if she was about to add something more but changed her mind. "We'll leave it at that. Maybe sometime I can explain, but let's leave it at that, shall we?"

It wasn't the sort of question that expected an answer. Norman curled his lower lip inwards and bit down on it hard.

"Just to be on the safe side, I'll take this," Meg declared, waving the paperback as she stepped back through the doorway. "I'll check in on you later."

It was something she never said.

Lying on the bed, Norman felt his mind race. Somehow his mother knew he could get inside books. He'd always thought it was just him.

He'd thought it was a secret, but his mother knew it was possible. She had guessed it. Was it really not that unusual? Maybe everyone could do it. Maybe it was one of those things that everyone knew but never mentioned, something you were supposed to know not to do. There were lots of things like that. Maybe the bookweird was just another bad habit, like putting your elbows on the table or chewing with your mouth open. Or maybe it was a danger all normal kids understood, like getting into a car with a stranger. But surely if this were the case, there would be public service announcements about it, warnings. They didn't mention the bookweird in health class.

It couldn't be that normal. It had to be some weird disorder or mental problem. Maybe that was why no one mentioned it. It was something you were supposed to be embarrassed about, and that's why his mother wanted him to stop. She had said it was dangerous. Maybe you went crazy if you did it too much. He would stop, he told himself. He had promised his mom he would stop. He would give up the bookweird. Just as soon as he had sorted out the mess back at Kelmsworth and in Undergrowth, he was going to give up the bookweird for good—but there was a reason why he was lying in his bed with George's sweater and his running shoes on.

An hour ago, when he was sure that his mother had gone downstairs, Norman had slid the page that he had torn out of *Intrepid Amongst the Gypsies* from underneath his pillow. Methodically he'd folded and torn the page into six even vertical strips. There was now only one left. He brought it to his teeth and began to chew, drawing it in like a long string of licorice. He was actually starting to like the taste of paper pulp.

Maybe that was the first sign that you were addicted to the bookweird and that it was a real problem—just one more thing to worry about. He would be finished with the page soon, but he knew it would be ages before he fell asleep. There were too many thoughts churning in his mind to give himself over to sleep. For starters, how could he explain all this to Malcolm?

The New Master of Kelmsworth

Norman awoke on the couch in George's lodge. He was getting better at this, he thought. He had left from this same couch two nights ago and had been able to land right back here. The first rays of morning light were just seeping in through the wavy glass of the lodge windows. George would be up soon, frying eggs and boiling water for tea.

He stretched and thought how good it was to be back, until he remembered his mother's mysterious warnings. He felt guilty disobeying her, but he had to do this.

George appeared on the stairs in his blue-and-white-striped pyjamas and plaid dressing gown.

"You're back!" he cried, surprised to see his guest lying on the couch.

"I'm back," Norman declared with a smile.

The smile was not returned. "We thought the poacher had got you, or you'd run off."

The accusation stung. "I went back home," Norman replied, "to fetch something for Malcolm." He had no idea what Malcolm had told George about the bookweird and Undergrowth, but he needed George to know that he hadn't just abandoned them.

George's appearance had changed. His hair was longer, more

dishevelled. Norman had never seen George in his dressing gown, either. He usually appeared every morning with a freshly ironed shirt.

"You left Malcolm here," George admonished him. "He wants to know why you left him." George's old, easy confidence was gone. He was angry now, suspicious.

"I tried to take him. It didn't work." Again Norman found it difficult to explain without giving away too much about the book-weird and his *ingresso*. "I came back as soon as I could."

"As soon as you could?" George scowled. "You've been gone a fortnight!"

"Two weeks?" Norman translated for himself. He had been gone only two nights—but of course time passed differently in every book. "I'm sorry, George. I really did try to get back as soon as possible."

George raised a finger and opened his mouth as if to unleash a lecture he had been rehearsing, but a tap at the window interrupted him. Both boys' heads snapped quickly to the kitchen window. Malcolm stood on the sill, leaning jauntily against the pane, as if he had been waiting for them to open it. The sight of the little warrior there made Norman smile. He was decked out in his green hunting gear, a cap pulled low on his head and a quiver bursting with arrows slung across his back.

George glared at Norman for another second, then turned to unlatch the window. Malcolm bounded in and tossed his weapons and cloak aside.

"'Bout time you found your way back!" he grumbled.

"Sorry I left so suddenly. I couldn't take you with me." He hoped Malcolm wouldn't press for an explanation. "I came back as soon as I could."

"S'all right. It's been an adventure here, hasn't it, George?" He winked at the other boy. Norman felt a twinge of jealousy.

George didn't answer. His eyes flicked back and forth between Norman and the stoat, trying to guess the unspoken communication between them.

"Our friend stayed away last night," Malcolm reported, turning to George. "I tracked him out to one of the local farms, where he swiped some eggs and some clothes off a clothesline. Then he spent an hour at the pub in Kestleton."

"That's the first time he's done that," George mused. "Could you tell what he was doing there?"

"I dunno. Not getting drunk, at least. He nursed one small beer all night—small by your standards, at any rate. He met with some local types. Not farmers or townsfolk—ruffians like himself, if I'm any judge. I hid outside on the window ledge. I couldn't hear a word they said, but our man gave them some money and they shook hands, so they did some sort of deal."

George rubbed his chin. "You were right. He is planning something. What could he have been buying at the Book and Badger? Nothing legitimate, I'll say." He was silent for a long time as he considered this. "You'll be famished," he concluded finally. "Will it be bread and jam again this morning?"

Malcolm rubbed the white fur of his belly in anticipation. "And some of that tea," he replied. "It's colder than a Lochwarren winter out there at night."

While George boiled water and buttered toast, Norman beckoned his friend aside. The stoat bounded from windowsill to counter to Norman's shoulder and let himself be carried into the living room.

"Did you get the map?" Malcolm asked eagerly.

"My mother has it," Norman told him ruefully. "She's hidden it."

"That's great," the stoat king declared. "Ask her for it back, then."

What could Norman say to that?

Malcolm leapt from Norman's shoulder to a side table so he could look his friend in the eye. "She's your mother, isn't she? Why would she keep it from you?"

"It's complicated. She knows about the bookweird. She thinks it's dangerous and she doesn't want me to use it."

Malcolm remembered his own protective mother. "When I was a kit, Mum banned me from the tall ships at Rivernest when she found I'd been climbing the masts," he murmured.

"So you understand."

"But if I came with you," Malcolm insisted, tugging at Norman's sleeve, "if I explained, wouldn't that help?"

Norman had a vision of his mother arguing with the King of the Stoats. Malcolm might be royalty, but Norman had never seen his mother lose an argument to anyone.

"We need Fuchs's help," he said finally.

Malcolm cocked his head to one side, puzzled.

"Fuchs," Norman repeated, wondering why this was so confusing. "That's right ... you know him as the Abbot of Tintern. I know him as Fuchs."

"But that would mean going back to Lochwarren," replied Malcolm. "I'm not sure it's safe for me to do that without the map Besides, the abbot comes and goes."

"Didn't I tell you?" Norman interrupted. "He's here. I met him here, in London. He's George's lawyer, Mr. Todd."

The stoat cocked his head to one side as if he hadn't understood.

George interrupted them before Norman could continue. "That scoundrel!" he declared vehemently. George stood at the doorway to the living room, a breakfast tray in his hands.

Norman cast a quick, interrogative glance at his friend the stoat. "Who?" he asked quietly, unsure what George had heard and who he was accusing.

"Mr. Todd." Malcolm spat out the name like unpleasant food.

"What do you mean?" Norman asked.

"My trusted lawyer, the not very honourable Mr. Todd, has taken over administration of the estate," George explained. "He now lives in my house, occupying my father's rooms, using my father's study and spending my inheritance."

"What?" Norman repeated, utterly confused.

The knock at the lodge door interrupted his question. It was an elaborate musical knock that could only have been a secret Intrepids signal. George opened the door to let the Cooks in. They were dressed in their school blazers and ties, as if going out, and they looked especially glum about it.

George smiled grimly at them as they entered and slowly took their seats around the kitchen table.

"I am now officially a guest of the estate," George continued telling Norman. "I'm permitted to stay at the lodge only as long as it is convenient for the estate. Todd has already mentioned boarding school in Canada for the fall."

Behind him at the kitchen table the Cooks sighed. "Us too, and not even the same schools," Pippa added forlornly. "We're off to Kestleton to buy our books for the term."

Gordon threw his cloth cap on the table to express how he felt about it.

Norman tried to make sense of it all. "Does Todd know you're here?" he asked Malcolm.

The stoat shook his tiny head. "I've kept out of sight. I didn't know that Todd was—"

"I'll go talk to him," Norman interrupted.

"What good will that do?" George demanded bitterly. "If he won't listen to me, he's not likely to listen to you."

He looked to Malcolm for confirmation that Norman's idea was useless. George could not know that Norman and Mr. Todd had a history.

Malcolm shrugged. "Maybe he will tell Norman more than he'll tell you. Norman could trick him somehow."

George scoffed. "Or perhaps Norman will just disappear for a few more days."

Stung, more by Malcolm's silence than by George's rebuke, Norman protested. "I did what I could—" A boiling kettle began to whistle on the hob.

George held his hand up, as if he couldn't listen to this anymore. "Do what you like." He turned his back on them and stomped up the stairs to get dressed.

They watched him walk away, but no one protested. Pippa Cook rose and finally removed the kettle from the stove. They shared the tea in uncomfortable silence. Pippa and Gordon watched Norman reproachfully. Even Malcolm was sullen. They all blamed him, and they had every right to.

The more Norman thought about it, the worse he felt. Todd was breaking up the Intrepids. Could anything more go wrong?

"Did you get Malcolm's map, after all that?" Gordon asked. Norman was surprised that Malcolm had told them, but now he had to go over the story again.

"Did your mum not say anything about where the map might be?" Pippa asked hopefully.

Startled, Norman looked over at her. He hadn't thought she was listening.

"There ought to be a clue. There's always a clue," the red-haired girl continued. In her world there always was one.

Norman shook his head dejectedly.

"What exactly did she say?" Pippa pressed.

"She said," Norman began, imitating his mother's all-knowing tone, "'Your map is safely hidden away.'" It didn't sound right when he said it, so he repeated it: "'Your purloined map is safely hidden away.'"

"She said that? 'Purloined?'" Pippa's attention was piqued.

Gordon scratched his head. "I ought to know that word. It sounds familiar."

"I just thought it meant 'old' or 'parchment' or something." Norman had a habit of guessing what a word meant just by how people used it. He wasn't always right.

"It means 'taken,'" Pippa explained. "'Stolen,' but in a nice way, almost."

"Aye, 'pilfered,' 'nicked,'" Malcolm explained. He was, after all, an educated stoat. "Yer mum's purloined my map, all right."

Gordon seemed to wake up from his own thoughts. "It's from that story!"

They all looked at him.

"'The Purloined Letter'!" Pippa exclaimed. "Of course!"

No wiser for this information, Norman and Malcolm stared at the Cooks.

"It's a story by Edgar Allan Poe. The thief hides the letter in plain sight in his own letter box." Pippa's voice gained certainty as she spoke. "So it makes sense that the map will be in the map box with the other maps."

"That's not hidden at all!" Gordon protested.

"That's why it works," his sister continued. "No one would think to look there."

Norman and Malcolm exchanged a glance.

"I don't think my mom has a map box," Norman told them skeptically.

The Cooks fell silent. It had seemed like a good clue.

"There's a map cupboard in our library." They all turned to look at George. He must have just caught the end of their conversation as he descended the stairs with the dog, Nelson, at his side. Nelson gave Malcolm a wary look. They might have spent two weeks in the same house, but the border collie was obviously still at a loss as to how to treat the talking stoat.

Malcolm smiled firmly at the dog, acknowledging him, and Nelson gave him a reluctant nod of his snout back.

George grabbed a jam sandwich from the counter and beckoned the dog to follow.

"I'm off to Kestleton to ask a few questions at the Book and Badger. If you need a map to get home," he said, regarding Norman coolly, "you can ask Mr. Todd when you have your little talk with him."

Norman strode slowly across the lawn to Kelmsworth Hall wondering what he might possibly say to Fuchs—or Todd, as he supposed he should call him now. Norman tried to put a good spin on it. He wanted to hear that Todd knew what he was doing. Maybe he really was here to keep an eye on things. Maybe, just as he had before, back in the Conran thriller, he'd recognized that Norman was out of his depth. Maybe Todd just didn't understand that he was messing up this book. Norman reassured himself that he'd be able to explain it all.

He passed through the long shadow of the Rook and felt a chill go through him. His pep talk to himself hadn't really worked. He'd never trusted the man, not when he was the fox abbot of Tintern, not when he was the social services man in *The Magpie*, and especially not when he was the substitute librarian back home. Why should he trust him as Todd the lawyer?

He had never told Norman the whole story, had never explained anything. He'd helped him out with a few things—helped him escape that New York police station, helped him fix what he'd broken in Malcolm's world—but if he'd wanted to make things easier for Norman, there was a lot more he could have done.

At the back kitchen door Norman clenched and raised his fist to knock, then paused, his hand hanging in the air, while he composed himself. Perhaps he should go around to the front, he thought, rather than knocking at the back. He had the vague memory that the back door was supposed to be the tradesman's door. The peeling black paint didn't look all that impressive. Real guests would arrive at the front. He didn't even get a chance to lower his hand, though, because the door suddenly opened. Surprised, Norman took an involuntary step backwards.

A tall man dressed in grey trousers and rolled shirtsleeves peered down on him from the open doorway. "Who are you?" he asked. "What do you want?" His forehead wrinkled into deep horizontal frown lines.

"I'm . . . I'm Norman," Norman stammered. He hadn't thought this out. He must have looked like an insignificant schoolboy. If he were to ask to see Todd without a good reason, the servants would just send him away.

The man's face didn't soften as he watched Norman fidget and stammer nervously.

"I'm . . . I'm here to see Mr. Todd."

"And why would he want to see you?" the man asked, his face twisted with disdain.

"I have an important message for him, from London," Norman tried.

The man at the door scoffed, "You're no lawyer's messenger."

"No, it's important," Norman insisted. "He'll want to hear this message."

The man waved him away impatiently. "No doubt it's important to you, but the master has more pressing things to do than receive the neighbourhood children." He began to close the door in Norman's face.

"He'll want to see *me*," Norman insisted, raising his voice.

The servant relented for a moment, leaving the door open just a crack. "Why? What are you to him?"

"I'm . . ." Norman cast about for a plausible lie, something that would make him more than a strange child from the neighbourhood. "I'm his nephew. Mr. Todd is my uncle."

"Your uncle, you say." The man frowned and looked him over again from head to toe. "He didn't say anything about that."

"He's not expecting me, but he'll want to see me. I have a message for him."

The servant paused, perhaps weighing the dangers of annoying his master with a frivolous interruption. After a moment's thought, he appeared to decide that turning away his nephew was probably worse. He opened the door wider and waved Norman into the kitchen brusquely.

"Wait here."

Norman sat at the kitchen table and stared at the blue ceramic plates on the sideboard for what felt like half an hour. The servant looked no happier when he returned. He scowled and gestured for him to get up. Then he guided Norman to the great hall and pointed him to the stairs.

"Master says he'll see you. Second door on the left." He moved aside and watched Norman climb the stairs.

Norman had only read about the inside of Kelmsworth Hall. He wasn't prepared for its grandeur in reality. A broad stone stairway rose from the black-and-white marble of the hall to the upper storeys. Norman put one hand on the ornate banister and strode upwards. His steps echoed through the vast foyer. It made Norman feel small and insignificant. His steps became slower and less confident as he rose past gigantic paintings of historic Kelmsworths on horses, in uniform, posing in elegant costumes. The strong, confident features of George Kelmsworth were echoed in every face, the same dark hair growing to different lengths according to the fashion of the period.

At the top of the stairs, a large darkened area on the wallpaper indicated where a painting had once been. He stopped and pondered it for a while. Was this where George's father's portrait had hung? His anger rushed back into him.

"Come along," Todd's voice called from an open doorway down the corridor.

Norman stomped down the carpet and through the open doorway. He didn't wait to explain himself or even to say hello. "Are you putting your own portrait up at the top of the stairs?" he asked bitterly.

Todd, unperturbed, lifted his head from the papers he had been reading and smiled his annoyingly serene smile.

"I hadn't thought of that," he admitted, scratching his ear languidly with his fountain pen, "but it's an excellent idea. Do you have any suggestions for the composition? Me in armour? Or perhaps with one of those feathery admiral's hats. How about fox hunting? Is that too tacky?"

Norman scowled at him and surveyed the room. It was a library, like the one at the Shrubberies, only about four times as large. His eyes flicked over the dark-panelled cupboard behind Todd's desk, where Pippa had told him the maps were kept.

"I hear that you're my nephew now," Todd teased. "Why not go all the way and say that you're my son?"

"Would you have let me in if I'd told the truth?" He tried to avert his eyes from the cupboard. His map wasn't going to be there, of course—his mother could never have been here—but he didn't want to give this man any clues.

"Of course," the lawyer insisted in a patronizing tone. "I always have time for my poor, lost friend Norman." A smug smile wrinkled the lawyer's face.

"Do you really consider me your friend?" Norman challenged.

"Of course," Todd assured him. He placed his pen down and brought his hands together with theatrical emphasis. "We share a great bond. The bookweird binds us."

"Then give George his house back," Norman demanded. He stepped boldly towards Todd's desk.

Todd raised an eyebrow, genuinely surprised by this request.

"Why would I do that?"

"Because it's not your house," Norman replied, incredulous. He put both hands on the desk and leaned over to make his point. "It's his family's house, and you're wrecking this book."

Todd leaned back in his chair as if avoiding Norman's breath. "Well, you'd know all about that. You're quite the little book-wrecker yourself. How are you doing with the stoat map?" he drawled. "Have you found it? Young Malcolm's little kingdom will be in complete disarray by now."

"Why do you care?" Norman spat back. "Isn't it just another book for you to wreck?"

"I care very much about the little creatures," he replied in his usual mocking tone. "The map is a very important document. How could you have lost it?"

Norman clenched his fists in rage. Todd was getting right up there with Dora in his ability to drive him crazy.

"No, really, Norman," Todd continued to lecture, "you ought to be getting young Malcolm back where he belongs."

"You brought him here," Norman countered. "Why don't you take him back?"

"I honestly would like to." The lawyer's voice was all mock concern. "Things are not going at all well for the stoat faction back at Lochwarren, from what I hear."

Norman knew that Todd was just trying to distract him, but he couldn't help it. "What do you hear? How?"

"Ah, well, one reads things, here and there." He picked up some papers from his desk and began examining them.

"Why did you bring him here anyway? If it's the map he needs, why didn't you just bring him to my house? Why are you making things hard for us?" The questions tumbled out. "Why won't you help us now? Is it because you can't do it?"

Todd bristled for a moment, as if Norman had hit a sore spot, but he composed himself and regarded him earnestly. "I am trying to help. It's this business about the map. There's no use sending him back without the map. Only you can help him with that."

Norman stood, lowering his eyes to the floor. He looked for all the world as though he were studying his toes.

"I don't have the map," he finally admitted in a small, reluctant voice.

Todd stopped pretending to read and put the papers down on the desk. "But you did have the map? Isn't that correct?" He leaned over the desk and grasped Norman's hand insistently. "You had it in Undergrowth."

Norman pulled his hand away and answered, "Yes," sullenly.

"You haven't lost it, have you?" Todd pressed.

"I didn't lose it. It was taken from me."

"Taken, you say? That's quite a plot twist." His eyebrow twitched and he leaned in towards Norman again. "Who is the thief?"

"There's no thief." Norman paused, not sure how much more to say. "My mother took it."

"What?" the lawyer cried, his hand reaching up to his ear in an anxious gesture. "Your *what* took it?"

"My mother," Norman repeated more loudly.

The smirk perpetually lurking on Todd's face flashed out clearly now. "Your *mother* has it," he repeated. "Well, that is awful. She's what? A master criminal? A cruel queen? Dungeon master? Wait, wait. She's not a dragon or anything, is she?"

Norman wanted to grip Todd by his ridiculous mutton-chop sideburns and give him a shake. Instead, he just gave his own head a sullen shake.

"She's not a criminal, or a dungeon master, or anything else. She's just my mother."

"And did this nefarious mother of yours indicate what she might have done with the map?"

Norman gave up. He might as well tell Todd about Pippa's idea. "It might be in a map cupboard."

Todd glanced quickly over his shoulder and raised an eyebrow. "What makes you think that?"

"Because of 'The Purloined Letter.'" Norman wondered how much more he should say. "Mom said she hid it."

"Poe?" Todd said thoughtfully. "Edgar Allan Poe? And have you ever read any Poe?"

"He seems to have a thing for murderers. There's that story where the dead guy's heart is hidden under the floorboards. Then there's the cask of something, where the killer walls somebody up in his wine cellar. Pippa told me about 'The Purloined Letter.' But it's not like we have a map cupboard. If the map is anywhere, it's probably back at our house in America."

Todd peered at him intently. "Did your mother say why she took the map?"

"She took it to protect me."

Todd appeared to think about this for a moment. "To protect you from what, exactly?"

Norman stepped back away from the desk, unsure how much to tell Todd. For once he sounded genuinely curious, as though he didn't already know the answer. "From the bookweird, I guess."

"Did she say that?" Todd demanded. He leaned across the desk and peered into Norman's eyes, his pretense of disinterest gone. "Did she say the word 'bookweird'?"

Norman looked away, unnerved by the lawyer's unblinking golden eyes. They really were fox eyes set in a human face. "Not exactly," he replied. "But she said that what I was doing was dangerous, and that I was too young to understand how dangerous."

"Implying that she understood the danger . . . That's very, very interesting." Todd rubbed his palms together and peered upwards, as if the solution to the problem might be written somewhere on the ceiling. "Could it be? Could it be?" he repeated to himself.

Todd leapt to his feet and strode to one of the tall bookcases. "In a Poe story!" the lawyer muttered to himself, more agitated than Norman had ever seen him. "That's diabolical!"

Norman edged closer as the lawyer ran his finger along the spines of the leather-bound books until he reached the one he wanted. Removing it with a tilt, he scanned the table of contents.

"'Amontillado,' 'House of Usher,' 'Tell-tale' . . . A-ha!" He turned the book towards Norman. Norman took it from him eagerly and saw that it was opened to "The Purloined Letter."

"So you think it's a clue, too? You think Pippa's right?" Norman asked. "You think the story will tell us how to find the map?"

"No, no," Todd replied smugly, closing the book with a thud. "I think the story *is* where you will find the map."

"What?" Norman was confused.

"Think about it."

Norman blinked a few times as if trying to reset his brain. Todd was suggesting that his mother had hidden the map inside a book. That was crazy. Wasn't it crazy?

"How?" he stammered.

"How would *you*?" the lawyer countered. And then to himself, "In a Poe story . . . who would have thought? Looks like a knack for the bookweird might run in the family."

Was it really so absurd? If Norman could enter books, why couldn't his mother? She knew *something* about the bookweird. She knew it was dangerous. She knew enough to ban Norman from using it. Had she seen how dangerous it was with her own eyes?

Norman gaped at Todd, hoping that he would add more—say, perhaps, what Norman was thinking—but all the lawyer said was "I have work to do now, but you can borrow the book. Try to keep it relatively intact." He pressed the book of Poe stories into Norman's hand and pushed him gently towards the door, making it as clear as possible that he was being dismissed. "I think you have the itinerary for your next trip."

"I can't," Norman stammered. "I can't leave Malcolm here. It's too dangerous. You should never have brought him here. Didn't you know that the murderer is here, the one from *The Magpie*? He's the one who caught Malcolm."

"Well, you *have* made a mess of things. I'm glad Malcolm has turned up. I was wondering where the royal beast had got to. I put a lot of effort into training him up for him to just disappear like that. But why have you brought a murderer here? Rorschach and Darwin would have caught him eventually."

"I didn't bring him here on purpose," Norman protested. He didn't want to believe it was his fault. "It was an accident. We have to stop him."

"Stop him from doing what, exactly?" Todd asked, as if it were an annoying minor point.

Norman raised his voice. "From catching Malcolm again, from getting at George. That guy knows something's wrong. He knows I'm not from here. He thinks I can take him back."

"Well, can't you?"

Norman stared at him, full of inexpressible rage. "I don't know how this works. You're the expert, remember!"

"You'd better leave it to me, then. I'm not sure that you've got it all right anyway. Last time I saw Rorschach and Darwin, they had the investigation well in hand. Either way, it sounds as though this interloper is more interested in you than anybody else. You look after the map, and I'll see what I can do to set things in order around here."

"You'll give George his estate back?"

"Well, not right away, of course—that's books and books from here. It shouldn't make much difference to George who occupies his ancestral home in the meantime. It sorts itself out eventually. Trust me."

Trusting Fuchs-Todd was the last thing that Norman would ever do.

"You should be getting on. You'll want to read that story thoroughly. You'll want to know it inside and out." He edged Norman ever closer to the door.

Norman ran his hand over the black-and-gold cover of

the book. "And you'll protect Malcolm? You'll deal with the poacher?"

"Yes, yes," the lawyer soothed. "We'll sort that out when you get back. Don't worry about that. Better to turn your mind to the fiasco at Lochwarren first. Things are a good deal more out of order there. Trust me." And he shoved Norman firmly through the doorway.

Norman paused in the hallway outside. He was not entirely satisfied with this meeting. He could never be sure he'd gotten through to that man.

"My mom loves this book. She doesn't want it wrecked."

"Nobody does. Nobody does," Todd repeated, his face mockingly earnest. "I'll do my best to fix what you've broken here."

Norman grimaced. "Why is it all my fault? You brought Malcolm here. Why did you do that? Why *didn't* you bring him to the real world?"

Todd ignored the question. "By the way, what's your mother's name?" he asked casually.

"Meg," Norman told him. Why did he always seem to change the subject?

"Hmm. Meg. That would be short for Margaret, but Margaret what?"

"Meg. It's always just Meg, not Margaret," Norman corrected him. "Meg Jespers-Vilnius, like me."

"Jespers-*Vilnius*? That's quite an unusual name. I have a cat named Vilnius, you know."

Norman did know, of course. Todd's question made him wonder again what this might mean. He was still wondering when the door closed behind him.

Norman didn't descend the stairs right away. He stood quietly beside the door and listened. Inside the library he could hear cupboard doors being opened, drawers being slammed shut and Todd's frustrated mumbling. After a few minutes, the door swung open. Norman stepped back out of the way, but Todd didn't even look as he stormed out empty-handed. Norman waited for him to disappear down the stairs, then tiptoed down to the kitchen and let himself out.

As Norman rushed back to the lodge, his mind raced ahead of him. His mother knew something about the bookweird, but could she *use* the bookweird? Did she have her own *ingresso*? If she took the map, she must have known he had been dropping into books for some time now. Why hadn't she said something before? And would she really have concealed the Undergrowth map in a Poe story? Norman had never read "The Purloined Letter," but if it was anywhere near as scary as "The Tell-tale Heart," he didn't think he'd ever dare to go there, even to retrieve Malcolm's map. Was his mother that fearless? Was his mother that mean? All this speculation and doubt rolled though his head like so many rocks in a rock-tumbler.

Norman and Malcolm read the "The Purloined Letter" over and over together while they waited for George to return from the Book and Badger. Thankfully the story was short and easily digested. The purloined letter of the title was stolen from a French princess. The thief, a certain Minister D., was blackmailing the princess with the information it contained. The Parisian police had searched Minister D.'s apartment meticulously but could not find the letter. The hero of the story, the amateur detective Auguste Dupin, solved the mystery. Knowing that the police would search every secret compartment and hiding place in his house, the minister had hidden the letter in plain sight in his own letter box. Dupin discovered the letter and replaced it with a harmless copy.

"Do you think the map is in the minister's letter box?" Malcolm asked eagerly.

"That would make sense, I guess. Todd thinks the map is in this story, and that's the hiding place."

"You should let me go. I can sneak in without anyone noticing. It would be much harder for you."

"I don't think you can," Norman replied reluctantly. He would have liked to have his friend there for backup. "You needed help to get here, and my *ingresso* didn't work when I tried to bring you with me last time. I have to go myself. It says here that the minister is usually out at night, and the servants are drunk and asleep. The Paris police have searched the apartment twice without them noticing."

"Strong Arm," Malcolm reminded him wryly, "stealth isn't exactly your greatest attribute."

Norman couldn't help smiling. It was true that Norman's greatest contribution to the Battle of Scalded Rock had been making noise.

"I'll be fine," Norman assured him. "I'll go at night, when the servants are drunk."

"When whose servants are drunk?" It was George appearing in the kitchen doorway. When neither Malcolm nor Norman answered, he repeated the question. "You'll go where? When whose servants are drunk?"

Malcolm and Norman exchanged a confidential glance. They had agreed not to mention the bookweird to George. His life was in enough turmoil. He didn't need to find out now that he was a character in a book.

"Minister Deschamps's servants," Malcolm replied after a moment's thought. "Norman is going to retrieve something from the desk of Minister Deschamps."

George came closer, sat down and peered from human boy to stoat king. His face looked somehow different to Norman. Something about it had altered. When George spoke, Norman knew what it was. The glint of intrigue that had been missing from George's eyes had returned.

"I don't know this minister. What is it that he's got?"

"A map," Norman quickly replied. He didn't dare look at Malcolm. He just hoped that the story they were inventing together made sense. "It's a map that shows Malcolm's homeland back in the forest. The minister doesn't know it yet, but he'll learn sooner or later. We have to find it before the secret of Malcolm's people gets out. If people knew, they'd be destroyed."

George nodded. He understood the gravity of the situation. "When do we go?"

Norman hadn't counted on that. He should have known that George would want to be part of the adventure. He opened his mouth to speak, not sure yet what he was going to say.

Malcolm came to his rescue. "Norman has to go himself. He has the key, and he has to go at night while the minister is having dinner with Norman's father."

Norman thought this through. It made sense, but their lies were getting more and more complicated.

"We have to stay here and watch the poacher," Malcolm continued.

"Oh," said George, suddenly remembering something he'd meant to say earlier, "I have news of my own. I found out what the poacher was doing at the Book and Badger."

"What?" Norman and Malcolm asked in unison, relieved that he'd changed the subject.

"He was buying a gun."

Norman stared. Could things get any worse?

"A cannon, you mean?" Malcolm asked, perplexed because his medieval world didn't include guns that you could carry.

"We have to tell Todd," Norman said. Turning to Malcolm, he repeated, "You have to go to Todd. You have to tell him it's too dangerous now."

"Are you mad?" George sputtered. "You can't have Malcolm giving himself away like that. Todd can't know that Malcolm can speak. You've seen the way he's taken over the house. The man's a grasping schemer. You can guess what he'd do with a talking stoat."

Even if George didn't know the whole story, he was perhaps right. Fuchs or Todd or whoever he wanted to be known as today hadn't shown much sympathy so far. The only thing that interested him was the map. Once Norman got his hands on the map, he'd have a very different conversation with the lawyer and sometime librarian and abbot.

The Purloined Letter

The darkness was nearly complete. It took a moment for Norman's eyes to adjust, but slowly the outlines of the room began to emerge. He was on the couch. In the dim light he could make out the curved backs of two chairs and a small desk, perhaps. Norman brought himself up to a seated position and felt the thick carpet beneath his feet.

On the table beside him he saw the outline of something that looked like a lamp. He groped around the ornately carved base for a power switch, inching his hand higher until he caught something dangling—a pull cord? He yanked decisively. Something came off in his hand and the whole lamp erupted into a musical jingling. Withdrawing his hand, he felt the object in his palm. It was smooth, shaped like a lozenge with sharp, faceted edges. He closed his hand over it quickly, as if to make it go away. Only then did he remember the flashlight that George had given him.

Under the flashlight's beam, the object sent off light—it was a crystal bead. He turned the beam on the lamp and revealed a glistening tree of beads, a whole elaborate chandelier of dangling glass. It was impossible to tell where the bead belonged. He slipped it into his pocket.

Sweeping the flashlight around the room, he could make out the contents more clearly. The room was crammed with furniture.

There were tables everywhere, cluttered with lamps and statues and tiny boxes. Had Norman attempted to move around the room in the dark he would surely have knocked something over.

He ran the beam of the flashlight up and down the walls, following the vertical stripes of the wallpaper in search of a light switch. There was something there, just at head height—some sort of lamp with small glass globes. On his tiptoes he could almost reach it, but again no switch. He slid his hand across the wall until he touched a small metal dial. Turning it slowly between his thumb and forefinger, he expected a sudden burst of light. There was only a slow hissing sound. Norman smelled something foul.

"Jeeze . . . gas!" he cried out loud, and he quickly turned the dial the other way until the hissing stopped.

His heart was beating faster now, making the room seem less silent. He strained to hear any other noise, hoping that his cry hadn't awakened the servants in some other room. He swung the flashlight like a searchlight around the room again, seeking out the corners, the edges of curtains. This darkness was creeping him out.

Crossing the room to the largest of the curtained windows, he felt carefully along its smooth silk surface until his fingers touched the tassels of the centre parting. He stuck his head through at first, just to confirm that he was where he was supposed to be. Outside, Paris was asleep. He gazed across the roofs to the wet streets and the dim streetlights. The apartment was about four storeys up, but few buildings reached higher. Out of the black and grey only one colour stood out, a flash of red here and there from a lit sign in the distance or from gaslight shining through a closed red curtain.

He dared to leave the curtain open just a bit. The lights of Paris at night crept into the room, lighting up its floor with red and grey, but it was not only the lights cast from outside. The apartment seemed to have been painted with the same palette. The dark, wood-framed couch was upholstered in scarlet red. The two armchairs matched it. The wallpaper had an alternating pattern of black and red, an intricate weave of brambles and flowers, so thickly intertwined that they were dark stripes from afar. The whole room looked like an illustration from an old book, a black-and-white engraving enlivened by a single colour—red.

"Let's get this over with," he muttered under his breath.

A particularly strong beam of red light illuminated the small writing desk in the corner, and above it hung a bulletin board of some sort—the card rack. Norman inched closer and shone the flashlight into each of the four cubby holes. There were the visiting cards, little rectangles of thick paper with fussy inscribed names and addresses, and there in the top left compartment was a letter—the purloined letter itself!

It looked harmless, like a piece of junk mail. The paper was ragged and had been ripped nearly in half. Only the large crimson seal of the minister made it look at all imposing. Norman leaned in to read the minister's name from the address. He couldn't help it. It bothered him that in the book the minister's name was only ever written as "D—."

He read the name once and, startled, read it again slowly to make sure he'd got it right—Deschamps, the same name that he and Malcolm had made up for their story. How weird was that? Norman tried to think of another French name that started with D but couldn't. His curiosity was getting the better of him now. What exactly was in this letter? He reached in and touched the seal. He had time to read it, didn't he?

A creak in the floor as he reached up made him jump and reminded him otherwise. He didn't have time. The map was obviously not here in the card rack. Deschamps had left the purloined letter in full sight amongst other letters. That was the whole trick to the story. The stolen map would be hidden in plain sight amongst other maps.

Norman shuffled the papers on the desk. They appeared to be bills and legal documents, but then, Norman knew only about five words of French. Anyway, they certainly weren't maps. He turned and scanned the room again. There was a tall bookshelf in one corner and beside it another small desk. It was worth a try. The floorboards creaked as he stalked over there. He kept the beam of his light low along the floor to make sure he didn't trip . . . but then something stopped him in his tracks. Footprints—muddy sneaker prints. He gazed down at his grimy white sneakers. They were his own footprints. He cursed himself under his breath.

The library of Minister Deschamps resembled the more boring shelves of the cottage library back in England. The books were curiously sized, either ridiculously small—small enough to fit into the pocket of your jacket—or crazy big. They were all bound in black or deep burgundy leather and engraved with gold curlicues and arabesques.

The Undergrowth map was small, a single sheet of paper drawn by tiny weasel hands. Folded twice, it could be hidden in the pocket of Norman's jeans. It didn't need a huge book to hide it. Norman took a few of the smaller books and used the technique of the Parisian police as described by Dupin, shaking them vigorously upside down to see if anything fell out. Nothing.

The beam of the flashlight passed over the titles on the spines of the larger volumes: *Great Criminal Masterminds, Timeless Schemes and Conspiracies, An Atlas of Infamy.* "A-ha," Norman whispered dramatically to himself, "an atlas."

He slid it down from the shelf and, resting it on the table, opened it to the frontispiece, which was elaborately engraved with daggers, skulls and men hanging by their necks from trees. "Nice," he muttered as he turned the thick, yellowing pages. Page after page of maps revealed themselves—biblical Egypt, the Roman forums, Hadrian's Wall, the siege of Quebec—fascinating, but not Undergrowth. Again he turned the book upside down and shook out its pages.

A single red banknote wafted to the floor. Norman bent down to retrieve it. Only then, with the flashlight level with the floor, did he notice the black leather tube beneath the little desk. His mother used translucent plastic tubes like that to carry posters and display materials to her talks. Minister Deschamps's black leather one was just the sort of thing you'd put a map in.

The lid of the tube came off with a satisfying pop. Norman reached in and felt a tightly rolled set of plans inside. They were too large for the desk, so he spread them out on the floor and kneeled down to pore over them. They were not maps but architectural plans to some palace. He flipped the pages cautiously. Nothing was concealed between them. He was running out of options. If the Undergrowth map wasn't here, then where?

"Come on, come on," he muttered. "Be here. Please be here."

He rolled up the plans and was sliding the tube back into place when a cough interrupted him. Norman jumped to his feet defensively and trained the flashlight in the direction of the sound.

The two upholstered chairs had definitely been empty when Norman arrived. They were not empty now. One was occupied by a tall man, dressed entirely in black. His dark hair was swept back across his forehead, and he held his left arm across his chest, supporting the elbow of his other arm, which reached up to cradle his chin. His eyes narrowed under the beam of Norman's light, but he did not take them off the boy for a moment.

"I gather you have not found what you are looking for?" The voice spoke English with a thick French accent.

Norman gulped and shook his head. The Frenchman's eyes had apparently become accustomed to the light, as he stared unblinkingly back towards him.

"I had heard that the English secret service occasionally employs children for certain delicate assignments. A child, after all, can go safely where a man might quickly be detected. But wouldn't it be wiser, in France, to employ French children?"

Norman did not answer his question. His mind was racing for a solution. What advantage did he have here? How could he save himself?

"I know where the letter is," he blurted out.

"Indeed you do. Indeed you do," the man replied calmly. "This is the most interesting thing about you."

"But, Minister Deschamps," Norman said, the start of a plan forming, "someone else knows where it is. If you let me go—"

The man in the chair let out a low, chuckling laugh. "Oh, I am not Minister Deschamps. I doubt the minister would have received you so politely. The minister would have beaten you soundly and turned you over to the police by now."

"Dupin?" Norman asked.

"Indeed," the man replied, running the tip of his finger over his eyebrow as if just registering another interesting fact. "You are quite the perspicacious little *espion*, aren't you? May I ask," he continued after a pause, "what it is you are looking for?"

Norman resorted to his last trick, the truth. "I'm looking for a map."

"A map, you say?" A note of intrigue rose in Dupin's voice. "And the minister has this map?"

Norman shook his head slowly.

The detective leaned in ever so slightly. "And yet you believe it is here. Why so?"

Norman opened his mouth to speak but couldn't say what he meant to say. He couldn't tell Dupin that he believed the map was here because his mother had insinuated that it was in a Poe story. Dupin wouldn't believe that he was just a character in a story.

"Relax, my boy. The worst has already happened. You have been caught breaking into the chambers of a minister of the French government, and you have not even found what you were looking for. Come, I enjoy a puzzle. Let me help you. Why did you believe that your map was in this apartment?"

"I was told that the map was hiding in plain sight," Norman admitted finally.

"Interesting." Dupin ruminated, drumming his fingers on the arm of the chair. "And who told you this?"

"The person who took it," Norman said, hoping to avoid telling him exactly who that was.

"That," Dupin declared with some satisfaction, "is a clue in itself. It tells us a lot about the thief. It is possible to understand the *how* of almost any crime by understanding the *who*. We know that our thief is clever enough to use the same scheme as our Minister Deschamps, and is so overconfident as to tell you that he has done it. What else do we know about this criminal?"

"Erm . . ." Norman hesitated. He wasn't sure how much more he should tell Dupin.

"You can count on my discretion. I can assure you of that." Dupin sounded eager to help solve the mystery. "Understand the criminal and understand the crime."

"How is that?" Norman asked, edging closer and lowering the flashlight.

"Ah well, young sir, this is the first lesson in criminology. I understand that Compte Rochambault himself introduced his game to your George Washington."

"Roshambo?" Norman repeated, perplexed.

"Ro–cham–bault," Dupin repeated, making in turn the sign of a rock, paper and scissors with his fingers at each syllable.

"Oh, sure! Rock, paper, scissors," Norman guessed. Perplexed, he stepped closer to the chair so he could examine the detective's face. He appeared neither nervous nor angry. He might have been sitting in his own apartment having a chat with a friend.

"Do you have an older or younger sibling?" Dupin asked.

"A sister, younger." Norman wrinkled his nose reflexively at the thought of her.

"And do you usually win when you two play Rochambault?" Norman nodded his head emphatically.

"Because you can predict what she will pick," the detective summarized.

That was exactly it. "She always picks rock first," Norman said. "Little kids always pick rock."

The detective smiled knowingly. "And children your own age?"

"Smarter kids pick paper, because they expect you to pick rock."

"And yet more intelligent children, like yourself?" Dupin asked, raising a languid finger and pointing.

Norman smiled, finally getting Dupin's point. "You pick scissors, because the other person picks paper, expecting you to pick rock."

"So you see, understanding our opponents helps us to understand their methods." Dupin concluded his lesson with the same professorial tone that Norman's father used. "And who is our opponent in *l'affaire de la carte*?" he continued.

Norman whispered his answer hoarsely. "My mother."

Dupin leaned forward as if to say something, then leaned back and repeated the peculiar gesture of rubbing his forefinger across his eyebrow.

"Very interesting. Very, very interesting," he repeated. He thought for a moment before saying, "May I ask an additional, impertinent question?" When Norman assented cautiously, the detective asked, "Does your mother love you?"

"Yes . . ." Norman replied quickly, shocked by the question.

"Well, then," Dupin began as he rose from the chair, "I assure you that your map is not here in this apartment." He removed a large silver pocket watch from his breast pocket and squinted at it.

"Why?" Norman asked.

"Because if your mother loves you," Dupin explained, "she would not send you to such a place."

"But she didn't send me," Norman argued. "She told me not to come."

"Which to a boy of your age is as good as sending you. She would have imagined, at the very least, that you might try. No, you must think about the clue once more. She told you that it was hiding in plain sight. Correct? She alluded to the minister's ruse, which she has learned of somehow through the proverbial grapevine. No doubt the prefect has spoken incautiously," he grumbled.

That wasn't what Meg Jespers had said, but it was how Norman and the Intrepids and Todd had interpreted her cryptic use of the word "purloined"—a reference, they felt sure, to the Poe story "The Purloined Letter." And the trick of this story was that the letter was hidden in plain sight.

"Well, our nemesis the minister here concealed his letter where you would expect to find a letter—in the letter box." Dupin inclined his head towards the desk and the letter holder. "You have looked in that tube, and at the atlas, of course. This was well thought out. If your map was concealed somewhere within this room, then those places are exactly where I should look. However, since we have concluded that it is not in this room, we ought to consider where you are most likely otherwise to find a map."

Dupin removed a key from the breast pocket of his jacket and strode to the apartment door. He held his finger to his lips before turning the key in the lock. The lock clicked smoothly and Dupin pushed the door open. Norman's eyes widened as he saw the sleeping figure of a servant on the chair outside the doorway. Norman stepped back and suppressed a shout of surprise. But Dupin did not hesitate, striding forward through the door and into the hallway. With a wave of his hand he beckoned Norman to follow.

Norman tiptoed nervously down the hall, holding his breath and hearing the rush of his own blood in his ears. He couldn't keep his eyes off the sleeping guard as he tiptoed past. A hank of the sentry's oily black hair hung across his face and floated up with each exhalation. It tickled Norman's nose just to see it. How was it possible that it didn't wake the man? How was it possible that Norman's rummaging through the adjacent room hadn't woken him?

A hand tugged at Norman's sleeve. He leapt into the air, and his barely suppressed scream came out as a little yelp. Dupin, his hand on Norman's shoulder, glared at him and motioned down the corridor. Norman needed no further encouragement. He scampered down the hall to the stairway at the end. Behind him Dupin re-locked the door, and then he joined Norman at the top of the stairs.

They were silent until they were outside on the street. They walked side by side, keeping close to the buildings, striding only through the outer edge of the gaslight circles. After a few blocks a thought occurred to Norman.

"In the story . . ." he began without thinking. He stopped and corrected himself. "I thought that only the police broke into the apartment at night. I thought that you visited the minister during the day, while he was there."

"You are a very well-informed young man, aren't you?" Dupin broke his stride for a moment and turned to give Norman an evaluating once-over. What he concluded, Norman could only guess. He merely repeated the curious gesture of running his forefinger across his eyebrow and resumed his walk. "Very well. I shall confess. Perhaps I should not, but I find you a very compelling listener. You remind me of a friend of mine, a very receptive man. It is a delight to explain my inner thoughts and methods of ratiocination to him. If he should ever decide to write down the thoughts I so eagerly recount, I daresay he could reveal my entire method, and spawn a thousand imitators. I can only ask you to promise the same discretion, my young friend."

Norman agreed immediately. It was an easy promise to make. Who was he going to tell?

"It is merely curiosity, a weakness, I admit. But I simply must know how the story ends."

"So you were checking to see if he'd discovered the fake," Norman concluded.

"Indeed," the detective replied. "I confess that my curiosity gets the better of me. I return quite often to the minister's apartment, every few nights or so. To be the author of a fine scheme and not see its conclusion is intolerable. Monsieur G. of the Paris prefecture would never tell me, and I simply must know."

"And has he? Has the minister discovered the fake?" Norman asked. He was curious, too, to know how the story turned out.

"I believe I've told you enough, don't you think?" They had arrived at a wide boulevard lined with horse-drawn carriages. "Would you like to tell me about your map over a cup of hot cocoa?"

Norman hesitated. "Not really." He suddenly had an idea about how he could avoid wrecking this story. "In fact, I want to make a deal with you."

"A deal?"

"Yes. I promise not to tell anybody about your visits to the minister's apartment, but you have to promise not to tell anybody about me."

"That seems eminently fair."

"Not anybody. I won't even tell my mother. You can't even tell your friend, the one who is the good listener." Norman had a strong suspicion that Dupin's friend was the narrator of "The Purloined Letter." If Dupin could keep it to himself, the story would remain unchanged.

Dupin considered this clarification for a moment, as if he was reluctant to give up the pleasure of recounting his encounter with the strange boy, but finally assented with a nod of the head. They stood now in a dim circle of gaslight many blocks from the apartment they had separately broken into. Dupin raised a hand as if to shake Norman's and bid him adieu, but Norman stopped him.

"I have one more favour to ask," Norman said in a low, tentative voice.

"Ask away, young sir," Dupin replied.

"I'd like to sleep on your couch tonight. I promise that I'll be gone before you are awake. It's just that—"

"I very much doubt that you'd be able to escape my lodgings without my noticing. They are extraordinarily well secured," Dupin assured him with a chuckle.

"I'll bet you I can," Norman said with a sly smile. He raised his own hand now and took Dupin's to shake on the deal.

The Siege of Folly

Norman nearly fell asleep in the carriage on the way back to Dupin's apartment. Only the jolt of the wooden wheels along the cobbled street kept him awake until they had reached the quiet street where Dupin lived. Even after the detective had brought him a blanket, Norman had to fight to stay awake longer. It was a close thing, but he managed to stay awake long enough to nibble through half a page of *Intrepid Amongst the Gypsies*.

The other half of the page was still in his hand when he woke up on the couch in Kelmsworth Lodge. Norman would never get used to falling asleep in one place and waking up somewhere else, but it helped that it was still dark outside. He let himself wake up slowly. When he finally sat up there was just a smudge of daylight on the horizon behind Kelmsworth Wood.

Should he wake George and Malcolm? he wondered. It probably wasn't worth it. It wasn't as though he had anything worth telling. Perhaps Malcolm was still out in the woods anyway, stalking the poacher who had once captured him. In the dim light, Norman looked around cautiously. Everything appeared much the same here. There was no evidence that the poacher had dared to try to break in.

He got up and walked about. There was no use trying to sleep.

It was a little brighter in the kitchen. The sun would be up in half an hour. That was one thing he could count on in the Intrepids' England—at least the sun shone here. Norman was eyeing the kettle, wondering whether he should make tea for George, when he saw movement at the edge of his vision, something outside, just a hint of motion blurred by the thick, uneven glass of the leaded windows. Norman leaned closer to the window and peered out through the clearest of the diamond-shaped panes. The figure of a man carrying a long pole on his shoulder moved across the woods. The figure became clearer. It was the poacher.

"George! Malcolm! Wake up! He's here!" Norman yelled. His eyes followed the poacher's progress towards Kelmsworth Hall until the angle became impossible. Norman rushed over to the other side of the house, to the sitting room, and leapt onto the couch. He pulled aside the thick curtains of the window behind it.

The poacher lumbered across the lawn, bent beneath the weight on his back. From this angle Norman could see that the poacher was carrying not a pole but a ladder. In his other hand he dragged a long, rectangular piece of corrugated tin.

"George! It's him, the poacher! He's going to try something!"

Where were they? Malcolm might have been the sleep-in type on most days, but he would usually snap awake at the first sign of alarm. George was always an early riser. Norman closed the curtains hastily and jumped from the couch. He took the stairs up to George's bedroom two at a time.

"George, you have to get up! He's heading to the hall!" Norman banged on the door and twisted the knob as he shouted. The door burst open to an empty bedroom. The room was tidy and the bed was made, and there was no sign of its occupant. Norman stood stunned for just a moment as he tried to imagine where George might be.

Norman risked a quick peek out the bedroom window. Sure enough, the poacher was still making his way towards the house. He walked brazenly upright, not bothering to duck behind the garden walls or dash between clumps of shrubbery and trees.

What was he doing? Where was he going with that ladder and sheet of tin? Norman scanned the second-storey windows of Kelmsworth Hall. None appeared open. He checked the poacher's progress across the lawn. Something caught his eye, a flash of yellow in the green of garden and the grey of stone wall. There, at the top of the folly. He didn't need George's telescope. He knew what it was—the same sleeping bag he had used the night of the stakeout. George had retreated to the folly.

Norman smiled to himself, admiring George's resourcefulness. The folly might be just a scaled-down replica of a castle tower, but for one boy and a stoat it would do the job of a castle. There were no windows to smash, no easy access from below.

Norman stopped there. That's what the ladder and tin sheet were for. George and his folly were under siege!

He pelted down the stairs and into the kitchen. He was at the door before he had a second thought. He had to warn George at the folly. He couldn't let the poacher sneak up on him like this.

Norman was no expert at battle strategy, but he had been in more medieval battles than the average modern twelve-year-old. Back in Undergrowth he had helped take Lochwarren Castle back from the wolves. At Scalded Rock he had helped to break hundreds of stoats out of the prison camp, even if his only real job had been to provide the distraction to allow the stoats to sneak in.

Norman cast his eye around the kitchen, hoping something would leap out, some sort of weapon, or at least a way to warn George in the tower. His eyes lit upon the copper pots hanging from hooks over the stove. It had worked at Scalded Rock . . .

Norman snatched the two handiest pots and dashed out the door. He bounded across the lawn, a copper pot in each hand. At the greenhouse he stopped to catch his breath. The big poacher was already far ahead of him, swinging the ladder and corrugated tin beside him as though they were the lightest of loads.

Norman let his heart rate settle for another moment. If the poacher came after him, he'd need every bit of energy to escape. He took one more peek around the corner of the greenhouse. The poacher had nearly reached the Rook, and there was still no sign of alarm in the tower. Suddenly a movement in the woods caught his eye, a flash of white. Norman ducked instinctively, but there was nowhere to run. Frozen between the woods and the poacher, his mind raced. Had the poacher recruited an ally? Who was out there in the forest?

His senses were sharpened by fear. He could hear the wind through the trees now, but no sound of footsteps. Whoever was out there wasn't moving. Then he heard it, a sort of quiet whimpering, like a wounded animal.

Malcolm! he thought. The image of his friend flashed through his mind. He imagined him lying there wounded and vulnerable—just as he had been at the battle with the ravens, when Norman had first rescued him. And just as he had that first time, Norman suddenly forgot all fear and dashed towards the woods.

He hardly looked where he was going, just crashed through the brush, gripping his only weapons, the copper pots and pans, in his fists. He nearly tripped onto the path, but just managed to stay on his feet, pulling himself up into something like a fighting stance and wielding his copper pots like short ninja swords.

He was alone on the path, except for the whimpering animal. It was too big to be Malcolm, its white and sable hair much longer. When it saw Norman, it stopped struggling against the ropes that tied it to a nearby tree and looked up.

"Nelson!" Norman whispered. "What happened to you, boy?" He bent down and began to loosen the ropes. "Are you on watch? Were you supposed to sound the alarm?"

Even if the dog had been able to speak, he couldn't have answered. A mean leather muzzle was strapped to his snout. When he was finished with the ropes, Norman saw to the muzzle, too. The dog licked his hand in gratitude. He was too smart to make any noise unless ordered to.

Norman patted him, feeling for an injury, but Nelson seemed to be okay. The dog pointed his muzzle to a pile of ground beef on the ground and growled.

Norman understood immediately. "He tried to poison you."

Nelson's eyes blinked in agreement.

"Come on, boy," Norman urged, his adrenaline still pumping. "We've got to help George."

They raced down the path to the edge of the woods and dashed for the cover of the greenhouse. The poacher was nearly at the base of the tower, and still there was no movement on the ramparts.

Nelson whimpered, desperate to sound the alarm. Norman spread his arms, holding the pans out wide. He held his breath for just a second, then swung the pans together in front of him three times in quick succession. They made a pure, bell-like sound that rang across the lawn—*gong, gong, gong.* Nelson barked liked he'd never barked before, then both of them ducked behind the greenhouse again.

Norman took a deep breath and waited for the echoes to subside before sticking his head out again. The poacher had dropped his ladder and stopped in his tracks. The big man ducked low and lifted the sheet of tin up over his head like a shield. Crouched under his shield he turned in a slow circle, trying to locate the source of the din. There was something about his stance, squatting low and wary, ready to pounce, that made him look more animal than human. Norman could see the whites of the poacher's eyes. He could only bear to look for a moment. They were a killer's eyes.

With a gasp Norman ducked back behind cover. His chest pounded as if he'd just run a race. But the race hadn't even started. The next time he banged the pots together, the poacher would know exactly where the sound was coming from. Norman's plan had been to draw the poacher into the woods and lose him there, but he was losing his nerve. He knew he couldn't outrun the big man. The poacher knew the paths through the woods better than he did. Norman wasn't sure it was a race he could win.

He breathed deeply, closed his eyes, raised the pots and counted to three again. He couldn't do it. His arms trembled in front of him and he could not bring himself to bang them together again. He wasn't brave enough. It was so quiet out there now. The poacher could be creeping towards him across the lawn. He could be just around the corner of the greenhouse.

Cringing, Norman placed the pots down on the grass, willing them not to make a sound. Slowly he dropped to the ground, lying on his belly in the dirt. With the smallest of movements he crawled to the edge of the greenhouse and peered fearfully around the corner. He fully expected the poacher to be there, looming over him. He expected it to be over in a blink.

But the poacher hadn't moved. He was still there in the middle of the lawn, huddled under his shield, turning this way and that, trying to figure out where the din had come from. Behind him in the tower there was a stir of motion and colour as the yellow sleeping bag was flung away and George poked his head over the parapet. That part of Norman's job was done. George had been warned.

Within seconds there was the whistle of missiles in the air—arrows, two of them. Norman saw Malcolm's tiny head pop up behind the parapet. Behind him the unmistakable bright orange hair of Pippa Cook flashed for a moment in the morning sun, then it too disappeared behind the stone parapet. There was the sound of two arrows *ting-tinging* off the tin shield.

There was nothing Norman could do by himself now. He needed help. "Stay here," he told Nelson. The dog blinked his understanding. He seemed to know what his job was.

Norman waited another second and then dove behind the low stone wall that led across the lawn. He could do this, he told himself. He could make it across the lawn without being seen, just as he had that first night with George.

Beyond the greenhouse there was enough stone wall, garden hedge and shrubbery to conceal him all the way to the back door of Kelmsworth Hall. He moved as quickly as he could, running bent over, scrambling, almost crawling when he had to. Behind him Nelson started barking again, drawing the poacher's attention. Norman did not look back, at least not until he heard George shout the command "Pull!"

Above the tower's parapets, a small red ball about the size of a softball was tossed straight into the air. Behind it George's body flashed into view, his shirt-tails untucked and his face tightened in a determined grimace. George wielded a cricket bat, and he swung it in a huge, wide circle in the air. It connected with the ball with a solid *thock*. Norman followed the arcing flight of the cricket ball and watched it strike the poacher's shield with a clang. The sound of reverberating tin echoed across the lawn. George had brought out his artillery.

Norman burst into a full run now. At the kitchen garden he leapt the low wrought-iron gate and rushed up the path to the back door. Behind him he could hear the ringing of arrows off the poacher's shield and the shouts of the combatants.

"Be gone with you. It's no use. We could stay in here for weeks!" George shouted from the tower. His words were brave but his voice was thin and unconvincing.

"Just give him to me and I'm outta here," the rough American voice growled back. "No one needs to get hurt."

The tower's answer was delivered with another shout of "Pull!" and the deep, echoing *thock* of the cricket bat connecting.

Norman clenched his teeth. The poacher wanted Malcolm back. That's what he was after. Norman was not going to let that happen. The poacher was not getting into that tower. Norman hammered on the back door of the hall and yelled, "Fuchs . . . Todd! Let me in!"

There was the sound of shuffling feet and the slow scrape of chair legs across the floor inside.

"It's me, Norman. You have to let me in now. Hurry up!" He banged again on the door.

Norman paused and glanced over his shoulder towards the tower. The poacher peered towards him, squinting. At this distance, and in the dim light of dawn, it would be difficult to recognize him. There was another shout of "Pull!" from the tower. The poacher ducked and raised his shield to protect his head. The cricket ball sailed over its target. He was getting closer; George had lost the angle.

There was the whistling sound of more arrows sent down and then a *ting* as they rebounded off the shield. The Intrepids were fighting back, but as long as the poacher had his shield, he could creep ever closer.

Norman raised his hand to pound on the door again, but the door swung open. Had he swung to knock he would have landed his fist in the smug, ever-smirking face of the lawyer, Fuchs-Todd.

He greeted Norman breezily. "Good morning," he said. "How can I help you?"

"Are you kidding?" Norman screamed. "Don't you notice anything?" He ducked under the man's arm into the kitchen. "Do you have a gun?" he demanded. "Something to help us?"

"To help you with what?" Todd sounded neither surprised nor especially interested.

Norman threw his hands in the air. "To help us get rid of this guy. Is there a phone? Do they have telephones in this book? How do we get the police?" Norman rushed on, looking around the big kitchen for a telephone.

"Who do you suggest we telephone?" Todd asked, holding his hands out helplessly. "The author, perhaps?"

"Well, the gun, then. They have guns, don't they?" Norman shouted. "Hurry!"

Todd put his hands in his pockets. "What's the hurry? You're in no danger."

"I'm not, but George is and Malcolm is. He's got them trapped up in the tower out there."

"Well, this *will* be interesting." Todd craned his neck out the open door towards the tower. "A full-blown siege, right here on the lawn. It's the sort of thing that only happens in books."

"It's not interesting. It's dangerous, and it's all your fault."

Todd turned and stared at Norman. Totally unmoved by Norman's pleas and accusations, he merely raised his eyebrow. "It's my fault, is it? I'm sorry, but I thought you had a little something to do with this."

Norman stared back. He seethed with anger, but there was no retort. Todd was right. A lot of this was Norman's fault.

"Help me fix this. You obviously don't care about George, but you don't want anything to happen to Malcolm, do you?"

Todd leaned against the door frame casually. "Oh, I'm sure the little furry warrior can handle himself. You've seen him in battle. He can hold his own."

"Against other animals. People from his world. Not against some New York psycho murderer."

Todd arched an eyebrow. "That makes it all the more interesting."

Norman couldn't believe his indifference. Todd, as Fuchs, had saved him once. He'd pulled him right out of the *Magpie* mystery because it was too dangerous. Why wouldn't he help now, when the *Magpie* murderer was right here? What had changed? Norman stood with his mouth agape for a moment before speaking.

"You want the map." He wasn't sure where the thought came from. It just popped into his head. "You want the map, don't you?"

"I believe Malcolm is after the map. I really couldn't care less. I'm going upstairs to watch." He closed the door, turned his back and started out of the kitchen. Norman followed him out into the grand hall.

"No, *you* want the map," Norman repeated. He was sure of this now. "You're willing to let Malcolm die out there in a book that isn't his own because you want the map."

Todd had one foot on the bottom stair, but he turned and regarded Norman with an appraising look. He wasn't angry. If anything he was amused. If he'd been trying to conceal something from Norman he wasn't troubled.

"If you ever want to see the map," Norman warned, "you'd better help me now."

Todd just smiled a thin little smile and continued up the stairs. "Come on, then. I believe there's something up here that might be of use."

Norman scrambled up the stairs after him, passing Todd and encouraging him on. "Hurry up."

Todd led him to a small study on the second floor. It was decorated with hunting trophies and black-and-white photographs of various Kelmsworths in foreign lands—wide African deserts, Indian jungles, the American Rockies. Their moustached faces stared out sternly as they posed with various dead animals. Norman shrank back as he scanned the rows of mounted animal head—gazelles, buffalo, a mountain lion. A full stuffed bear stood in one corner, its arms raised in pathetic threat. Norman averted his eyes. You looked at animals differently when one of them was your best friend.

"Here we are," Todd declared, opening a large glass case on the wall. He lifted an insanely large gun down from the case and handed it to Norman.

Norman's arms sank as they took the weight of the huge rifle. Todd rummaged through a desk drawer for a few moments, then handed Norman a box of cartridges.

"And there you go. That's an elephant gun, I think. I'd be careful if I were you. It's probably got quite a kick."

With a flourish Todd opened the French doors at the end of the study and held them open for Norman, standing back and waving him out like a butler. Norman stepped out onto the balcony beyond.

Below, the siege was coming to a close. The poacher had managed to make it to the foot of the tower. He crouched low, tight to the tower wall, holding the sheet of corrugated tin to protect his head from any shots from above. But the *ting* and *thock* of arrows and cricket balls had stopped. Malcolm and the Intrepids had realized they were wasting their ammo.

The poacher had already propped the ladder up against the side of the tower, its top rung well above the level of the ramparts. Protected by his shield, the poacher waited beneath the ladder, holding it tight with one arm. He only needed to swing around now and start his climb.

Norman felt powerless as he watched. "We have to help them," he pleaded.

Todd leaned on the carved stone balustrade and watched intently. "Well, help them," he murmured distractedly.

"I can't," Norman whispered hoarsely.

"You've got a gun, don't you?" Fascinated by the siege, he didn't even bother to turn around.

"I can't," Norman repeated insistently. Even in a book, he didn't think he could actually shoot someone.

"Your choice," Todd replied, seemingly indifferent. "Be quiet, then. I want to see how this turns out."

There was a strange silence below as the poacher paused and prepared his final assault. Above him on the battlements, the tiny figure of Malcolm appeared. He braced himself against the stone castellations and drew his bowstring back to fire, just waiting for a clear shot. He would have only one chance. When the poacher came out from beneath the ladder, he would expose himself for just a moment. Malcolm would have to take that moment.

Norman gripped the balcony with one hand and the ridiculous gun with the other. His knuckles were white with tension. He wanted to do something, but he couldn't bring himself to raise the weapon.

"Please," he begged Todd. "Can't you do it?"

Engrossed in the battle unfolding below, Todd didn't answer.

The sound of rattling tin at the tower turned Norman's head. The poacher had decided the moment was now. For a quick second he let go of the ladder, switching his shield to his other hand, and swung around from beneath the ladder. Norman caught a brief glimpse of his face. His beard had grown thick and his skin was burnt from the sun and his eyes seemed to glow with anger. Norman had seen faces like this before, the faces of real medieval warriors when he'd faced the Viking hordes at Maldon.

Malcolm saw the face, too, and recognized his opportunity, because the *twang* of a bowstring now resounded across the lawn. Norman never saw the arrow. He only heard the resulting *ting* as the arrow hit the poacher's tin shield.

The poacher was too fast. He'd managed to grab the ladder and get the shield back over his head. Already he had his foot on the first rung. At the top of the ladder, four white human hands had grasped the rails, attempting to push it back, but George and Pippa too had missed their moment, and they weren't strong enough now. With the poacher's weight on it, they'd never be able to push the ladder back.

What made the whole thing strange was the silence. It was like watching the television with no sound on. The poacher wasn't shouting threats. Malcolm and George worked just as silently up in the tower. Norman himself wanted to shout, to say something, but he was finding it hard enough just to breathe. His whole body had tensed up and he was frozen on the spot.

Suddenly this silence was shattered by an immense boom. Norman felt the sound as much as he heard it. It was like a huge sound wave knocking him backwards. He groped around on the stone floor of the balcony, trying to get his bearings. What had happened? Had the Intrepids sprung a surprise for their attacker? Or was it the other way around? Norman scrambled dizzily to his feet and focused his eyes on the scene below.

The poacher had leapt or fallen to the ground and had taken refuge behind his corrugated metal shield. The ladder was still leaning against the tower. As Norman watched, four pale hands reached out from behind the stone parapet and began drawing the ladder up, over the tower wall.

Norman glanced towards Todd for an explanation, but the lawyer only stared back, his look of perpetual amusement never more emphatic. Norman followed the lawyer's eyes to the floor of the balcony, where the gigantic elephant gun lay smoking. He looked back up in shock. Todd had fired the gun . . . no, that was impossible. It had been in his own hands. He looked down at his trembling fingers. They were covered in a fine black dust. *He* had fired the elephant gun.

Only now did he feel the pain beginning to radiate from the spot on his arm where he had held the gun. He rubbed it slowly and turned again to the siege. The ladder was disappearing behind the tower battlements. Norman strained to hear George and Malcolm's voices, but all he could hear was a shrill ringing in his ears.

The poacher retreated from the tower, cowering beneath his shield as he watched the walls of Kelmsworth Hall. When he spotted Todd on the balcony he stopped to shout.

"You! Was that you?" He called Todd a name that Norman had heard in the schoolyard but did not dare repeat. "Stay out of this!" he warned.

Todd said nothing in reply, just stood there staring down at the furious poacher.

He brandished his shield as he screamed, "You're a big man up there with your gun, ain't ya? How 'bout you come down here, then? We'll see who's the big man!"

Again Todd did not reply. A small smile of amusement uncurled across his face. He was enjoying this.

On the tower ramparts Malcolm again emerged and, pulling back his bowstring, drew a bead on their besieger. The poacher was focused on the balcony. He had spotted Norman.

"Hey, kid! Rams fan! It's you. Is that your dad who shot at me?"

Norman shook his head silently.

"Kid, I don't want to give you or your ferret any trouble. Just show me how to get back to New York and I'm outta here. Okay?" His voice cracked as he threatened and pleaded. "Just show me how and we're done. Right?"

Norman was about to open his mouth to say something when Todd finally decided the situation merited his attention. "I believe the steamers for New York leave from Liverpool. If you catch the 2:10 train, you could be in Liverpool tonight," he called down.

Todd's condescending reply sent the poacher into a fury. "Smartass limey, aren't you? You know which New York I want. The *real* New York. Ask Rams boy about it. There ain't no St. Louis Rams in this place, and you both know it. I want the New York where the Rams play the Giants." His anger became a desperate plea. "All I want is to get back. I don't want no trouble."

Norman tugged the sleeve of Todd's black coat. "You need to send him back."

Todd paid no attention. He was more interested in goading the poacher. "I don't believe there are any giants in New York. The place you are talking about sounds like a fantasy land."

"Don't you tell me what's fantasy!" the poacher howled. "I know what's real and what ain't, and what ain't real is talkin' weasels. You better get me back unless you want me to come up there and kick your ass." As he got angrier his shield dropped ever lower, and he shook his fist at Todd.

Todd remained unbothered. "Sir, I'm going to have to ask you to leave the premises," he replied.

"I'll leave the premises when I'm ready, punk," the poacher growled. "I'll leave the damned premises when I leave this whole place, and you're going to help me. Whether you like it or not!" He lowered his shield arm and brought his two hands together in a choking motion.

Malcolm didn't miss his moment this time. The poacher heard the *twang* of the bowstring, but it was too late to protect himself. The missile flew unerringly down towards its target. It struck the poacher in the shoulder. He dropped the shield to the ground and let out a howl. Norman flinched, imagining the pain.

Up on the tower, Malcolm nocked another arrow but held his fire.

The poacher howled and swore as he grasped the tiny arrow in his arm. His face was contorted in pain. He braced himself to remove the arrow but could not bring himself to do it. He turned in a frenzy, like the wounded animal he was. Finally, with one violent tug, he grunted and pulled the missile from his arm. He slumped to his knees, panting and wheezing. When he looked up, his face was twisted with pain and hatred.

Norman willed Malcolm to fire. *Finish him off*, he thought, but the shot never came. The poacher rose to his feet and grabbed the metal shield. Turning like a hammer-thrower, in one smooth motion, he hurled the shield up towards the tower ramparts.

The Cooks and George poked their heads above the folly's walls. They swivelled in unison, following the path of the sheet as it wobbled and clattered against the tower, then fell noisily to the ground.

Norman never took his eyes off the poacher. Before he staggered away across the lawn, he turned once again to glare at Todd

149

on the balcony. His eyes took on an insane white gleam as he stared up at his new enemy.

By the time Norman reached the lawn, the poacher was gone. His corrugated tin sheet lay abandoned on the grass. There was a small spatter of blood on it. Norman stared down at it, mesmerized. It was weird how blood made everything more real.

"By the Maker, Strong Arm, you left it late this time!" Malcolm called down from the ramparts.

Norman waved up to him apologetically. The stoat rappelled down the tower wall.

"Where've you been?" the stoat asked, exasperated, when he reached the lawn. "We were nearly done for there."

"The big lout has attacked us every night for three nights," Pippa recounted breathlessly. Her face was flushed from the excitement of the battle, and her words tumbled out rapidly. "He surprised us by coming in the morning. Lucky we collected our ammunition last night rather than going straight to sleep."

"Lucky you had that bloomin' great big gun of yours," Gordon added, rubbing his unruly red hair out of his face. "Crikey, where did that come from?"

Norman didn't have time to answer. George Kelmsworth moved between the two Cooks to confront Norman. "We could have used that last night, and the night before."

Norman blinked, unsure how to explain. "I came as soon—"

"That's what you always say," George cut him off. "'I came back as soon as I could.'" He mimicked Norman's accent. "We could have all been killed." He lunged towards Norman, who stepped back, alarmed by George's belligerence.

"Steady on, George," Gordon began. But it was Malcolm who stayed the older boy's hand. The stoat leapt onto George's shoulder. George patted the stoat's sleek head and relaxed.

"Let's hear what he has to tell us," Malcolm weighed in. "Norman has always stood by me. Let him have his say."

Norman was confused. Even though Malcolm was standing up for him, it was difficult to see him there on George's shoulder. Why hadn't he leapt immediately to *his* shoulder? He felt a twinge of jealousy and then hopelessness.

"I sounded the alarm . . ." he tried to explain. He looked at the faces of the defenders. Gordon's freckled face was frank and curious, while Pippa was frowning intently and George's eyes were blazing with anger. Norman just raised his hands helplessly.

"What were you doing in there?" Gordon asked, motioning towards the balcony of Kelmsworth Hall. "What were you doing with *him*?" He said the word "him" as if it left a bad taste in his mouth.

Norman turned to see the tall, dark figure of Mr. Todd looming over him. The lawyer placed a hand on Norman's shoulder and smiled his smarmy smile.

"Well done, boys," he congratulated them, as if they'd won a soccer game or done well on a quiz, rather than just escaped with their lives.

Norman grimaced and shrugged the lawyer's hand off his shoulder.

"Why were you in the house, Strong Arm?" Malcolm asked, "Todd's the enemy as much as Baldy is."

"We need his help," Norman insisted, looking from stoat to boy. Their eyes were hardened against him.

"You keep disappearing on us, Strong Arm," Malcolm pleaded. "It's hard to know if we can count on you."

"How far is your house, anyway? How long does it take to get there?" Gordon asked, scrunching an eye as if trying to work it out. His sister pulled him back. Norman gave her a hopeful look, but Pippa just curled her lips, as if suppressing her own rebuke.

"It's complicated. My dad . . ." Norman didn't know where to start, without getting into the bookweird.

"Are you even trying to get Malcolm's map?" George asked.

"Of course I am!" Norman protested. "It's just not easy."

"He's not your stoat, you know," Gordon railed, catching George's anger, as if it were a fever. "You can't own a talking animal."

Getting it from all sides now, Norman just sputtered, "I know that. Listen—"

He felt Todd's hand on his shoulder. "Now, now, children," the lawyer cooed patronizingly, "let's not squabble."

Norman snapped. "Get off!" he shouted, shoving Todd away again. "This is all your fault. Either help us or stay out of it."

Todd stepped back and shook his head, almost like a shiver, in surprise. For a moment he was too stunned to say anything. They all turned to stare at the lanky lawyer now.

"So are you?" Pippa asked finally. The look she gave him wasn't pleading or threatening or even indignant, but there was a sort of impatient force to it. "Are you going to help us?"

Todd continued to stare.

"Or is it war?" Gordon muttered pugnaciously. It would have been funny if they hadn't just barely won a battle for their lives.

A Deal with the Fox

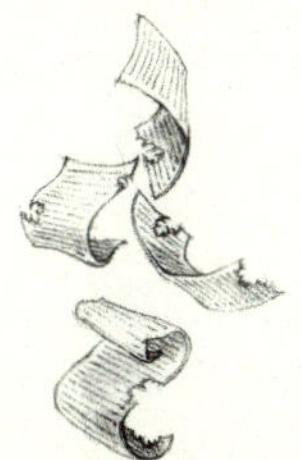

"I don't know why you won't just send him back." Norman stared at his plate in weary disbelief. They had been arguing about this for half an hour, but he always returned to the same question.

Todd placed his knife and fork in a cross on his empty plate. Leaning back in his chair, he intertwined his fingers in front of him and let out the smallest of sighs. "Perhaps you think I'm a magician or something. I'm sorry to disappoint you, but I don't have the power to send people back and forth between books at will."

Norman looked across the table to Malcolm for some support, but the stoat king was distracted by his lemon cake. He peered intently at it, but he hadn't yet taken a bite. The battle at the tower had made him sombre, but he was not as distracted as he appeared. In truth, he was watching Todd covertly. He wasn't convinced that this man was also Abbot Reynard of Tintern Abbey and the Royal Chapel of Lochwarren. The abbot might have used the power of the bookweird to bring him here to this strange world, but he'd said nothing about transformation. If the abbot had come with him to Kelmsworth, wouldn't he still be a fox, just as Malcolm was still a stoat?

"But you could send him back to his own book," Norman insisted. "You sent me back to my own book when we were in New York."

"If you remember correctly," Todd lectured, "you sent yourself back. You have your own peculiar little *ingresso*. I doubt very much that our criminal friend has the same aptitude."

It was true. Todd, in his guise as Fuchs, had only supplied the book. Norman had brought himself back from the New York police station by eating it.

"But it must be possible," Malcolm reasoned. "He got here, didn't he?" He took a distracted bite of the lemon cake. "He must be able to go back."

"Oh, I'm sure it's possible," Todd replied. "But it would take someone who knows a great deal more about the bookweird than I do."

"Do you know anybody?" Norman asked hopefully.

"No one comes to mind." A servant had come in with a pot of tea and all talk of the bookweird ceased for the moment.

"Thank you, Jenkins," Todd murmured.

The servant poured tea in Malcolm's cup. Todd watched him enviously as the servant continued to pour, serving Norman, then Todd.

Jenkins had expressed polite surprise when he'd first learned that some sort of talking weasel was joining them for dinner. He had bowed ever so slightly when Todd had introduced him as King Malcolm of Lochwarren, but Malcolm's first act to Jenkins was to send regards from George. That Malcolm was a friend of the young master was more important to the old servant than his royal status.

Jenkins had asked if His Highness had any special dietary requirements. Malcolm had replied that yes, he did indeed. He needed to eat often and in great quantities, he'd said, letting out one of those peculiar stoat snickers that rippled his white belly. Jenkins had merely bowed and replied, "Of course, sir."

Malcolm raised his head from inside the teacup and licked his lips. He squinted over the rim of the cup and regarded Todd as though he was a man who might try to steal the silverware. This could have been because Todd was the sort of man who *would* steal the silverware, and the entire house that contained it.

"Answer me this one question," he demanded, as if it were a royal command. "Are you actually the Abbot of Tintern?"

Todd smiled and waved his teacup. "Can you ever really know who anybody is?" he asked mysteriously. "Is there a book somewhere that explains exactly who is who?"

Malcolm scowled at Todd's evasion.

"You are George's lawyer, Mr. Todd, but Norman here knows you also as Fuchs. Which are you?"

"Oh, I am most definitely Mr. Todd," he replied solemnly, holding his teacup high in the air as if taking an oath.

"But was Mr. Todd always a thief and a usurper?" Malcolm asked, showing some fang.

"Well, I should take offence to being insulted in my own home," Todd replied, but his face showed that he was anything but insulted. He looked merely amused. "I assure you that everything is as it should be. How could it be otherwise?"

Malcolm leapt from his chair to the table and strode across the tablecloth so he could stare Todd directly in the eyes.

"And if I were to sneak into Kelmsworth Hall tonight"—he paused and tapped the hilt of the rapier in his belt—"and sliced your throat, would we find your dead body at Lochwarren tomorrow morning?"

The lawyer blinked, taken aback by the suddenness and sincerity of this threat.

Norman was glad to see him ruffled a bit. "How about we just tell our friend the poacher out there that you are the one who bookweirded him out of New York?" he said.

The lawyer looked at Norman sharply. He quickly regained his composure, but kept glancing back and forth between the stoat and the boy, assessing them in a new light.

"I'm afraid the bookweird, like the law, is rather complicated, and I can't expect children and stoats to understand it." He smiled while he insulted them. "But perhaps there *is* something I can do to help."

Norman and Malcolm exchanged wary glances. Neither was ready to take Todd at his word.

"Why'd you send us off after the map?" the stoat pressed. He focused his sharp woodland eyes on Todd, scrutinizing his face for signs of the fox abbot he knew. "Is it what Uncle Cuilean says? Is it really a treaty map?"

"Ah, yes, the map." Todd tented his fingers again and pretended to remain uninterested. "You have retrieved the map?"

"First tell us why you want it," Norman countered. "You don't care about Malcolm's treaty with the weasels. If you cared about Malcolm, you wouldn't have let him get caught, and you'd have helped us out there." He gestured towards the window and the folly outside. "You'd have fought with us."

Todd looked down and fiddled with the stiff white cuffs of his shirt, making them even under his coat sleeves.

"Tell us why you want it," Norman repeated.

"Or you'll never see it," Malcolm growled

Todd stopped playing with his shirt-sleeves and scanned the stony faces of the boy and stoat.

"Let's just say that it's an interesting artifact," he began guardedly. "It has some peculiar properties." There was another long pause. "I'd be interested in studying it." Malcolm's ears twitched with interest before the lawyer added, "If you'll permit me." He smiled obsequiously at the stoat.

The king's lip lifted at the side to expose a fang, rather than returning the smile. "How 'bout you stop talking," he warned, seething through his teeth.

Todd attempted one of his smirks, but it did not have its usual effect.

Malcolm reached over his shoulder for his bow. He twanged the string experimentally.

Norman had never before seen Todd, in any of his forms, look at all rattled, but he flinched now. Everything Norman knew about dealing with adults he'd learned from his parents, and he knew that when adults looked weak or indecisive, you pressed your advantage.

"Return Kelmsworth Hall to George and send this poacher back where he came from, and maybe we'll let you see the map." It wasn't really within his right to offer this. He cast a glance to Malcolm, who colluded with the sort of quick wink that only a stoat can wink.

"Let me see the map first, then we'll talk terms," Todd replied snippily.

Norman hesitated just a moment too long in replying.

Todd drew himself up to his full height and placed his hands in front of him on the table. His moment of doubt had passed. "You don't have the map." The all-knowing smile returned to his long, pale face. "You didn't find it."

Norman didn't reply. He didn't have to. Todd read him easily.

"You know where the map is. You know where this person called Meg Jespers-Vilnius has hidden it. What seems to be the problem?"

"The problem is that this person called Meg Jespers-Vilnius is my mother," Norman replied, suddenly tired of this and exasperated.

Todd dismissed the argument. "Interesting, but neither here nor there."

"And Dupin says that if the clue is right, the map isn't in 'The Purloined Letter,'" Norman continued, happy to show Todd that he'd been wrong. "It is hidden *like* the purloined letter, with other maps."

"Yes, of course," Todd mumbled, annoyed that he hadn't thought of it himself. He drummed his long fingers on the table, deep in thought. Suddenly his eyes widened. He pushed his chair back from the table and rose to his feet.

"Could it be . . . ?" he asked, speaking to no one in particular. He began to pace. "Of course!" he concluded, answering his own question. "It's so obvious." Turning to the table again, he surveyed the two faces that looked up at him. "I believe we can come to an arrangement."

Norman and Malcolm exchanged wary glances.

"Shall we use my *ingresso* this time?" the lawyer asked. "Yours doesn't seem to allow passengers." His eyes flicked from Norman to Malcolm, who scowled identical scowls.

"Right, then," Todd continued. "If you'll excuse me, I'll bring some writing materials."

Boy and stoat sat quietly and waited, both impressed with their performance.

"I won't let him send me alone," Norman told his friend earnestly once Todd had left the room. "I'm not going anywhere without you."

The stoat just nodded, his jaw set and his face full of conviction, as if he'd never doubted it.

The lawyer sauntered back into the dining room.

"How are your hands feeling? All loose and ready for a bit of dictation?" he asked breezily. He slid several sheets of thick writing paper across the dining table.

Norman frowned when he read the letterhead: Radisson University, the university where his father taught. This was paper from Norman's world. He looked up to see Todd smirking back at him.

"I think six copies of the following paragraph should do the trick," Todd continued. As he slid a glossy catalogue across the table to them, he sounded like a schoolteacher handing out punishment in detention.

Norman picked up the catalogue and began reading out loud.

"Listing number 202, the Shrubberies. Lovely traditional English cottage nestled in the woods adjacent to a well-stocked river. Easy commute to university and to National Trust–listed stately homes . . ."

"Norman, it will help if you think of someone back home as you write. Think of your dear old mum, perhaps. As for you, wee Malcolm," Todd advised, changing his voice to the croaks and growls of the Abbot of Tintern, "just concentrate on your pal Norman here. He's your connection. If you're ready, the text today is a rental listing. I'm sorry we don't have anything better."

Norman had a few questions to ask. Where had Todd got this house catalogue? How did he know about the Shrubberies? Most of all, he wanted an explanation. He had always wanted to know how the trickster's *ingresso* worked. But Todd interrupted him before he could ask anything.

"By the way," he added, in that knowing way of his, "the book you are looking for is called *A Secret in the Library*."

Malcolm just whispered the name of the book to himself, committing it to memory, as he licked the tip of his pencil eagerly.

Norman gave Todd a long, hard look before he too picked up his pencil and began to write.

My Favourite Book in the Whole Wide World

"This looks a lot like George's book. Are you sure we're in yours?" Malcolm asked.

They lay beside each other on the bed in the Shrubberies. The orange fleece blanket was the same. The same pictures hung crookedly on the wall. Norman's books lined the windowsill. Outside, beyond the flowered curtains, he could see the steady drizzle of a grey English morning.

"I'm sure," Norman told him, regarding the rain outside. "This is my book," he added for the stoat king's benefit. It felt weird to say it, but Norman did not want the discussion about who was more real at this moment.

The stoat perked up. "Something smells good." He stood up and sniffed the air. "Let's hurry up and get that book, and then we can have some breakfast."

"Smells like pancakes," Norman replied. He could tell already that it was going to be difficult to keep Malcolm out of sight.

"Come on, then. Which way is the library?" Malcolm licked his lips with his tiny pink tongue. "I'm hungry, so let's get the job done." He leapt from the bed to the dresser and then to the floor.

"Wait!" Norman cried. "You have to be careful. They can't see you."

"Why not?" Malcolm sounded offended.

"Because stoats don't talk in this book, and neither do mice or rabbits or anything."

"Are you sure?" Malcolm asked, his nose wrinkled skeptically.

"Very sure," Norman assured him.

Malcolm rolled his eyes as if such a thing were preposterous. "Oh well, George and Pippa had never seen a talking stoat before either, and they got over it."

"I tried to stop you then, too," Norman argued. "If things get mixed up, it gets complicated. We could wreck the whole book."

"Did you wreck my book?" Malcolm asked impatiently.

"I nearly did, didn't I? It was because of me that you got stranded at Scalded Rock. It was because of me that Simon Whiteclaw died."

Malcolm blinked and started to say something. "All right," he conceded reluctantly. "You check if the coast is clear."

Norman dashed down to the kitchen to find his dad at the stove. Edward Vilnius knew how to cook two things, and only one of them was suitable for breakfast.

Norman verified that there was a pot of coffee on the counter beside his dad before inquiring, "Pancakes?"

"You know it, Spiny." He turned around to offer Norman a plate. "But with a twist. These are *English* pancakes, in honour of your mother and her rediscovered Englishness. Apparently you eat them this way." He spread jam on the thin crepe and rolled it into a tight tube.

Norman took the plate of pancakes from his father but did not sit down. "Where is Mum?" he asked, as casually as he could.

"Gone for a jog," said Edward.

So that was his mother accounted for. It just might be safe to sneak into the library.

Norman picked up the crepe and took a tentative bite from one end. "Hmmph. That's actually pretty good," he mumbled through a mouthful of pancake.

"Full of surprises, these English," his father said, his back turned. "You want to tempt fate and wake your sister? She's supposed to be up by now."

Norman didn't need to be asked again. He bounded back upstairs, stopping by Dora's door to listen for just a moment. Once he'd confirmed that all was quiet inside, he tiptoed down the hall and opened his own door just a crack. "Malcolm, the coast is clear. We can search the library."

There was no answer. He opened the door wider and poked his head inside. "Malcolm?" he repeated in a loud whisper as he scanned the room for his friend. The stoat had vanished. Why couldn't he just stay put?

Norman hurried down the hall to the library. The door was gapped just wide enough for a stoat to squeeze through. Norman opened it wide and whispered Malcolm's name again.

"Over here," the stoat replied, from somewhere in the shelves.

Norman ducked inside and closed the door behind him. "Where are you?" he whispered hoarsely.

"That's the biggest pancake I've ever seen!" From somewhere over Norman's shoulder, Malcolm whistled appreciatively. Norman turned in time to see the pancake snatched from his plate in one lightning-quick movement.

"I told you to wait for me."

"There's no time to be wasted. We have to get that map and get back to George." He stood on a shelf chomping on the rolled-up pancake voraciously, as if he were biting its head off.

"Okay, let's get going," Norman urged him. "My mom might be back any minute. I'll search the shelves from my head down. You search the higher ones I can't reach.

Malcolm stuffed the pancake in his mouth crossways, like a buccaneer's dagger, and leapt nimbly to the top shelf.

Norman knelt down and began his own search on the row where he'd located the Intrepids books. He pulled out the biggest encyclopaedia volumes and stacked them beside him on the floor so he could examine the second row properly.

Up on the high shelves, Malcolm chattered while he searched. "This Fuchs-Todd fellow seems to know an awful lot about you and your family, don't you think?" he mumbled through the pancake.

"I suppose," Norman replied. He wasn't really listening. He was thinking about finding the book and getting out of there without anybody seeing the talking stoat.

Malcolm pressed the question. "Don't you think it's a bit strange that he knows what books are in your library?"

"I guess so." The same thing had been bothering Norman. He just didn't want to think about it yet. He finished rifling through the shelf of Intrepids books. There was no *Secret in the Library* amongst them.

The stoat was making swift progress on the top shelves, darting from book to book and scanning them as rapidly as he spoke. "He must have been here, right? You saw how he got us here. He told us to think about someone in this book. He told you to think about your mum. He told me to think about you. Same as last time back in Lochwarren. The abbot told me to concentrate on you."

"There was something about the paper, too," said Norman without looking up from his search. "That paper was from my dad's university. Was there anything special about the paper the abbot used to get into George's book?"

The stoat stopped his search and replied eagerly, "Yeah, there was! It was a contract. Abbot had me write on the back of it. I didn't understand a word of it, all lawyer gibberish, but it was something about Kelmsworth Hall. Abbot told me it helped for beginners to have something from in the book. Said paper was best, but any old thing would do in a pinch. He told me he could fetch you using your shoe."

"He said that?" Norman stopped, alarmed by the thought. "He said he could *fetch* me?" Norman had left a sneaker behind in Undergrowth. It was now bolted to the wall of the grand hall of Lochwarren Castle.

The stoat nodded grimly.

"He needs something from inside that book," Norman concluded. "Or maybe he needs to follow someone else. He followed me into *The Magpie*."

"So how did he get here?" Malcolm asked again. "How does he know about your library?"

"He could have followed me. He knew me from before, from the library back in America. He could have nabbed something of mine. Some of my papers. Maybe he's got some of my school notes. It would explain how I lose so many of them."

It left one big question. Norman had been trying not to think about it, but Malcolm wouldn't leave it alone.

"How'd he get here the *first* time?"

Norman waved the question away. "Maybe he met someone here. Maybe someone from here visited his book and left her shoe," Norman muttered. He was thinking all of a sudden about his mom.

Malcolm finished another shelf and leapt to the next. "I think he's from here," he said. "I think he's from the same book as you. That's how he knows about the library and everything else." Malcolm had convinced himself, if nobody else

"Shhh," Norman hushed him. The problem of Fuchs–Todd was just a distraction now. How *did* he know about the library here at the Shrubberies? How did he know anything? How had he known where Norman would be to rescue him that time in *The Magpie*, and why was he not helping more now?

"And another thing," Malcolm continued, getting it all off his chest, "if he could send us here, he could come here himself. Couldn't he? Why didn't he?"

"I suppose he didn't want to get caught. If he got caught taking the book out of the house here, he'd be taken in as a burglar. Right? If I do it, it's just me not doing what I'm told again."

"He's got us doing his dirty work," the stoat grumbled.

"He won't get the map from me. And he's not getting this book, either," Norman snapped. "I'll make sure of that."

"What book? And who's not getting it?" a stern voice demanded.

Norman jumped at the sound. It wasn't Malcolm's voice at all. It was his father's. "Who were you talking to?" he asked.

"Myself." Norman's eyes darted to the shelf where Malcolm had last stood, but the animal had vanished.

"Aren't you supposed to be waking Dora up?" Edward Vilnius's voice was deep and strained. Norman never could tell when his dad might be cheerful or annoyed. Sometimes his mood changed without warning. Mom usually put it down to how well his work was going. Norman thought lack of coffee was a more important factor.

"Did you leave that book out?" Edward frowned and indicated the encyclopaedia on the floor.

"I was just about to put it away."

"Yes, you were," Edward declared firmly. "Do it and get downstairs and finish your breakfast. When you're done you can go outside and play. I'm trying to write this morning, and I don't want you hanging around the house."

Norman twisted to look over his shoulder. There was no sign of Malcolm. "I'll just put the encyclopaedia away."

"I'll deal with it." Edward Vilnius put a firm hand on Norman's shoulder and ushered him out the door.

Norman didn't go outside after breakfast, even after his father had returned upstairs to work and Dora had begun rummaging frantically for her riding gear. All Norman could think of was the library and what Malcolm was doing up there by himself. He was still moping around the kitchen table when his mom came in from her jog.

Her hair and running cap were wet from the morning rain, but she didn't seem to care. She was her old self, relaxed and happy after her run. It was hard to imagine that yesterday she had given him a lecture about the bookweird. It was as if it had never happened, but Norman was still nervous when she climbed the stairs, carrying two cups of coffee. He craned his neck to watch her go up and prayed that she didn't go into the library.

Upstairs he heard doors opening and closing and the low, muffled conversation of his parents. He had no idea what they were saying. It was several minutes before they both came down. His mother's face was hard to read, but his father raised a warning eyebrow.

Had she been to the library?

"Your father tells me he's had to lock you out of the library."
Meg flashed Edward a smile, but Norman wasn't fooled. He was
being set up.

His father's stern face softened, as though he saw the humour
in this. "Wasn't the trouble last time being locked *inside* the library?"
he asked.

That was true. The last time he'd returned from Undergrowth,
Norman had woken up in the public library.

Meg took a sip of coffee and regarded him coolly over the rim
of her mug. "What were you looking for in there, anyway?"

Norman couldn't think what the best answer was. Should he
just say he was looking for an Intrepids book?

"He was looking something up in the encyclopaedia, apparently," Edward offered. "Seems the boy's trying to educate himself
now that we've forbidden it."

166

His mother gave his father an indulgent smile and took the
empty coffee cup from his hand. Something in her glance told
Norman that his father didn't know the whole story either. But the
idea of his mother keeping a secret from his father was even more
far-fetched than her being able to tap into the bookweird.

"What were you looking up?" she asked breezily, putting both
cups in the sink and turning on the tap.

"Actually, I was just looking for something to read."

"What? More Intrepids?" she called over her shoulder. She
handed a dish towel to her husband, who joined her at the sink.

It was as if they had never had the other conversation. Not two
days ago she had forbidden him to touch the Intrepids. Maybe this
was a trap.

"No, no, not the Intrepids," he reassured her. "I didn't much
like it. George Kelmsworth is a bit of a know-it-all, and it's obvious
that the lawyer is ripping him off."

"He's a know-it-all, is he?" Meg repeated with a wry smile.
"He seemed like the perfect boy to me. Intelligent. Brave . . ."

"Obedient?" Norman couldn't resist the poke.

"Respectful," his mother replied pointedly.

Norman relaxed a little. This was more normal: his father amusingly grumpy, and his mother cheerful and teasing. It was impossible to imagine her now as his opponent in a game of hide-and-seek inside books. He'd feel whole lot better, though, if he knew what Malcolm was getting up to in the library.

What he needed to do was change the subject. "Mom, can I ask you something?"

"Of course."

Norman began hesitantly. "It's about another book."

"Yes?" she turned warily to face him.

"About that book you were reading last year, the crime story, *The Magpie*."

She looked at him sharply now. "What about it?"

"Did they ever catch the killer?"

"Of course they caught the killer," she replied. "They always catch the killer."

"Are you sure?" He was frowning now, as if the question deeply concerned him.

"Why are you asking?"

"It's just something that has been bugging me. I read a bit of it last year. You told me not to, but I did, and I sometimes dream about it." He pulled the pathetic face he used when he was trying to get out of going to school.

His mother's face softened. "This is a Conran book, right? With Rorschach and Darwin?"

Norman nodded.

"It's the one that gets weird. A body disappears from a crime scene and there's a horse there instead." Meg thought for a while, trying to remember the details. "It wasn't very good. I stopped reading Conran after that."

"It was the big bald guy, right?" Norman gulped. "The one who steals credit cards and works out at Vito's Gym?"

Meg didn't reply. That look of suspicion returned, as if Norman's question had suddenly given her an idea of where that horse might have come from.

Drying dishes at the counter, Norman's father was oblivious to his wife's wary tone. "No, that's not it. That's that Wentz guy, Rorschach's snitch," he interrupted. "Bit of a sad character, really— kicked out of the army, became a small-time crook and informant. Remember, Meg? He was in the movie version, too."

Meg coughed, interrupting him. "Why are you asking this again?"

"Wentz," Norman repeated, wanting to hear it confirmed. "He's the killer?"

"Why would you think that?" she asked, avoiding the question.

"I guess he was in the part of the book I read, and I dreamed the rest."

"That," she admonished, "is why you should keep your nose out of books that aren't meant for you."

There was a long silence that was broken only by Dora's arrival. Norman wondered how long she'd been standing at the bottom of the stairs.

"Can I get a drive to Penny's? I'm going to be late now."

"You can walk the back way," Meg replied, but she didn't take her eyes off Norman. "If you hurry, you'll get there on time."

Perhaps it was something in Meg's tone, but Edward Vilnius turned to look, placing a dried plate on the counter behind him. Something over Norman's shoulder caught Edward's attention. He stepped towards the back window and peered out. "Norman, is that your book again out there on the lawn?" His tone had turned grim.

Norman stood up and looked out. "I don't think so." He had learned that just because he didn't remember doing something, it didn't mean he hadn't done it. "I'll go see."

"You stay where you are," his father told him. He strode to the door and let himself into the backyard.

Dora followed her father to the doorway. She watched for a second while he fetched the book, turning back only to mouth, "You're in trouble," her ponytail bouncing in rhythm with the singsong taunt.

"I thought you were late," Meg reminded her.

Dora managed to pull one more face before slipping out the door.

Norman opened his mouth to respond, but his mother's voice snapped him to attention.

"You didn't listen to my warning, did you?"

Any trace of a smile had vanished, and her eyebrow was arched like a taut bow. Her eyes looked about ready to fire arrows.

Norman could not reply. He bit his lip and glanced anxiously from his mother's angry glare to the scene outside.

"I can't tell you how much you remind me of your uncle Kit sometimes," she muttered. Norman could tell this was not a good thing.

On the lawn Edward waved goodbye to Dora and stooped to pick up an open book from the grass. He looked around as if he expected to catch the reader somewhere in the garden, and then glanced up towards the roof or the second-storey window. Apparently seeing no one, he returned to the kitchen with the book. As he walked, he turned the book back and forth in his hand and brushed bits of grass from the cover.

"*A Secret in the Library*. Ever heard of it?" he asked, closing the door behind him.

All Norman could do was shake his head slowly from side to side. He knew he looked guilty, but he didn't know what sort of noise would come out. He didn't dare open his mouth.

Meg Jespers-Vilnius fixed Norman with the full power of her motherly stare. She waited for him to blink and look away.

"Strange thing is that it's perfectly dry. The rain only just stopped before you came in from your run." Edward turned the book over in his hands, perplexed.

"Can I see that, Edward?" Meg asked gently. Norman wasn't fooled by the evenness of her voice. He was in big trouble.

"Have you heard of it?" Edward asked as he handed her the book.

She turned the pages carefully, smoothing them out with her fingers. "It's probably my favourite book in the entire universe." She ran her fingertips across the blue cloth cover and opened it gently. She did not raise her head for a long minute. "It is also extremely, extremely rare." She clapped the book shut and regarded Norman evenly. "You're very lucky that there's no damage. When your grandfather gave this to me, he told me that it might just be the only copy left."

She watched Norman and let the seriousness of the situation sink in. He gulped.

Her face softened, but not completely. Norman knew he was being warned. "I don't think we need an inquisition on this. I'm sure you didn't mean to leave my book out on the lawn, and you had no idea how valuable it was, but it was careless. Until you show us you can be a little more careful, your ban from the library stands. Now go outside and get some fresh air."

Norman's father scowled as if he thought his son had got off lightly.

Norman knew better. He understood that tone of his mother's, when she spoke slowly and clearly, enunciating every word. It was worse than being shouted at. He rose quietly and headed to the door. What could he say? He'd been wrongly convicted but lightly punished. It was best not to argue.

"Norman," his mother called brightly as he headed out the door, "thank you for finding this. I'd almost forgotten it. I can't wait to read it again."

As she put the book in her purse there was a hard glint in her eyes. She knew he was up to something. She'd said that to make a point. He was to keep his hands off that book.

Norman just muttered, "You're welcome." It was the craziest thing to say, but she had said thank you.

Norman dangled his legs over the little bridge that spanned the brook behind their cottage. He didn't even bother throwing pebbles. He just watched his feet sway beneath him. He might as well give up now, he thought. The bookweird had brought him face to face with some fearsome enemies. He'd been attacked by heavily armed ravens and pursued by wolves bent on killing him. He'd been in the clutches of a ruthless murderer. He'd snuck into the private apartment of a notorious blackmailer and political schemer. And he'd have happily done any of these things again, but he did not think that he could really defy his mother. There was no way he could get that book now. *A Secret in the Library* was truly off limits, and with it so was Malcolm's map. He was going to have a hard time explaining that to the stoat.

"So did you get my little present?" The question made Norman jump. He turned to find Malcolm beside him on the bridge. The stoat chuckled, obviously pleased to have startled him.

"No, I did *not*," Norman replied sullenly.

Malcolm lifted his arms in helpless outrage. "After all that? That's an enormous book even for a powerful stoat like myself."

Norman exhaled exasperatedly. "You left it on the lawn!"

"Left it on the lawn? That's not the half of it!" The stoat leapt onto the bridge railing so he was eye to eye with Norman. His whiskers twitched as he tried to convey the heroism of his actions. "It took me ages to find it. Then I had to get it down and out the window. Do you know how hard it was to manhandle that thing out of there?"

Norman's jaw dropped open. "You threw *A Secret in the Library* out the window?"

"Like a yeoman chucking boulders down from the ramparts." He puffed out his chest proudly.

Norman couldn't hide his disbelief. "You could have damaged it. That's my mother's favourite book in the whole world, you know."

Malcolm sat down on the railing. "That figures," he concluded. "She hid my map in her favourite book." He put a paw on the boy's shoulder. "Are you ready to ingress?"

"I can't," he muttered sulkily, staring down at the water in the brook. "My mum took it back."

Malcolm rolled his tiny black eyes comically. "All right, where did she put it this time?" he huffed. "Nowhere too hard for me to break into, I hope."

"She put it in her purse," he muttered. "She wants to reread it."

Malcolm leapt up, ready to go. "Easy as lingonberry pie, then. She'll have it with her tonight when she's asleep."

Norman shook his head warily. He knew he'd already pushed it too far with his mother. "Maybe there's another way we can prove your claim to the throne."

Malcolm shrugged. He knew he'd convince Norman somehow. "Listen, Strong Arm, I was just talking to some rabbits—"

"What throne?"

The shrill voice behind him startled Norman. He turned around to see Dora standing at the other end of the bridge. He snapped his head back to warn Malcolm, but the stoat had already ducked out of sight.

"Who are you talking to?" Dora asked, wrinkling her nose.

"Myself," Norman replied defensively.

"*I* stopped having imaginary friends a long time ago," she said. Norman bit his tongue.

"Are you playing knights and castles?" she continued.

Norman just stared, hoping that ignoring her would make her go away.

"You were talking about a throne. Can I play?"

"I thought you were going to Penny's."

"I was too late. They've already gone on their ride. You made me miss it."

Norman found it hard to accept that this was his fault. She should have woken up on time herself.

Dora stood and looked at him, placing her hands on her hips as she worked out a way to annoy him. "You're wrong about that book, you know."

Norman stared at her silently, hoping that she would just go away, but she carried on.

"That murder book. Wentz isn't the murderer."

"How would you know?"

"I saw the movie. Pippa and I watched it at her house. Wentz isn't the murderer. He's just a robber, but he works for one of the police guys. He's an informal. The police guy gives him money for information."

"You mean he's an *informant*?" Norman said, trying to piece it together.

"That's what I said," Dora replied petulantly. "Anyway, he's not the murderer."

Norman just looked at her and thought about what this meant.

"Do you want to play Clue, then?" she asked, almost plaintively.

"Later," Norman told her, eager to get rid of her. "You go set it up."

Dora regarded him warily for a moment, then decided to believe him. She twirled and skipped off back towards the house.

"She seems all right," Malcolm said, appearing again as quickly as he had disappeared. "Is she coming with us to help?"

Norman rolled his eyes at the thought.

Malcolm took the hint and returned to the problem. "So your mum has the map. We can get it tonight."

Norman turned to the stoat, his eyes pleading. "You .don't understand. My mother explicitly told me not to touch the book. I can't defy her. Would you have defied your father?"

The stoat paused and thought for a long moment, his eyes darkening and his furry brow wrinkling into a sombre furrow. Norman knew he must be thinking of Duncan, his father, who had died on the battlefield during the long war to wrest the highland kingdom from the wolves.

"Have you another plan?" he asked finally.

They sat on the bridge and schemed for a long time. Norman was for going directly back to Undergrowth, but Malcolm wouldn't hear of it.

"It's not just about me anymore," he declared. "I could go back to Lochwarren and fight. My people will fight with me, with or without the treaty map. But we can't leave George. You can't do that to a friend. You can't abandon him." The stoat looked directly into Norman's eyes before continuing. "You didn't abandon me."

Norman was already nodding his agreement. Malcolm was right. They would stick by George.

"We'll do it tonight," he declared firmly.

A Secret in the Library

The cold, wet touch of the stoat's nose woke him. Norman looked around to see where he was. It was a habit now—you could never be sure. But he was still in the room where he and Malcolm had fallen asleep hours earlier. He blindly patted the pillow beside him to reassure himself that the stoat was there, but the indent in the pillow was cold.

He blinked the sleep from his eyes to open them. Moonlight shone in through the gap in the curtains, lighting up the face of the stoat, who stood beside him.

"Wha—?" Norman asked in a groggy voice.

"I've done your booknapping again," Malcolm whispered.

Norman rubbed his eyes and saw that the stoat's foot was planted proudly on the blue cover of a book.

"Malcolm, did you get this from—?"

"Yer mum's room? Yes," the stoat replied. "Let me tell you, it was no easy thing."

Norman sat up in bed. "If she'd seen you—" he began.

"If she'd seen me she'd've thought some wild animal had got into the house." He paused and grinned, exposing his sharp teeth. "I suppose one has." He removed his foot so Norman could pick up the book.

"But this is dangerous. You could've been caught." Norman didn't even want to imagine it. He ran his fingers across the woven cloth cover. "So this is it?" he whispered.

"You remember what else your mum said? It's *Intrepid Amongst the Gypsies* that changes everything for George. If we let Todd take this over, George'll lose it all. Let's just find the map and I'll take the book back. You wouldn't let George down now, would you?"

Norman gave the pages an experimental flip, catching a few of the chapter titles: "The Sultan's Arabian," "In the Dungeons of Acre," "The Oasis of Agadir."

"Looks exciting," Malcolm murmured in his ear.

"Uh-huh," Norman agreed. He was already reading the first paragraph.

"You want me to take it back?" Malcolm asked mischievously.

Norman rubbed the stoat's head, ruffling his hair in reply. The stoat squirmed away, grinning.

"No need to say thanks," he said. "I can see you're busy."

They both settled back on the pillow to read, Norman holding the book so they could both see it. Despite it all, Norman couldn't help feeling just a little bit happy. It was like old times, the two of them together again.

As the fiery orange sun came up over desert dunes and a low wind began to howl through the turrets and arrow loops of St. Savino in the Desert, a lone rider appeared on the horizon. Silhouetted by the rising sun, horse and rider were clearly on their last legs. His progress was slow, his mount tiring. Few would have suspected that this was one of the finest knights in the Holy Land approaching, nor that he was riding the pick of the sultan's Arabians. They looked a sorry pair, far from their majestic former selves. The man's armour was tattered and bloodstained. The horse's mane was ragged, and its jet black coat was smeared with red sand. But a weaker man and a weaker horse would have succumbed days ago to the heat, the marauding attacks of the Saracen and the relentless speed of their escape. They should have been two piles of bones in the desert by now, food for the vultures and the wild dogs, but instead they were alive and within two arrow shots of safety in the refuge of St. Savino.

The clang of the portcullis chains and the strained creak of the drawbridge gears were already echoing across the dunes when the sharpest eyes in the lookout towers realized their error. It wasn't that there should have been two piles of bones in the desert—there ought to have been three. Seated on the horse behind the knight, slumped and unmoving, was another figure. Much smaller than the first man, he wore no armour. His body tossed and jerked with the motion of the horse. It was only a boy, but perhaps he would be a pile of bones before the other two. As the horse and riders reached the gate, the defenders of the desert refuge realized their other mistake. From a distance, the battle grime had obscured the crest of the knight who approached. Only now could they see that he wore the distinctive sea blue cross of the Livonian Knights.

That evening, when Sir John of Nantes and two dozen knights arrived at St. Savino, there was no hiding the black stallion that raged in the stables. The horse had been fed and watered, but no stable hand within those walls could calm him.

"Where is the knight who rode this horse?" John of Nantes demanded.

The governor of St. Savino, Hugh Montclair, answered the great man calmly, if not truthfully. "The horse arrived alone. It came across the desert, fleeing this morning's sandstorm. There was no rider." Hugh Montclair knew the risk he was taking in lying to Black John. John of Nantes was possibly the most powerful man in the Holy Land, a man who answered only to the King of France, and only when it suited him.

"There is a fresh grave in your cemetery, unmarked," John of Nantes continued, undeterred. "Whose body lies there?"

The prior of St. Savino, Father Lombard, took his turn to lie. "Those are the bones of Tachino the leper. He died last night of his affliction."

John of Nantes curled the nostrils of his noble nose at the very thought of such a disease.

The body they'd buried might as well have been that of a leper. They'd burned his clothes as quickly and as completely as they would if he'd had the plague.

Sir John and his men spent the night searching St. Savino. They scoured the kitchens, the dungeons, the stables, the armoury and the priests' cells. They even took a short, perfunctory look around St. Savino's dusty little library. But they did not find the rider of that horse, or the boy he had brought with him.

The men who saw the ragged pair ride through the gates that morning expected to be digging a grave for the boy, so sickly and exhausted had he been, but those were not the boy's bones that lay in the fresh grave outside the walls. It was the knight whom they had buried, the knight whose name they never knew, but whose sea blue cross they feared. The nameless warrior had collapsed as he'd dismounted and was dead within the hour. By noon he had been sent to whatever afterlife he deserved. His leather armour and the tunic bearing the offending crest were nothing but a pile of grey ash in the kitchen hearth.

Of the boy even less was known. He wore no armour and no crest. He had not spoken because he had yet to awaken. Brother Godwyn, the archivist and herbalist, did his best to treat the boy's visible wounds and left him to sleep in a tiny cell behind a wall of scrolls in the library.

The next morning, Black John and his knights rode out of St. Savino. He might not have known about the secret in the library, but John of Nantes had a feeling, as he turned back for a final glance at St. Savino's single tower, that he would be returning one day for a more satisfactory visit.

Malcolm said what Norman was thinking: "This is a great story."

"Uh-huh," Norman agreed. "That boy must be a prince or something."

"Or the son of Black John's enemy," Malcolm suggested excitedly.

Norman put the book down, his arm sore from holding it for them both.

"It's weird, though. This doesn't seem like a book my mom would read. It's . . . well . . ." Norman couldn't find the right word. "It just seems too exciting for a girl."

"Well, didn't you tell me she reads mystery books, books where someone has been murdered? That knight has obviously been murdered."

Norman murmured a skeptical "Hmmm."

"Keep reading," the stoat king urged. "My bet is that there's a girl in it soon, someone to fall in love with the boy in the library."

Norman turned on his side and let the stoat settle in the crook of his neck, where he could see the book. As a precaution Norman angled the lamp beside his bed so it shed less light towards the door. If his parents discovered him now, he'd be in huge trouble. If that happened, it might almost be worth introducing them to the talking stoat, just to distract them.

The opening of *A Secret in the Library* was a little bit misleading, but by the time Malcolm and Norman had realized it, they were too far into the book to care. There were none of the Crusader battles and knights in armour that they had been led to expect. It was mostly about the boy growing up in the desert outpost of St. Savino.

Two days after his arrival at the desert fort, the boy woke up. He remembered nothing about his ride across the sands. He didn't even remember his own name.

He remained in his tiny cell for a week, cared for by Brother Godwyn. Only three men visited him there: Godwyn, Father Lombard and Hugh Montclair himself.

After a week's convalescence, the skinny, pale-skinned boy was able to walk about and speak both in French and in a strange northern tongue that startled and worried anyone who heard it. He also had a smattering of German and Latin, so he was obviously high-born, probably the son of a crusading knight, but that was all that they could determine. It was enough. The blue Livonian cross on his rescuer's surcoat told the most important part of his story: the boy was both dangerous and in danger himself.

Only Father Lombard, Montclair and Godwyn knew that he was alive, concealed in Godwyn's library. When he was well enough to walk, the boy was allowed the freedom of the archives and a small hidden courtyard. His entire life was constrained to the tiny space of the courtyard and the library. He spoke only to the three men who protected him. Each of them grew to love him. Each tried to teach him, to protect him and to replace the father who was no doubt dead on some battlefield somewhere.

The boy studied history with Sir Hugh and scripture with Father Lombard, but it was the books of Godwyn's library that he loved the most. They took to calling the boy Jerome, after the saint who had first translated the Bible into Latin. The boy answered to that name, but as he lay in the tiny chamber behind the bookshelves each night, he prayed for his real name to come back to him in a dream, the name that his dead father had given him.

The boy whom they called Jerome was not unhappy in the library. The library was the most important part of St. Savino. The fort existed only because of it. A hundred years ago the hermit St. Savino had unearthed this trove of ancient scrolls in his desert cave. The Crusaders had come, built the walls and the tower and enlarged the church, but the heart of St. Savino remained the hermit's collection of scrolls. Scholars across Europe coveted its treasures: sermons of ancient prophets, diagrams of temples and palaces, and maps to lost cities and treasure mines. This archive was kept in the highest tower of the fort and jealously guarded by a series of archivists, the latest of which was Brother Godwyn.

Brother Godwyn had been a young man when he'd arrived in the Holy Land, but he was now old and grey and bent by years. When Hugh Montclair had brought the boy to him, Godwyn had rolled his ancient eyes and arranged the hiding place. Charged with the boy's education, the archivist had bowed slowly and taken on the burden, but it soon became no burden at all. Jerome was bright and attentive, cheerful without being boisterous. He learned quickly and eagerly and soon became Godwyn's assistant, copying texts that the old man's failing eyes could no longer read and asking the questions that prodded the old man's sluggish mind to solutions.

The young foundling became the Holy Land's youngest scholar. Godwyn finished off the boy's foundation in Latin and added Greek and Aramaic. When Jerome had mastered these, they turned to English.

Brother Godwyn had almost forgotten the language of his own homeland. It was decades since he'd spoken it regularly. Only in his dreams, when the desert wasteland of the day was replaced by the green hills of his youth, did he speak and hear English. It was a pleasure to be able to speak it out loud again with the strange boy with the prodigious facility for languages.

As Jerome grew older and the archivist's eyes grew weaker, Brother Godwyn enlisted him in his great struggle to maintain the archive at St. Savino. For years the kings of England and France had tried to get their hands on the St. Savino scrolls. England and France agreed that the scrolls were not safe in this far-off desert outpost. The kings disagreed only on whether the scrolls would be safer in London or Paris. Brother Godwyn's campaign of letter writing had kept the courts of England and France at bay and at each other's throats for years. The boy now acted as his scribe.

Jerome and Godwyn worked together during the warm desert days at the top of the tower that housed the library. It was just a few small rooms, tightly packed with shelves, but it contained documents of incalculable value. Every cubbyhole was stuffed with scrolls. Brother Godwyn and Jerome had hardly begun their quest to catalogue them. There were scrolls there that no hand had unravelled for hundreds of years.

"That's where your map is," Norman declared.

"Sure as Stoats," Malcolm agreed. "When are we going?"

Norman shook his head reluctantly. "We can't both go. My *ingresso* works only for me." He knew his friend wanted to be part of the action, and to tell the truth, he would have liked to have the little warrior at his side.

"Then let's get back to Kelmsworth. We'll make Todd send us both."

Norman had thought about this already, but he had realized the limitations of the lawyer's *ingresso*. "He can't either. He was bluffing. He needs more than just the book. He needs something from it. He needs a piece of paper, something, or else he can't get in. He didn't think we'd figure it out, but that's why he needs our help."

"But you can't get in either. You can't eat a page of this book. You know what your mum said. It could be the only copy."

Malcolm was right. He couldn't eat any part of *A Secret in the Library*. "I don't know what would happen if I ate the last copy. Probably its whole world would disappear. But I don't have to. I can just copy part of it and eat it."

The stoat started to say something, but instead he sighed and snarled, showing his little fang in frustration. "I don't like being put out of the action like this. At least if I were back in Kelmsworth, I could be helping George."

"I wish you were coming too. I don't like the looks of this Black John guy."

The stoat just stared back silently, his whiskers rippling with a frown. But there was one thing about Malcolm you could always count on—he never stayed down for long.

"Right, there's no use moping about it." He bared his teeth determinedly. "You fetch a pen and paper. I'll find that page about the library."

The section about the library was almost perfect, a full page, four paragraphs, describing its location at the centre of a maze of chambers, how it could be reached only by a flimsy wooden stairway, its rows of shelves and cubbyholes for the scrolls.

Norman sat down at the desk and slid out a blank piece of foolscap. Malcolm held the book open for him with his small paws while Norman copied it out in the tiniest letters he could manage.

He was going to have to eat it, and he wanted to keep it late-night-snack size. The result was just barely readable.

Malcolm huffed and tutted as he looked it over. "You should have let me do it. I could have written it much smaller and tidier. This looks like it was done by a palsied giant."

"We didn't have all month," Norman shot back.

Malcolm held up his paws and grimaced. They were not made for holding a pen. "All right, then," he conceded. "*Bon appétit.*"

"Promise me you'll put the book back when I'm gone," Norman pleaded between chewing, swallowing and ripping another strip of foolscap.

"Sure," replied the stoat. He wasn't convincing. "When I've read some more."

"No, right away. You have to put it back," Norman insisted. "If my mom wakes up and finds it gone . . ." That was certainly part of the reason, but something else bothered him about Malcolm reading on without him. Maybe it was just that he didn't want his friend to know more of the story. Part of him felt weird about Malcolm reading a book when he was in it. "You need to get it back as soon as possible. I've no idea what time my parents get up in the morning."

"Okay, sure," Malcolm assured him.

Norman wasn't assured. "Promise?" He looked him in the eye.

Malcolm's glossy black eye stared back for a long time before blinking. "Just be quick and bring back that map."

They lashed one of Norman's belts around the book to make it easier for the stoat to carry. It was still an enormous load for the little animal, but Malcolm just winked and hoisted it over his shoulder. Like all stoats, he was enormously strong for his size. He left by the bedroom window and promised to be back within the hour. Norman lay in bed waiting, imagining he could hear his friend scrambling up the drainpipes and across the roof, but sleep finally came, and he never felt the stoat return and curl up in the crook of his arm beside him.

More Secrets in the Library

It was more than dark. It was the dark of a windowless room. He could tell without opening his eyes. The dark seemed to seep in through Norman's closed eyelids. The air was thick and hot and heavy on his skin. He had to fight the panic that made him want to flail his arms around to find a light switch. There would be no light switch here.

There was a scent in the air that Norman recognized, that peculiar scent of old books. It reminded Norman of the library at his father's university, a sort of dusty, homey smell that made you tired but not sleepy, just the right mood for reading books. But Norman was not waking up at the university library. He knew with absolute certainty that he was waking up in Brother Godwyn's library in the desert fortress of St. Savino.

His eyes opened, but there was nothing to see. The dark was absolute.

"Jeeze," he admonished himself with a whisper, "you could have brought a flashlight."

Slowly he rose to his knees. The rough-hewn planks beneath him creaked as he shifted his weight. Cautiously he reached out into the dark, his fingertips grasping for something to grab onto and pull himself up. They touched nothing. He waved his hands, but they just wafted in the air. It made him dizzy, kneeling there in the dark with nothing to brace himself with. He could be on a high balcony or at the top of the stairs. The bookweird didn't really think about safety when it set you down somewhere.

"Okay, Norman," he whispered, "just relax. Close your eyes." He screwed them closed, as tight as he could. It was a trick you used when sneaking downstairs to inspect your presents on Christmas Eve. Closed your eyes tight so you got used to absolutely no light. When you opened them, your eyes would be ready to take advantage of the smallest amount of illumination.

His eyelids opened slowly again to absolute darkness. He could hear his breathing now, ragged and scared, panting as if he'd just run a race, but only his mind was racing. Where was he? Had he woken up in a sealed chamber? Was this the dungeon instead of the library? He cursed himself for his lack of preparation. The bookweird could get you into a locked room, but you needed a book to get yourself out again, or at least a page. Norman had counted on writing himself home. How could he do that now without any paper and no light to read or write by?

"Stop it. Stop thinking like this. Just relax," he hissed.

"Who are you talking to?" a voice asked. It wasn't an especially deep voice or a threatening tone, but Norman jumped anyway. He wasn't alone here in the dark. He stayed as still as he could, not answering. If Norman couldn't see the owner of the other voice, the other voice couldn't see him. He thought of Bilbo Baggins falling into Gollum's cave in *The Hobbit* and his heart raced a little more.

"Who are you talking to?" the voice repeated. It was a curious voice, not an angry one. It sounded thoroughly unsurprised that Norman had arrived here in the middle of its darkness, but still Norman did not answer.

"Shall I open the skylight so you can see? Your eyes will never adjust to this dark. I can only do it because I live here. Brother Godwyn says I have the eyes of *felis lybica*." The voice stopped for a moment and repeated the strange word "*felis*" to itself, as if trying to remember something.

"*Felis*—cat. Desert cat. He says I have the eyes of a desert cat."

It was not a man's voice. It was a boy's voice, a boy who normally spoke another language—Jerome. Norman had not wanted to meet anyone here in the desert fortress. He'd just wanted to get in, get his map and get out. But if he had to meet someone, Jerome was at least the safest option. Still, he sat there speechless.

"You speak English," the boy whispered. "Are you from England? Like Meg?"

"What?" Norman asked, unable to stop himself.

"Do you know Meg?" Jerome asked excitedly. "Did she send you?"

There was the sound of movement as Jerome shifted from whatever location in the darkness he inhabited. First there was just a crack of light somewhere above him, then suddenly it was blinding. A trap door had opened somewhere in the ceiling. It was like being in the hull of a sinking ship when the hatch finally burst. Norman squinted and yelped. He couldn't help it.

"Sorry," Jerome apologized hastily. He must have reached up and closed the hatch a little because the light eased back. Still, Norman dared not look up into it. He had never seen a sun so bright. His eyes adjusted slowly to the brightness, but finally, through the dust that floated on the shaft of light, he was able to see his surroundings.

He was indeed in the library. On three sides of the room tall, rickety shelves rose up. They were lined with small, cylindrical cubbyholes. Each hole held a scroll, some of them attached to wooden handles, others just rolled up like an architect's blueprints. A small wooden table was pushed against the fourth wall. A tiny three-legged stool was pulled back from the table. It looked incapable of supporting anything, but it did support something. It supported a boy.

He looked to be about fourteen. Norman had expected him to be younger for some reason, but he had to be Jerome. He wore a short white tunic cinched with a length of rope. Norman had seen something like this back in England, the first time he'd visited, which was back in the ninth century. Unlike the Anglo-Saxon boys he had met there, Jerome wore no hose or jerkin. His feet were bare, and it was too hot to wear much more. Norman was already starting to sweat in his jeans and sweatshirt. It was difficult going from a rainy English summer to the desert.

"You are English, aren't you?" Jerome asked in a soft, curious voice. He looked like a little monk with his simple robe and his hair trimmed so short.

"Yes, I am. Well . . ." Norman started to qualify his statement, but he realized that he'd have to explain about the New World and Columbus and all that. "Yes, I'm English," he repeated.

Jerome's bright blue eyes lit up, and he pulled his stool towards Norman. "Did Meg send you?"

"Uh-huh," Norman replied. He rose to his feet, his head scraping against the low wooden beams of the ceiling.

Jerome's forehead wrinkled in confusion. "Pardon?" he said.

"Yes," Norman repeated, more correctly. "Meg sent me. She sent me to find something."

Jerome rose from his stool and approached Norman with his arm outstretched. It was a strange moment for Norman. This was a fictional boy who knew his mother. She had probably known Jerome longer than she had known him. He halted and shook away the strange feeling of unease that this gave him. He couldn't find a word for it. It took a moment to gather his wits and shake the offered hand.

"You must be Jerome," Norman said.

Jerome held Norman's hand resolutely and stared at him for a long moment.

"You're not Christopher, are you?" he asked, stepping back and eyeing him warily.

Norman didn't understand the question. "What?"

"Are you Kit? Meg's brother?" Jerome narrowed his eyes and assessed Norman.

"Unc— uh . . ." Norman stuttered. "No, no, I'm Norman."

Jerome continued to stare.

"Why would you think I was Christopher?" Norman asked.

"You look like her," Jerome replied. "Like Meg. You could be her brother. She said he might come."

Norman could tell by the wariness in the other boy's face that his mother had not said anything kind about Uncle Kit, but then she rarely did. Why would she expect Uncle Kit to come here? Why would he? Could he even? Could everybody do this?

"People say we look alike, but we're not related," he began hesitantly. "We're friends from school. We read the same books."

Jerome looked skeptical. Norman wondered for a moment how to convince him. Really, there was nothing he could do to prove who he was. A bead of sweat darted past his eyelashes into the corner of his eye, making it sting and blink. The heat was getting to him. He pulled his sweatshirt over his head and looked around for somewhere to put it down. No, that wouldn't do. He had already lost too many clothes in books.

Norman had a sudden inspiration. Losing his clothes had reminded him of something. "I don't suppose this will convince you?" he asked. He held out the label for Jerome to see.

Jerome leaned over and read Norman's name from the label.

"My mom wrote it in there so I wouldn't lose it. It doesn't seem to help, though. I lose everything."

"Your mother can write too?" Jerome asked, curious again, his suspicion apparently easily assuaged.

Norman tied his sweatshirt around his waist by the arms and nodded. Why was that surprising? he wondered.

"Meg is the first girl I've heard of who could read. I mean, I haven't actually met anybody, since I never leave this part of the fortress, but I know that none of the serving girls or wives or even the nuns here at St. Savino can read. Brother Godwyn tells me that noblewomen are often taught to read. Is Meg a noblewoman?" Jerome answered his own question. "You must be nobility, too, if you have enough clothes to lose them. Of course, you both must be. She never will say. I always thought she must be. Her hair is always so well combed and her hands are perfectly clean and soft." Jerome's tone changed completely when he talked about Meg. His voice softened and trailed off. He sounded a little bit like Dora when she talked about the pony she rode.

Now it was Norman's turn to regard the other boy suspiciously. Did Jerome have a crush on his mother? That was crazy. Jerome was just a boy. Meg Jespers-Vilnius was a grown woman now. Maybe he hadn't seen her since she was a girl his age. Maybe she'd given up coming here after she grew up. Would Jerome have noticed this, or was it always the same time to him? Norman had not yet worked out the relationship between normal time and book time.

"Has Meg sent a message?" Jerome asked. He'd moved closer and joined Norman in the square of sun under the skylight.

Norman thought for a moment about how to approach this. He thought better of trying to trick Jerome. It seemed best to be as honest as possible.

"I've come for the map. My . . . Meg left it here for safekeeping. She sent me to get it."

Jerome regarded him studiously for a few more seconds. He appeared to be trying to make a decision.

"The map?" Jerome pretended half-heartedly that he knew nothing about it.

"Yes, the map of the realm of Undergrowth. It shows the Northern Kingdoms and the Obsidian Desert." Norman didn't know if Jerome had read the map, but if he had, he wanted the other boy to know that he'd read it, too.

"Yes . . ." Jerome answered. It was half a question, half a statement.

"At the centre is the Castle of Lochwarren. That's my friend King Malcolm's castle." Norman hoped this would impress the apprentice monk. He failed to mention that his friend was a member of the weasel family.

Whether this impressed Jerome or not, it finally burst the dam that had been holding back his curiosity.

"This is in the land of Scotia, yes?" he asked eagerly. "Or is it Hibernia, or Kernow? I could never place it on my maps."

"There are lots of names for these places," Norman replied warily.

"Of course," Jerome agreed. "Map-making is an imperfect art.

I should like to make a comprehensive atlas one day. Have you really come all the way from Lochwarren?"

"Yes," Norman replied, making this up as he went along. "I left from the port of Cuaderno, one of the Five Cities. Let me show you."

Jerome's cautiousness had completely disappeared now. He tugged at Norman's elbow, and Norman followed him to a wall of scrolls. He paused for just a moment, scanning the rows of tiny cubbyholes, and then drew out a wrapped cylinder. Norman recognized his map right away.

Jerome unravelled the scroll and held it up to the intense light that flooded in through the skylight.

"This is how I guessed that Lochwarren was in the British Isles."

Norman squinted at the unravelled parchment, unsure what he was supposed to be seeing.

"The watermark," Jerome explained. "It's from England, so it stood to reason that Lochwarren was close."

Norman took the map from Jerome's hand and held it to the light. The pale outlines of the watermark glowed through the thick parchment, the emblem of a sailing ship encircled by the words "Waterford & Sons, Est. 1867 London."

"Strange how the zero looks like an eight in the date. That confused me at first."

Norman didn't have to convince himself that the date was wrong. The whole thing was wrong. How could the treaty map of the stoat princes have been made on paper from London?

"Is this your friend Malcolm's crest?" the boy asked, pointing to the red-and-gold insignia of the stoat princes.

Norman scanned the map eagerly. "Here is where we fought the Battle of Scalded Rock," he mumbled distractedly. He was trying to make sense of it all. Was the map a fake? Was it drawn by Malcolm's ancestors on paper brought from the real world? Had it been drawn in the real world? Who could have done that?

Jerome was more interested in Norman's story of Scalded Rock. "You fought in a battle?" Jerome asked in wonderment.

"I didn't do much." Norman traced his finger across the map. "Assassins tracked us across the wilderness here. They caught us just before we reached the borders. Malcolm's bodyguard, Simon, died to protect us." Norman stared in wonder at the map King Duncan had given him. It was a stoat heirloom, but it was an heirloom from outside, like that sneaker of Norman's that hung up on the wall at Lochwarren. When and how, Norman wondered, had the map gotten into the story?

Jerome's eyes widened as he listened to Norman's tale of Scalded Rock. "I've hardly been out of this library. The courtyard out there is the farthest I've been in my life."

Norman tried to put aside the mystery of the watermark and concentrate on the mystery of Jerome. "Except when you were a kid, right?" he pointed out. "You travelled through the Holy Land before you came here."

"No, I was born here in St. Savino," Jerome replied firmly. "I've never been outside the castle."

Norman couldn't help prying a little. Just how complete was Jerome's amnesia? "What was it like here when you were small?"

Jerome furrowed his forehead. "It all blends together. I remember the library, playing in the courtyard, the kindness of Brother Godwyn."

"You don't remember being out of the castle at all?"

The other boy paused for a moment before replying. "Only in dreams." There was a distant, wistful tone in his voice. "I dream of the desert, of riding horses or lying in the shade of great white tents, but that is just dreams."

"Hmmm," Norman murmured, rolling up the map and sticking it in the pocket of his jeans. This was the biggest temptation when you went into books. You wanted to tell characters secrets. You wanted them to know what you knew.

"What about your mother and father? Where are they?"

"They died," Jerome declared quietly. "They were pilgrims on their way to Jerusalem. They were very sick when they arrived here at St. Savino. Brother Godwyn couldn't save them. I don't remember them at all."

"What does Meg think?" Norman prodded.

Jerome looked confused again. "About what?"

"What does she think about your parents?"

Jerome pursed his lips, then looked away. "We don't talk about that anymore, not since she first came."

Norman was curious. Had she told Jerome about the bookweird? "What do you talk about?"

"About England, about what it would be like if I came back with her to England, about how I could live with her family and study at the university nearby."

"Her family? She talks about … does she talk about her husband?"

Jerome turned suddenly and stared at Norman, his expression woefully pained, as if Norman had just kicked him in the gut. "Husband? Is she married now? She didn't even tell me she was betrothed." He shook his head ruefully. "I should have known, a girl of her age and position. Her father must have already chosen someone for her. Still, I would have thought they might have waited a few years. Sixteen is the usual age."

Norman saw his mistake. Jerome knew only the young Meg, the Meg who had first come here.

"No, no," he protested. "I just thought . . . when you said she talked about her family and the future . . . I mixed the two up. I guess she talks about her parents. The house in Summerside, and her brother."

Jerome's shoulders and forehead relaxed just a little. "Yes, she talks about Summerside, how peaceful it is, and about Christopher." He frowned again before asking, "Is it still the same with them? Do they feud still, or are they reconciled?"

"It's still the same," Norman told him.

"I thought since you were here that perhaps they had found some way, some way to make the magic safe." He sounded disappointed.

Norman just stared back at the other boy. He was learning the hard way that the bookweird was anything but safe.

"I thought it was some devilry when she first appeared, but such an angel could never be the work of the devil."

Norman still didn't like the wistful tone Jerome took when he talked about Meg. "Have you told anyone about her?" he asked.

"What would I tell them?" Jerome grinned. "I have tried to ask Brother Godwyn slyly about it. I used some English word once that he didn't know. I told him an angel came to me in a vision and spoke to me in English."

"What did he say?"

Jerome crinkled his brow seriously. "He told me to be careful of blaspheming and said not all dreams are visions."

The sound of heavy boots in the rooms beneath them alerted both boys.

"I have to be going," Norman whispered. "Do you have any paper?"

Jerome smirked and held his arms wide. He was surrounded by paper.

"Paper I can write on," Norman clarified.

Jerome coughed and laughed at the same time. "Do you think I am a baron or a bishop with scrolls lying around for my own use?" he sputtered.

"Just a scrap, anything. I can write on the back of something. It doesn't need to be new. I need it to, you know, get out of here."

Jerome regarded him skeptically. "Sir Hugh may have some old letters in his chamber . . ."

"Where is his chamber?" Norman asked more urgently. The footsteps sounded as though they were directly below them.

"Down below. I could look there tonight if you like," Jerome offered eagerly.

Norman smiled inside. So Jerome wasn't such a goody two-shoes. He did get out of the library sometimes, sneaking around at night by himself.

"But I can't wait until tonight. I need to get back quickly."

"Don't you get back the way Meg does, by reciting the homing narrative?"

Norman looked at him quizzically, and Jerome started reciting: "Beside the river Goodwood in the valley of the Thames, in the lands once governed by the trustees of Lincoln College, there is a stretch of meadows and woods that feeds and supports the tiny hamlet of Summerside."

It certainly sounded like the countryside around the family's home in England. This had to be his mother's *ingresso*. She recited this story. She must have read the description somewhere and memorized it. It would have been convenient to have an *ingresso* that didn't require the book itself. Just then it would have been very convenient.

"That won't work for me," Norman told him. "I need to write my story."

Jerome paced away from Norman and stroked his chin. "All right, tonight I will go down to Sir Hugh's chambers. We will find some paper."

Norman was about to object that he was in a hurry, but the sound of footsteps on the stairs below made both boys start and stare at each other silently.

"Jerome, boy, I have news," a tired old voice called up. Norman heard the steps creak as someone made slow progress up them.

Jerome motioned with his head for Norman to hide. While Norman scampered quickly behind a large, iron-ringed chest, the other boy lowered the skylight so that only a tiny sliver of light shone through.

The stairs continued to squeak as the voice came closer, wheezing and coughing more and more as it climbed higher. "Jerome"—*huff,*—"my boy"—*huff and cough*—"what do you say to a little journey?"

Jerome could not contain his surprise or excitement. "Where, Father? When? Outside St. Savino?"

"Outside St. Savino, yes." The voice began to laugh, but it descended into a coughing fit. "You and I are going to England. What do you think?"

"England?" Jerome asked. "But the scrolls . . . our library?"

"Ah, but that's just it. The library is coming with us," Godwyn announced mysteriously.

Norman couldn't resist peeking over the top of the trunk. A small, elderly man in a monk's habit held Jerome by his shoulders.

Standing straight he might have been as tall as Jerome, but with his back bent by age, he was in fact smaller. Jerome supported the old man. There was a look of incomprehension on his face, as if he could not imagine that it was possible to leave St. Savino, as if such a thing couldn't actually happen.

"Why, Father?" he asked. "What has happened?"

Here the old monk paused and breathed deeply. "Pass me the stool, son, will you?"

The little wooden stool scraped across the floor. Brother Godwyn wheezed as he lowered his weary frame onto it. "Our old friend John of Nantes has returned. He has papers making him overlord of St. Savino. Sir Hugh is arguing the case, but he has told us to leave now while we can. We are taking the library to London."

Norman caught sight of Godwyn's face. It was pale and sallow. Norman couldn't imagine this frail old fellow travelling to London even in a world of taxis and airplanes. How would he manage it now?

Jerome and Godwyn whispered conspiratorially. Norman could barely make out a word. Perhaps it was better, he thought, to take this opportunity to find some paper. Jerome could tell him about the trip later, or Norman could read about it when he got home. He couldn't get bogged down here. He needed to get back home and then return with Malcolm to Kelmsworth.

Making as little noise as he could, Norman slipped out from behind the chest and tiptoed towards the stairs. The floorboards creaked ever so slightly, but the old monk did not turn around. Jerome's eyes flicked towards Norman as he began to creep down the steps. Norman could not read the message that flashed there.

The rickety wooden stairs descended in countless short flights down the wooden tower into the baked mud fortress of St. Savino. The stairway was incredibly narrow—too narrow for two people to pass.

Entering the fortified walls of the castle, the steps turned to stone, still narrow, and twisted to fit inside the stone walls. Finally they emerged at a small balcony. Though Norman had been descending for minutes, he was still quite high up. Below, the bald pate of a monk was bent over the rows of a tidy herb garden. Norman didn't stop to gawk. He crossed the long balcony to a door at the end. Pushing on it gently proved ineffective, so he gave it a good shove and nearly fell into the hall beyond.

He was in a much wider space now. The floor beneath him was worn terracotta, the walls thick, stuccoed stone. It was dark down here, too, but cooler. The thick mud walls of the fort must have had something to do with that.

Malcolm Alone

In the smallest bedroom of the house called the Shrubberies near the village of Summerside in England, the bedside light was still on. It was late for the occupant of this small room to be reading. If the parents of Norman Jespers-Vilnius had known that the light was on, they would have stormed in there and confiscated his books, and possibly his light bulbs. Fortunate, then, that they didn't know, because it was not their son who was up so late reading.

Curled up in the folds of an orange blanket in the warmth of the light cast by the bedside lamp was a small red-brown creature with whiskers and a white chest. He, too, to tell the truth, should probably have been sleeping now. He should have long ago completed his mission and been curled up somewhere safely out of sight. He should have carted the book across the red-tiled roof and down the trellises and downspouts to the open window on the other side of the house. The book should have been closed and sitting on Meg Jespers-Vilnius's bedside table. But the red-brown creature with whiskers had never been one to do what he was supposed to do, and since he'd become King of the Stoats he was even less apt to do what he was told, when he was told. And the book he was reading could not be put down so easily.

It was hard to say what was so compelling about *A Secret in the Library*. Not much had happened since Jerome's arrival at St. Savino. Brother Godwyn had taught him history and languages and how to take care of the scrolls, but the boy had learned nothing about his father. Malcolm had lost both his parents in the long battle to save his homeland. He would have done just about anything to see his own father, Duncan, one more time, to hear his deep voice bellow out orders or laugh at some joke he'd made. He couldn't understand why Jerome didn't seem to care about his own father, why he never once asked Brother Godwyn or Sir Hugh.

There was another reason Malcolm could not stop reading. The first sentence of the second chapter made it impossible to put down the book there.

"Johan of Vilnius had languished unrecognized in the dungeons of Acre for years," it began.

Malcolm's whiskers rippled as he read the name. How could he not read on?

Johan of Vilnius had languished unrecognized in the dungeons of Acre for years. It had taken him two years to dig the tunnel, scraping away at the hard dirt and mortar with his broken shackles, but the leader of the banned Livonian Knights was free again at last. He pushed a floor tile up from below and emerged at night into the castle kitchens, where he helped himself to a loaf of bread and the key to the kitchen door.

In the dark of night, Johan of Vilnius made his way through the dark back alleys of Acre to the spot where he had buried his armour two years before. Now, disguised as an Arab fruit merchant, he passed through the citadel's gates with his arms and armour hidden beneath a cartload of dates. He was heading to the oasis village of Amadir and he was in a hurry, because there he would be reunited his son.

He would go there alone. His Livonian Knights would not ride again. Black John's betrayal had finished them. But Johan's son had lived. He had made sure of that, entrusting the boy to his most steadfast knight, his best friend, André. Johan had given André his own horse, the stallion Nacht, and instructions to take the boy to the oasis town of Amadir. Together, André and Nacht would have protected the boy and brought him to safety.

Malcolm was beginning to understand now. Jerome was the son of the head of the Livonian Knights, the order that John of Nantes had sworn to crush. Hugh Montclair must have suspected it. He knew the boy had something to do with the Livonian Knights. That's why he had kept Jerome hidden and discouraged him from speaking that "strange northern tongue."

Once he'd read about the escape of Johan of Vilnius from the dungeons of Acre, Malcolm was hooked. Johan had to be Jerome's father. Malcolm promised himself he'd just read until the point where Johan arrived in Amadir and then he'd take the book back. So it was frustrating when the action switched back to St. Savino and the boy.

For page after page, Jerome picked weeds and catalogued scrolls in the library, but Malcolm couldn't put the book down. He was waiting for it to switch back to Johan.

It wasn't just the story of a father looking for his lost son. It wasn't just the thought of the captive returning triumphant, of Johan of Vilnius riding up to the gates of St. Savino at the head of a long column of Livonian Knights. The knight's name was bothering him more and more. He was no expert in the bookweird, but he knew enough now to suspect coincidences. So he read on, following Jerome's life in the library of St. Savino while the moon rose in the English night around him and the peculiar calls of English animals began to fill the darkness.

Then Norman appeared and changed everything. It was on page ninety-eight. Malcolm leapt up in surprise and gave his whiskers a shake. He had never expected anything like this. He'd known that Norman was going into the book, but he'd never imagined seeing them there, being able to read what Norman and Jerome were saying to each other and to see what they couldn't see going on around them in the castle. It was the strangest thing. There was no way he could put the book down after that.

Norman and Jerome couldn't see that down below in the castle, John of Nantes was delivering his ultimatum to Hugh Montclair. The old warrior wasn't caving in to the blustering tyrant. John of Nantes could bring as many knights as he wanted. He could raise a siege if he liked. "I'm an old man," Hugh declared. "I hate to go outside of the castle walls anyway. A siege will give me a reason to stay in and read."

The more calmly Montclair replied, the more Black John stormed and raged. He uttered threats that would have made the river pirates of Malcolm's childhood proud. Malcolm wasn't nearly as calm as Montclair. He was only reading the confrontation and his nerves were on edge. He turned the pages eagerly, racing through each of them. If only he were there with a good strong bow and a quiver full of well-fledged arrows. He'd brought down larger prey.

It only got worse when Norman decided to creep down the stairs. "Don't do it, Norman," Malcolm kept whispering to himself. "Don't do it. Stay up in the library out of the way. Wait until Black John and his thugs have gone." Norman couldn't hear him, of course. Ignorant of the danger waiting for him, he kept creeping down the stairs and out into the hall.

At that moment there was a sound outside his own door. Malcolm was startled to attention, closing the book reflexively and pricking up his ears to listen. Yes, that was a footstep outside on the creaking floorboards of the corridor. This was embarrassing, to let a creature as big as a human sneak up on him. He clicked the switch of the bedside light, but his woodland eyes were still sharp enough to see the giant bare feet beneath the door.

He tensed his muscles as the doorknob turned. He would have to make a dash for it. The window was still gapped, so he could escape, but he couldn't take the book. It would slow him down. He slid it under the covers and crouched, ready to leap for the window ledge.

The door opened just a little. From his hiding place in the tangled mound of blankets, Malcolm could make out the shape of Norman's mother. He knew that human eyes were not as sharp as

stoat eyes, but surely she must see him there. How well camou-
flaged was he?

"Norman, darling?"

Malcolm's muscles were tensed, ready to leap, but he remained
perfectly still.

"Norman, I know you're awake," Meg whispered. "I saw your
light on." She opened the door a little more.

If she took one step in, Malcolm promised himself he would
bolt. She watched silently for a long while but came no farther.

"Norman," she began with a sigh, "I just want you to know
that I know about . . . about the bookweird." She paused before
continuing. "You have to trust me when I tell you that it's dangerous." She waited for a response.

Malcolm coughed and mumbled at the same time. It was as
close as he could come to making a human sound.

"Sometimes when people fall into the bookweird," Meg whispered, "sometimes they don't come back." Her voice wavered a
little, as if she was remembering something painful now. "Sometimes
they come back changed."

What was she saying? Who had she lost? Who had been
changed? Norman would know. When he didn't respond, Meg
finally gave up and started to close the door again, slowly.

Malcolm didn't relax. He wasn't going to be tricked. Outside
the door he could still see Meg Jespers-Vilnius's bare, furless feet.
He could even hear her deep human breathing.

"I couldn't live with myself if I lost you that way, too," she
said finally.

Malcolm heard her hand brush across the door as she moved
away. He let out a small, stoat-sized breath of relief. That had been
too close. He had to do what Norman had told him and return the
book. If he kept this up, he was going to get caught. But what about
Norman? Norman was about to get caught, too. He had no idea that
Black John and his knights were just around the corner.

Malcolm didn't need the night light to read. Now that the
moon was up, that was enough light for him. He slid the book from

under the pillow and flipped hurriedly to the place he'd left off. Norman was about to turn the corner into another of St. Savino's long corridors, unaware that Black John's knights were marching the other way.

Malcolm didn't have time to read this through. He needed to figure out how it ended. He skipped forward a few pages to see how bad things got. What he saw made him very, very nervous. The pages weren't blank. But they weren't readable, either. The letters blurred as if viewed through rippled water. He flipped the pages to the end of the book. They were all like that. It was as if the book had unwritten itself.

He returned to his spot in the book. The first unread words were fine. Norman was just about to step around the corner. The sentence finished on the next page. Malcolm flipped the page to see that this one was ready to read. The book was rewriting itself, but only as fast as he read it.

The stoat stopped himself, looked down at the page again and blinked his shiny black eyes once before closing the book. This was no good at all. The more he read, the worse he made it. He had to stop. But now, of course, there was no way he could return the book to Meg's bedside table. Norman was going to have to sort this out from the inside, hopefully before his mother woke up.

The Chambers of Hugh Montclair

Norman could hear voices echoing from somewhere, but the twists of the fortress corridors made it impossible to tell from which direction. It was like being in the coils of a giant conch shell. The sound of boots on stone thumped in and out. There could be a whole army marching around these corridors. They could be coming up behind him now, or they could be just around the corner.

Norman sprinted down the passageway, glad of the rubber-soled sneakers that scuffed the floor silently. At each bend and twist of the mazy fortress he stopped to peer around. He had seen no one yet, but those voices and those footsteps did not seem to get any closer or any farther away.

All of a sudden they were on top of him. A loud conversation in an unknown language burst down the corridor behind him. He couldn't help looking back. Turning the corner were three men. Norman immediately noticed the black surcoats they wore over their chain mail and the white arms of Nantes on their chests. Even if he hadn't read the opening chapters of *A Secret in the Library* he would have known that these were not the good guys. This was exactly the sort of book where the bad guys wore black.

And now the black knights had seen Norman. Nantes's men

paused for a moment, confused perhaps by Norman's strange clothes and sudden appearance. But their hesitation was momentary. The lead knight tapped his companion's arm and pointed at Norman.

"C'est lui! C'est le garçon que nous cherchons!" he cried in a surprised, creaky voice.

Norman turned and ran.

They launched after him with hoarse shouts in a jangle of chain mail. He had no idea what they were saying, but it didn't sound very friendly. He took off down the hallway, skidding around the corner and flailing his arms to keep his balance, then careened down the next hallway. At the next turn he grabbed the iron torch stand that jutted out of the wall to catapult himself around. Behind him the black knights struggled to keep up with him in their heavy armour. He could hear them scrambling behind him, but after five or six turns they were out of sight. Now he needed a hiding place.

He tried every door that he came to, jiggling each handle hurriedly. Not a single door was unlocked. He cast about for curtains, boxes, furniture—something to hide behind or inside—but St. Savino was a remarkably empty fortress. Where was he supposed to hide? The best hiding place in St. Savino was the library, but he wasn't about to lead Black John's men to Jerome's hideout.

Suddenly the clank of their armour and the thud of footsteps came closer again, ahead of him in the hall now. Had he gone round in a circle? He turned in the other direction, ready to double back on himself, but no . . . he heard the rising shouts of another party of knights coming the other way.

He was caught. They were closing in on him from both sides. Soon, both chase parties would be in the corridor. There was nowhere to run. This was a corridor like all the rest—plain stone walls, iron torch stands, just a single door that would inevitably be locked like all the others. Norman pushed on it in desperation. He was more surprised than relieved when it gave way. He fell into the room, his weight on the door carrying him through as he stumbled in. He had just enough sense and just enough time to push the door closed behind him.

Voices argued in the hall outside. Norman stood still and strained to listen, but again they spoke a language he could not understand. Any moment he expected to hear the clank of swords. He had better hide.

He surveyed the room he'd taken refuge in. The chamber was furnished like an office, with a long table surrounded by eight weighty chairs and a massive wooden desk covered with letters and scrolls. A tall wardrobe stood behind the desk. It would easily conceal him. Norman started towards it but was distracted by what he saw on the desk—a small stack of papers beside a quill and an ink pot, just what he needed. He snatched the quill and the inkpot and riffled through the papers for the one that looked most edible. The crest on the topmost letter caught his attention: three lions. He had seen that same crest all over England. It had something to do with Jerome's trip to England, perhaps. Norman was about to put it down when he heard the door creaking. It opened just a crack.

A large man stood in the doorway with his back to the room. His arms spanned the open space as if barring the way. His broad back was covered in a dull grey jerkin. A sword was belted to his side, but he wore no armour, and no helmet covered the grey hairs of his head. Norman knew, as if he had read it somewhere, that this was Hugh Montclair. Had Montclair been alone, Norman might have stayed and tried to talk his way out, but the men whose way he barred wore the black uniform of Nantes's men.

Norman's eyes darted around the room. There was no time to jump in the wardrobe. Too noisy. The desk was no good. Nor was the table. It would have to be the curtains.

He had just managed to pull the curtain back in front of him when the voices filled the room. Black John's knights piled into the room after Sir Hugh.

It was a cacophony of noises that Norman struggled to interpret by sound and intonation. There were perhaps three or four voices, most of them indistinguishably gruff and aggressive, like a pack of barking dogs. One voice stood out, measured, even, but strong, arguing back against the dogs. That would be Hugh Montclair's. They were arguing about him, Norman guessed. Black John's men would be insisting that they had chased a boy down this hall. Montclair would know that this was impossible. Jerome would never have left his hiding place in the library.

There were more men now in Hugh's chambers. Norman heard the jangle of their chain mail as they circulated, mumbling to each other. As they passed by his hiding spot the motion of their bodies rippled the curtains, wafting them against Norman's trembling hands, but he stayed rooted to his spot. He closed his eyes and tried to imagine he was back home, sneaking down on Christmas morning to shake presents, nothing more daring or dangerous than that.

But he was not at home, and this was not Christmas morning. He was in the chamber of Hugh Montclair, governor of St. Savino. He heard the squeak and click of a key being turned and the creak of an opening door. Somebody had opened the wardrobe. The door slammed shut again, and Hugh Montclair's voice rose up in protest. Norman still couldn't understand a word, but something about the tone made him feel that he understood the governor's speech. The intruders went silent and stood still while he lectured them and then commanded them to leave. He punctuated his command with a shout and let it echo around the empty room.

There was no reply from Nantes's men. In fact, once Montclair had finished speaking the room was unnaturally quiet. Norman held his breath and waited for them to leave. He willed them to leave. Instead there was an eerie stillness. Then came the sound of a single set of boots. One man moved, while all the others stayed silent. Likely they all watched him as he strode confidently, not to the door but to the curtains where Norman hid.

For some reason Norman glanced down at his feet. His blue sneakers stuck out beneath the edge of the curtain. He inhaled sharply as the footsteps on the other side of the curtain stopped. Then there was a cry. It did not sound like his voice. It sounded like an animal screaming in pain. He never knew if it was him. It was all a mess of sound and sensation.

The curtains pressed hard against him. A sharp pain shot through his ribs, like a stitch when running. Something cold trickled down his hip. He felt his feet give way beneath him and his stomach roll. His hands grasped at the mud wall behind him, but there was no strength in his fingers. He felt the grit of the baked mud wall slip along his wet palms. The edges of his vision went grey, and then suddenly black and gone.

Escape from the Crusades

207

The howl of some desert animal woke him. He shivered and clutched his knees to his chest. Since Undergrowth, Norman had been terrified of wolves. The thought of being outdoors at night surrounded by desert predators filled him with an awful panic.

There was another long, desperate wail. It was answered by the high-pitched yaps and barks of nearby companions. What would they be—hyenas or wild dogs? Fear sharpened Norman's senses and made him fully awake. It was late in the day. He could see the sun hovering over the dunes through the open flap of a tent. The sand glowed under the sunbeams, a deep, incandescent yellow. Norman blinked and saw purple spots from staring at it.

He was alone in the tent. Whoever had taken him clearly didn't think he needed to be guarded very closely. He made to rise and had got halfway up when something yanked at his feet, sending him diving forward. He winced as he hit the ground. A sharp pain stabbed in his side and he started to remember.

He had been caught in Montclair's chamber. John of Nantes's men had found him. There had been a blade thrust through the curtain. He'd heard it hack through the thick tapestry, and he'd felt blood dripping down his side. He prodded the side of his ribs gently, his fingers seeking out the centre of the injury. His skin seemed intact. There was no gash where he'd expected one. It felt more like a bruise than a cut. Where was the wound? Where had the blood come from?

Slowly he ran his fingers over his body, starting at his ankles. There was a sharp pain there, too. His fingers grasped the band that encircled the pain. A thick leather manacle was strapped tightly to his ankle. The manacle was attached to a chain that ran to a small chest. This was what had pulled at him and brought him to the ground with such a jolt.

Norman continued searching for the source of the blood. He rubbed his fingers along his calves and up his legs to his hips. His jeans felt stiff near the belt line and were coated in a flaky substance where the blood had dried, but still no wound. Confused, he frisked himself more vigorously. How was it possible that there was blood and no cut?

In the front pocket of his jeans he found the answer. The sharp edge of broken glass grazed his fingertip. He removed it carefully and placed it on the ground beside him. It was a piece of the ink pot.

His first thought, as he gingerly picked out the rest of the glass shards, was relief. He wasn't cut. He wasn't going to bleed to death in the desert and be left to feed the desert dogs. A second thought cut his relief short.

"Please," he whispered to himself, "let there be some ink left." He turned his pocket inside out and removed the last splinters of glass. One large, curved piece, the thick base of the broken vial, was still sticky with ink. There might still be a way out of this.

Had he managed to keep the quill and paper, or had he dropped them when they'd brought him here? He reached into his back pocket and withdrew the pieces of the quill. He was rifling through the folds of his sweatshirt when a shadow passing across the flap of the tent alerted him.

Norman curled up again on the ground, keeping as still as he could. Through the slit of one barely opened eye he saw the dark silhouette of a man lean into the tent and peer down at him for a moment. Norman lay as still as he could, counting the seconds. The figure loomed silently for what felt like an eternity but came no closer. Finally he closed the flap and turned away with a snort.

Norman was not left alone for long. Within moments the tent flaps were thrown open wide and an armoured figure appeared in the triangle of light. He was smaller than Norman had imagined, his face wrinkled and tanned by the sun. The black hair that gave him his name curled around his ears, nearly touching the gleaming epaulettes of his armour. He snarled as he entered, flaring his nostrils as he spat out an order in a language Norman couldn't understand.

Two men-at-arms trundled over to Norman and lifted him roughly by the arms. Norman winced as they hoisted him up, but he tried to keep his eyes on the dark knight in front of him.

Black John stared over the hump of his crooked nose, taking the measure of his captive. He looked disappointed. Norman guessed that he didn't look like much of a prize.

The knight barked a question at him. At least Norman thought it was a question. Norman didn't understand a word. He guessed it was French.

When Norman didn't answer, Black John stepped forward, shaking the metal gauntlet he held in his hand, and repeated his question more loudly and more harshly.

Norman felt his hands trembling at his sides. "I don't understand," he said meekly.

His captor's dark eyes flashed from Norman to the men-at-arms at either side of him. There was a short, muttered conversation that served only to stoke Black John's fury. Norman looked down, unwilling to meet the French knight's glinting eyes. The Frenchman lifted his chin so Norman could not look away.

"Please . . ." Norman began, but Black John's tightening grip on his chin stopped him.

"So you play a game wiz us?" He sneered. "You think to fool us by talking only the *Anglais*?"

Norman shook his head slowly.

"The *petit* Vilnius is afraid." He let out a short, cruel laugh.

Confused, Norman blinked and narrowed his eyes, surprised to hear his name.

"No need to be afraid, little desert rat," Black John mocked. "The worst has happened. But I won't harm you. John of Nantes does not harm children, even the children of his enemies."

The vicious gleam in his eye told Norman otherwise. If he thought he had to, Black John would hurt anyone.

"You look like your father, you know," Black John said. "How sad that he cannot be here to see how you've grown."

So they thought he was Jerome. Black John thought he had captured his enemy's son. Norman wasn't sure whether to correct him.

"Now tell me about your protector, the stubborn Hugh. Why won't he give up the fortress? Why does he insist on provoking me?"

"I . . ." Norman stammered, "I don't know."

"Has he told you about his letter from the English king?"

Norman started involuntarily.

"He has spoken of it," Black John concluded ruefully, seeing the answer in Norman's face. He turned and muttered something to the henchman behind him.

John turned back to Norman, his face taking on a forced calmness. "It is not true. It is a ruse," he said. "Have you seen such a letter?" he asked, daring Norman to contradict him.

Norman wasn't sure what to say. If he said yes, would Black John leave St. Savino alone?

"Just tell me and we'll be done here. It would have his crest," the French knight pressed. "Three lions rampant."

Norman was looking away again, peering at the sand at his feet, or else Black John would have seen the realization in his eyes, the shock of understanding. The king's letter—the letter that guaranteed Hugh Montclair's rights to St. Savino and the safe passage of its books to England—it had been in his hands when he'd been caught.

"I knew it," John spat. "There is no such letter. If the old fool had such a letter he would have produced it. The King of England cares nothing about that old pile of baked mud." He gave Norman one last, dismissive stare before turning. He pulled the gauntlet onto his hand and motioned to the henchman who held his armoured helm. "Raze it to the ground," he ordered as he strode to the entrance of the tent.

The men who held Norman's arms released him, and he slumped to the ground.

"No!" he cried, looking up from where he lay. "There is a letter. I saw it."

Black John kept walking.

For a moment Norman was about to produce the letter, but that would have been a disaster. Black John would destroy it.

"Take me back to St. Savino," he pleaded. "I'll show you where the letter is."

Black John paused beneath the tent flaps and sneered. "Now he knows about a letter, now he thinks it can save his precious friends. He'll tell us anything, even if it isn't true. Living with the monks has not been good for you," he taunted. "Your father would have taught you to be a better liar."

With that he let the tent flap fall, and Norman was alone once more.

Norman slowly shifted on the ground, his hands rifling through his clothes for the paper. He was almost convinced that he'd dropped it. Finally, in the folds of the sweatshirt tied around his waist, he found the smooth scroll of paper he'd pilfered from Sir Hugh's desk. He glanced again to the entrance of the tent. The shadow of the lone sentry was still there, growing duller as the sun sank into the dunes. Norman could do little while the guard stood there.

Outside, he could hear orders being given, horses neighing and the squeak of heavy wheels turning. Black John's army was on the move. Would they really raze the desert fortress? Did it mean that much to Black John?

What, Norman wondered, were they doing in St. Savino tonight? Would Jerome have told Sir Hugh about him? Surely not. Jerome wouldn't have given away Meg's secret—his mother's secret.

Norman almost thought of them as two different people, his mother and this Meg girl who could slip into a book about the Crusades just to talk to an orphan librarian named Jerome. It was hard to imagine them as the same person.

He had to forget that now. He had to get out of here. He hauled himself up to a seated position and grasped the leather manacle around his ankle. If he could cut through the leather or somehow pry it off, he might be able to escape. He pulled off his sock and sneaker and tried to tug the manacle past his ankle. He was skinny, but not that skinny. He pulled until he couldn't stand the pain. That was not going to work.

He rubbed some feeling back into his ankle and pondered his next step. The leather manacle was fastened to a thick iron chain. Its links were firmly joined. There would be no prying them apart. He ran his finger over each link, searching for some weakness, following the chain to where a thick ring of steel fastened it to the trunk.

Norman examined the trunk. It was a firmly constructed little box, reinforced with iron bands and studs. It was almost exactly the size of a breadbox, which Norman thought was funny. Very few things are exactly the size of a breadbox. He gave it an experimental shove. It didn't move. It was a lot heavier than a breadbox. Norman looked around for something with which to pry it open. If he emptied it, he might be able to carry it.

There wasn't much in the tent that could be used as a pry bar. It wasn't like Black John's thugs were going to leave a sword lying around for him, but that's what he needed.

He wracked his brain. At the beach once he'd seen seagulls pick up shellfish and drop them on rocks to smash them open. Maybe that would work. Norman crouched down beside the chest, wrapped both arms around it and muscled it up on top of his knees, resting it there for a moment, then jerking it upwards and straightening his legs. He'd just about raised it over his head when the chain jerked at his ankle, throwing him off balance. He pulled his vulnerable toes out of the way as the chest fell with a thud into the soft sand, half burying itself there. That was not worth trying again.

There was nothing to it. There was only one thing left to try. He hated leaving Jerome, but he was going to have to bookweird his way out of this mess. He just hoped that there was enough usable ink. He retrieved his broken quill and ink pot and placed them on top of the wooden chest.

Norman unravelled the letter he'd stolen from Sir Hugh's desk and eyed it warily. He could, he guessed, just eat it as it was. That would be the fastest way out. You didn't always have to eat the story you wanted to fall into. Once you'd started falling into books you seemed to get to most other books by way of the real world. Norman had once escaped a Viking attack by eating a bicycle-safety pamphlet.

He fingered the letter nervously, running his fingers across the red seal of three lions. He shouldn't destroy it. This letter was his best chance of saving St. Savino and its inhabitants. Besides, it seemed to help if you ate a page from the book you wanted to land in. Maybe he was fooling himself, but Norman felt more in control of the bookweird if he targeted his landing that way.

The king's letter was short. It took up only two-thirds of the page. After the signature and the seal, there was still a slim margin at the bottom of the page. If he wrote a story for himself in that remaining bare space, he could save the letter. Even a few sentences might be enough.

Norman folded the letter, making a crease above the small, precious rectangle of bare paper. As carefully as he could he tore along the line. It didn't tear easily. This wasn't like the paper he was used to. It was thick and flexible, almost like cloth. That was another reason to keep it small.

Ink was the next problem. It wasn't completely dry, but it wasn't exactly liquid either—more like glue than ink. He spat experimentally into the biggest piece of the broken ink pot and stirred it around with the sharp end of his quill. The quill wasn't much of a pen at all, just a whittled stick with a thin metal nib. Norman's penmanship wasn't very good at the best of times. His grade three teacher had told him that calling it chicken scratch was an insult to chickens. With his spit-diluted ink and his blunt, broken quill he was glad that the bookweird didn't seem to give points for neatness. What counted for the bookweird was that you got it right. You couldn't just write, "My bedroom in England," and zip back there. You had to describe it. You had to make it so that someone reading it could imagine it perfectly.

He hesitated, the quill poised inches from the surface of the square of paper. He was finding it hard to visualize the little room and the cottage. The pressure of getting it right made it harder. What colour were the curtains? Were the flowers on the sheets yellow or pink? Was the floor still covered with laundry or had someone picked it up?

He started with the bed. He knew he'd left it a mess.

"Norman's bed was a mess," he wrote. It was a mess because it always was a mess. He never made it.

Norman's bed was a mess. There were plates underneath it. The red one was from when he'd brought the pancake up for Malcolm. The teacup and the bowl were there from lunch, when he'd brought Weetabix and milky tea up to his friend. Malcolm had slurped all the milk from the cereal and eaten the rest with a souvenir gift spoon from Windsor Castle. He'd waited for the tea to get cold, then slurped it, too, dripping tea onto the bedsheets from his whiskers.

Norman found himself describing Malcolm more than his bedroom, but he guessed it didn't matter.

Malcolm might have been a king, but he ate like a slob. There was always food in his whiskers for hours after a meal. Sometimes, if the meal happened to be lingonberry pie or jam tart, there would be food in his ears, too. It wasn't unusual for there to be a dark stain of blue or purple on the tufts of hair in his round little ears. When he was finished a meal he liked to lie back and rub his belly. That's how jam got on his belly, too. He didn't look so fierce when you saw him like that, lying back on a pillow with jam on his white belly and ear-tufts, but he could change in a second. Just like that, he could leap up, bare a fang and focus his sharp eyes and you'd know he'd fight to the death for you.

Just writing it was almost like escaping. It was like being there. Norman would have gone on writing all night if he could have, but he quickly ran out of paper. The lines of writing got more cramped as he wrote, trying to cram it all in. He couldn't go back and make it more about home and less about Malcolm now. He didn't even dare try to correct any mistakes. He took a handful of sand and shook it over the sticky ink to dry it. Then he sat down to the unappetizing task of eating his composition.

It was even tougher than he'd imagined. The paper didn't dissolve in his mouth. He had to chew it to break it up, tearing it into ever-smaller pieces. The pieces just stuck to the roof of his mouth. He needed some water or something. He rummaged around the tent, dragging the chest around after him like an anchor. Amongst some blankets in one corner he uncovered two dark green bottles stoppered with cork. He opened one and took a whiff, blinking away the tears as his eyes stung. The second was better, a dark red fluid, wine maybe. He hesitated for just a moment. Of all the rules he'd broken today, taking a few sips of wine was probably the least important.

He swilled each sip around in his mouth, letting it soak into the fibres of the paper, breaking them down as much as he could before swallowing, but even then it didn't go down easily. It was the toughest paper he'd ever eaten, but he somehow managed it.

When he'd completely eaten the strip of paper, he lay down and tried to fall asleep. The sun had set, but there was a new light outside. The canvas walls of the tent had begun to glow orange. Already it felt cooler. Norman put on his sweatshirt.

Fall asleep, he told himself. *It's nighttime. Just go to sleep.* But it wasn't that easy. His stomach gurgled and twisted as it tried to deal with the paper he'd sent it. He imagined his stomach working at breaking down the story in his belly. Just how eaten did the paper have to be? Did the story get sent to a particular gland or organ that made the bookweird happen? His stomach groaned, and he belched. He didn't feel well at all. If he puked right now, he wondered, and spewed the bits of paper onto the sand, would it still work?

He rolled over on his side and tried to put it out of his mind. He tried to imagine himself at home with Malcolm, but it only set his mind racing again. There was so much to do. Malcolm had to get back to Undergrowth with the map, but first they had to get Todd out of Kelmsworth Hall and the poacher back to his own book. When all that was done, he'd have to come here and put Sir Hugh's letter back. That was a lot of bookweird to do and undo. Thinking of everything he had to put right made it hard to get to sleep.

Outside the tent, the shouts of Black John's knights were louder. The light had changed again. It was no longer the orange glow of sunset. There were just spots of light, smaller but more intense—campfires?

216

He rolled closer to the edge of the tent and lifted the canvas experimentally. It wasn't hard. The canvas wasn't pegged tightly. He made a gap just high enough to stick his head out. The cool night air pricked his face. He had to blink to make sure he was seeing what he thought he was seeing.

There were fires all right, but they weren't for warmth. The flames lit up the desert night. Men-at-arms and archers were silhouetted in their flickering light. Some of them carried armfuls of arrows that they carefully placed beside the fires. Others shuttled burning torches to two skeletal wooden towers closer to St. Savino's walls. The towers were about as tall as five or six men, a crisscross of beams lashed to the ground by ropes. Norman shivered, but not from the chill of the desert night. He had seen and read enough to know exactly what these machines were—trebuchets, siege engines that could catapult projectiles over and through thick fortress walls. Black John was not waiting for Sir Hugh to produce his letter from the King of England.

Already archers were sending single arrows across the night sky in huge, illuminated arcs. The first arrows fell short, burying themselves in the sand and extinguishing like matches tossed into water, but they slowly crept towards the fortress as the archers found their range. Soon they were smashing into the thick outer walls, exploding in sudden sparks like fireworks. The archers adjusted again, and their next arrows flew high and far, launching almost vertically into the air and plummeting in an arc just as steep, this time into the heart of the fortress.

No sound from the fortress reached Norman in the tent, but surely the defenders would be busy inside, running buckets of water to the danger spots, trying to douse the fires before they spread. It would be just possible now, with only one or two fire-arrows finding their marks, but could they keep it up?

Without warning the archers stopped firing. That would give the defenders time, but surely the archers were just waiting for an order to fire again. That was not all they were waiting for. Orders were barked and men scrambled to the trebuchets. They took torches and lit the huge oil-coated rocks that sat at the end of each catapult arm. There was silence as the soldiers stood back and gazed at the blazing projectiles.

A single voice rang out in the night. Shouting out a countdown, he barked five times before giving the order to fire. With a jolt one of the machines was unleashed. The trebuchet shuddered under the whiplash motion of its firing arm. The soldiers stood back in silent awe, following the flight of the blazing missile.

Norman held his breath, watching the fiery ball hurtle towards the walls. It smashed against the mud fortifications with a thud. Norman exhaled—the walls would hold. But a cheer went up from the gathered soldiers, and they soon began to reload. This was just a practice shot. The trebuchets had found their range even faster than the archers.

Norman scanned the roofs of St. Savino, looking to the tall wooden tower that jutted into the sky above the mud walls at the north-east end. That was the library—Jerome's hiding place, the most vulnerable part of the whole fortress.

"Get out of there," Norman whispered. "Just get out of there now."

The second trebuchet creaked and shuddered, launching its blazing rock through the bleak desert sky. Again the soldiers stood back in awe of their war machine, and again Norman held his breath. The missile skimmed the top of the fortress wall, sending chunks of hardened mud careening through the crumbled wall into the heart of the fortified town.

Again Black John's soldiers cheered—it was an ugly, violent sound. They knew who was in there. It wasn't full of soldiers. It wasn't a military outpost. It was just a fortified village full of families, elderly monks, gardeners, scribes, librarians.

"Get out of there," Norman whispered to himself again. He meant all of them, not just Jerome. They should all just get out of there. He had no idea what Black John's men would do if they came out. Maybe they would die just the same. But if they stayed inside it was certain death.

Norman waited for any sign that the inhabitants of St. Savino might escape. The gate remained resolutely shut. Maybe, he dared to hope, they were leaving by hidden passageways, sneaking away into the night unseen. He clung to this thought as the arrows flew again in earnest, whole flights of fire-arrows screaming across the sky like falling meteors. Then the trebuchets resumed, an uneven rhythm of creak and whoosh and thud, sending huge balls of fire into the heart of the peaceful fortress.

What could Sir Hugh and his people do against this? They might rush with pitiful wooden buckets to the site of one fiery arrow or swarm hopefully into the wreckage where the giant projectiles had crashed, but it would be useless. Too many arrows plummeted into the dry straw roofs of St. Savino. Too many fires sparked and raged. And there were too few defenders, with limbs too old and too few buckets.

An orange glow ascended from behind the walls of St. Savino. The buildings were ablaze, the timber-framed houses, sheds, their thatched roofs and canvas canopies. Norman couldn't look away. He was desperate to see some movement, some evidence that Sir Hugh was sending his people out of the conflagration to safety. But now the flames themselves were visible. The wooden tower had taken a direct hit from a trebuchet missile. Flames were licking up the side of the tower and flickering in its tiny windows. All those scrolls would be perfect kindling. The library was like a huge torch waiting to be lit.

It finally became too much to watch. Norman closed his eyes and buried himself in the canvas of the tent. "Let me go to sleep now. Just get me away from this," he muttered, desperately wishing to be away, out of this terrible book. But it was not to be. Now that the only useful thing he could do was fall asleep, he couldn't manage to do it. Even with his eyes closed the sound of the fire was terrible. The whoosh of arrows and the shuddering recoil of the trebuchets had stopped, but the sounds of the fire continued. Timbers crackled and creaked. Norman couldn't stop himself from looking when something crashed or snapped. He opened his eyes to see the tower lean and fall in on itself. He shut his eyes again and covered his head with the canvas of the tent, but even that could not muffle the crackle and spit of burning timbers, the sounds of St. Savino and its library burning to the ground.

At some point late into the night or early the next day, he must have finally fallen asleep, but not before seeing St. Savino's final destruction. The towers fell. The massive gates gaped open, charred and black. Even the mud walls crumbled under the pressure and the heat of the fire. No one could have survived this.

Sleep was no escape for Norman. In his dreams he still heard the desert fortress burning. He saw the blackened faces of Jerome and Brother Godwyn as they raced frantically through the library, trying to save their precious manuscripts. These were terrible nightmares because they were true. That's exactly what Jerome and Godwyn would do. They wouldn't think of themselves first. They would think of the scrolls, and they would die in there.

And once again it was all Norman's fault. He had let himself be caught. He'd let Black John believe he was the boy he was looking for. They wouldn't have burned the place down if they'd known

Jerome was in there, or if Sir Hugh had been able to show his letter of protection from the king.

Should he have admitted that Jerome was still in there? Would Black John have believed Norman? Would it have been different if he'd shown them the letter? His mother was right. The bookweird was too dangerous. People were dying now because of him, and he didn't know if he'd ever be able to make that right.

The Poacher Poached

Norman knew Malcolm was there even before he was fully awake. He could feel the rhythm of the stoat's breathing as Malcolm slept in the crook of his arm. It made everything right. He was back. His best friend was here. Everything would be fine. He allowed himself to sleep in. His mom would call up when it was time for breakfast.

The sound of rain blown against the window by the wind finally made him open his eyes. He tried pulling the sheets up to cover his head, but that only disturbed Malcolm, who growled in complaint. By then their sleep was wrecked.

Malcolm stretched and smacked his lips dramatically. "Is your dad going to make us some pancakes?" he asked drowsily.

Norman snorted and rolled over, trying to hold on to that last bit of sleep. "Breakfast? That's what you're thinking about? How about the map? You don't want to know about *A Secret in the Library*?" He yawned. It was no use. He was awake now.

Malcolm didn't answer. It was unusual for the stoat not to have a sharp answer when called on, but Norman could no longer enjoy the silence.

"I did get it, by the way," he said, rousing himself and rubbing his eyes, "but I've made a mess of another book."

Norman sat up and tried to figure out where Malcolm had got to. It took about two seconds to realize that he was not at home in bed after all.

"Malcolm?" he asked hopefully. "Did you do this?"

"I was going to ask you the same question," Malcolm replied.

The room was familiar to them both. Here were the high-backed chairs where the Cooks usually sat. Beyond them was the kitchen where George made tea. They had not woken up in Norman's bedroom after all. They had woken up on George's couch, but the lodge was not as they had left it. It was not as they had ever seen it.

"Todd?" Norman asked. "Do you think Mr. Todd did this?"

Malcolm frowned. "He didn't make this rat's nest, nor did George."

Norman had meant the bookweirding, not the mess, but there was no point in clarifying. The lodge was a bigger emergency. It was a disaster area. Furniture had been dragged into the centre of the room, away from the windows. All the cupboard doors were open. The shelves were almost bare. Empty cans and cardboard boxes were strewn across the floor. There were dirty dishes everywhere, on the side tables, on the floor. The kitchen sink was piled high with filthy pots and pans, but no one had taken the extra step of actually washing them. Had it got that bad for George?

Malcolm answered his unspoken question, pointing to a pile of cigarette butts in the crystal bowl beside the sofa.

"The poacher," Norman declared in a wary whisper.

Malcolm asked the question they were both thinking: "Where do you imagine our George has got to?"

"Hopefully he's up at the main house. Todd would have let him in, wouldn't he?"

"Aye," Malcolm replied. "And that's where we ought to be heading. I don't think our bald friend expects to come home to houseguests."

They let themselves out as quietly as they could, leaving the door gapped rather than forcing it shut. Norman pulled the hood of his sweatshirt over his head. Malcolm leapt onto Norman's shoulder, sharing the cover of the hood as they set out across the grounds to Kelmsworth Hall.

They stopped at the greenhouse to reconnoitre. Norman put his hand on the wet glass and let Malcolm lean out around the corner to survey the lawns.

The stoat pulled his neck back in and shook his snout. "Nothing," he reported.

Norman hesitated before proceeding. "It's different here." And then he finally realized what was wrong. "It's raining. It never rains here. That's why I thought we were home."

Malcolm looked around at the rain. He considered it silently for a moment, then shook the rain from his wet fur. Neither boy nor stoat could put his finger on why it bothered him, but both felt it meant something wrong. The stoat king motioned for them to move again.

They made their way stealthily, dashing from cover to cover, from the greenhouses through the arboretum to the low stone walls.

"*Tsss*," Malcolm hissed, alerting Norman to danger. Norman ducked lower below the stone wall. "The Rook's fallen, too. Door's off its hinges." Malcolm let out a low whistle as he assessed the scene. "Must have been some battering ram."

Norman poked his head up to see for himself that the Rook's door hung loose, its top hinge pulled from the door jamb.

Malcolm jumped from one shoulder to the other to get a view of the main house. "I don't like the look of this open ground between us and the kitchen door. We're best to skirt the lawn from here, stay at the edge of the woods and take the long way round to the front of the house."

Norman admired his old friend's calm. This was the stoat's natural state, in combat, in command. It was like being back in Undergrowth again.

Malcolm tucked himself into the hood of Norman's sweatshirt and they made a dash for the edge of the woods.

"Wait," Norman whispered when they reached the first of the trees. "What if the poacher is in the woods, too?"

"He likely is," Malcolm affirmed, "so don't faff about. Let's get a move on."

Norman quickened his pace as he dodged through the trees.

They emerged around the front of the house. Kelmsworth Hall was even more impressive from the front. Two long reflecting pools ran on either side of a wide gravel path. The path ended in set of stone steps and a porch topped with four monstrous stone columns that reached a full three storeys to the roof. Between them was a huge, glossy black front door.

The gravel crunched under Norman's feet as he dashed up the path, making him painfully aware of how exposed they were.

Malcolm let out a low whistle of admiration as they leapt up the steps. "In Undergrowth this would be a wonder of the world," he murmured. "And to think that George's father is only a baronet. What must the king's castle look like?"

"Save your sightseeing," Norman told him, gasping for air. "Let's get into the house before the poacher sees us."

Norman was almost out of breath when they arrived at the massive front door. He cast around for the doorbell but couldn't find anything that looked as though it might be it.

"You're out of shape," Malcolm chuckled. He had a way of lightening the tension when the going got really scary. "I remember when you could run for a whole day without getting out of breath."

"Maybe you were lighter then."

"Aye, I've put on some muscle," Malcolm boasted, leaping onto the door handle and flexing a tiny stoat biceps. "Is that why you're waiting for me to knock?" He indicated the huge cast-iron door knocker beneath him. He needed two hands to lift it, but he swung it with all his weight behind it, rapping out three resounding knocks. When he was done, he turned to Norman and flexed his muscles again comically.

Todd answered the door in his housecoat—or somebody's housecoat, most likely George's father's. He held a book in one hand and an unlit pipe was clenched in his teeth. His hair had grown even more preposterously around his face. His moustache twirled in ridiculous curlicues that tickled the sides of his over-grown sideburns. On his head he wore his white lawyer's wig, but it was tilted and falling off the back, as if he'd forgotten it was there.

"Ah, the travellers have returned," he proclaimed. He stood at the top of the steps and regarded them with bored amusement. "Have you found our lovely map?"

"Never mind about that. Let us in. We've been knocking for five minutes. The poacher could be here any second," Norman remonstrated. He'd always thought that Dora was the most annoying person on the planet, but Todd was rapidly eclipsing even his sister.

The new lord of the manor put the pipe in the pocket of his paisley housecoat and craned his neck out the doorway. "I don't see any poacher out there," he drawled, "but if you two are frightened, please do come in and settle your nerves."

Malcolm bared a snarling fang. Sufficiently warned, Todd stepped back. The boy and the stoat ducked quickly past him into the house. Todd stayed a moment longer in the doorway, admiring the view before closing the big door behind him.

"Shall we discuss matters in my study?" He beckoned them with a wave of his pipe.

"You mean Lord Kelmsworth's study," Norman shot back bitterly.

Todd did not turn around to reply. He continued down the long corridor to an open door. "If you insist on using my title, go ahead, but I do find it a little formal," he replied, unperturbed.

Norman and Malcolm fumed as Todd took a seat behind a polished antique desk.

"What would you like us to call you, then?" the stoat asked, his words as sharp as his sword. "Do you still liked to be addressed as Abbot, or do you prefer Fuchs? Is it Todd these days? Or," he snarled, "shall we just call you usurper, if Lord Kelmsworth doesn't sit well yet?"

Even Norman flinched at this. In Malcolm's mind, "usurper" was the worst insult possible. His own father had lost his throne and had given his life to reclaim it for Malcolm. Todd knew all this but stared back calmly, unaffected by Malcolm's taunts.

"Shall we see the map, then? Did you have any trouble getting it back?" Todd began. "No, I don't imagine you did. Young Jerome isn't the quickest of souls. I'm sure you told him his long-lost love Meg sent for it, and he did whatever you wanted."

It was Norman's turn to snarl. He had met Jerome only once, but the boy seemed far braver and more honourable than the imposter lawyer. For all Norman knew, the young scholar might be dead now because of him, burnt alive in the fire at St. Savino. Norman was getting heartily sick of being manipulated by this man.

Norman set his jaw and replied, "We have the map, but we're not giving it to you."

Todd raised an eyebrow.

"It belongs to Malcolm. He's taking it back to Lochwarren."

"Oh, really?" Todd asked. He leaned back on his chair and put his arms behind his head. "You've got that worked out, then—how to get back to Undergrowth?" He looked so smug there in his housecoat and slippers that Norman wanted to kick the legs out from underneath his chair.

"I brought Malcolm to the Shrubberies with me. I can take him home to Lochwarren." Norman hoped he sounded more confident of this than he felt.

Todd brought his chair back down onto four legs. His lip twitched, and he dug out his pipe and put it between his teeth again as if to control that.

"Your *ingresso* isn't a particularly tidy one. It tends to leave a path of destruction in its wake," he countered. "Are you sure you want to be counting on that? I mean, just look at what's happened here."

Norman lost it. He pounded on the desk with both fists. "That's not me! That's you! It's *you* who wrecked it here! *You* came and took over the house! It's *you* who won't do anything about the poacher!"

A satisfied smile crept across Todd's face. "But who brought him here? Who started this whole mess?"

Norman had no answer. He was right. The poacher had escaped from the New York of *The Magpie* mystery.

Todd smiled his smug smile and started again reassuringly, satisfied that he'd put Norman on the back foot. "Now, let's not worry about who caused what and let's look at how to sort things out here. I'm happy that you've retrieved the Mustelid map. It's an important piece of stoat heritage, and I wouldn't dream of keeping it, but I would like to borrow it for a short while to study it. Perhaps I could accompany you back to Lochwarren and we could all examine it together there."

Norman couldn't forget what Jerome had shown him. The map wasn't made in Undergrowth at all. "You only want to study it. Why?" he asked suspiciously.

Todd appeared to think about this for a moment before answering. "Let's just say that I think it's a rather unique artifact."

Norman knew that. The map was a great mystery. It was definitely a map of Undergrowth, but it was on paper from the real world. Did that make it special? Did that give it some power over the bookweird?

"What about George?" Norman asked, not letting on what he knew.

"What about Kelmsworth? Are you going to fix things here?" Malcolm asked.

Todd furrowed his brow and placed his palms together in mock concern. "I'm afraid that's not in my control. I'm perfectly happy to stay in residence here and ensure that no harm comes to the boy, but I'm afraid this poacher of yours is stuck here, very much like certain wolves that ended up in the wrong story, too." He looked at Norman pointedly.

Norman shivered, remembering the wolves. He stared back at Todd with hatred in his eyes. The wolves had escaped from Undergrowth, just as the poacher had escaped from *The Magpie*. They had nearly killed two girls in one of Dora's horsey books. There'd been no way to send them back, either. They'd had to shoot them. Would they have to kill the poacher to save George's book? Norman considered it for a moment, but he knew he didn't have it in him. Now that he knew Wentz wasn't the murderer, he felt sort of sorry for him. It was confusing being ripped from one world and dropped into another. Norman knew that.

Malcolm stood on the desk. His glinting eyes never left Todd's face, but he could sense his friend's indecision, and the stoat king had learned a few things about negotiation in his time on the throne.

"Where's George?" he asked, barking it out like an order. "We'll have to talk to the young master first."

George, Gordon and Pippa were huddled around a table in the old nursery.

"You're back!" Gordon cried. "Have you brought reinforcements?"

"We are the reinforcements," Malcolm told him with a wink.

The Intrepids hurriedly explained what had happened, how they had lost the war with the poacher. The Rook had held out for four days, but the poacher had worn them down. After being on the wrong side of too many cricket-ball bombardments, he'd realized that the Intrepids had an ammunition problem. They had only one bushel of cricket balls. It was enough to beat back one attack, but they had to retrieve all the balls again before the next attack.

The poacher had figured this out eventually. He'd learned how to provoke them into firing while he stayed out of range, scooping up the cricket balls before the Intrepids could collect them themselves. A few days of this tactic had depleted their ammunition, and the Intrepids had had to abandon the Rook and retreat to Kelmsworth Hall.

"I don't like it," Malcolm declared. He stood on the windowsill staring pensively at the rain-soaked backyard.

The four children turned to him, surprised.

"What?" Pippa asked. "What don't you like?"

"The defensive situation, here in the hall," the stoat king explained. "It's too big."

"What do you mean?" Gordon asked deferentially.

George replied for him. "He means it's too hard to defend.

We can't watch all the entrances. I've been worried about that, too."

He and Malcolm exchanged a worried glance as they separately considered the strategic difficulties.

"There are five doors and thirty-two windows on the first floor," George continued. "The poacher could easily break in. We wouldn't know it until he was right on us."

There was a long silence as each of the children let the thought run through his imagination.

"Then why hasn't he done it?" Pippa asked. "We've been here three days now. He could have snuck in at any time."

"Maybe it's Mr. Todd," Gordon suggested. "Maybe he's afraid of Mr. Todd."

"Or maybe he's in league with him," George intoned in a low voice. "Maybe he's Todd's lackey."

Norman hadn't contributed much so far. He had hoped that Malcolm and the Intrepids would come up with a solution. He was just a reader, after all. They were the real adventurers. But the conversation became more and more resigned to failure.

"I think we should call the police," Norman offered finally.

George didn't even turn to face him. "We can't."

"Of course we can," Norman insisted. "He attacked us all. He broke into your house. Those are real crimes. The police can arrest him. You don't have to defeat every criminal yourself, you know."

"No, we *can't* call the police," Pippa explained. "The telephone wire was cut last night."

Malcolm gave Norman a searching look, as if to say, "What's a telephone wire?"

A sudden crashing noise below interrupted Norman's explanation.

The four children and the stoat stared at each other. Each wanted to imagine another explanation for the crash, but they all knew what it meant.

Malcolm was the first to react. He bounded from the windowsill to the floor, drawing his bow from behind his back. George was quickly on his feet. He gripped the door handle and clenched his teeth with determination.

Pippa and Gordon were not far behind. Pippa had grabbed her own bow. Gordon slapped the palm of his hand with the cricket bat, his eyes screwed up in a mask of ridiculous determination. Norman just stared. This wasn't a good idea.

"I really think we should go to the police," Norman urged. The Intrepids looked at him as if they didn't understand a word he was saying, but he kept trying. "If the poacher is here in the house, now's the time to get the police," he argued. "He's not out there to catch you, and if the police can get here in time, they'll catch him red-handed."

For once, the Intrepids actually stopped for a moment to consider one of Norman's suggestions.

"These police," Malcolm asked, "they are your allies? Reinforcements?" He thought about that for a second, then made a decision. "He's right. Now's the time to go. Lady Pippa, will you and Squire Gordon take this mission?"

The Cooks nodded their red heads in unison. They'd been against it when it was Norman's idea, but they would do anything the stoat king asked.

George, Malcolm and Norman watched from the study window as Gordon and Pippa slipped out the tradesman's door and dashed down the gravel road towards Kestleton. Gordon had left his cricket bat with Norman. He twirled it nervously in his hands.

"I think we should hide now. This place is big enough. We should be able to stay out of sight until the police arrive."

But Malcolm was already bounding down the hall, motioning them to follow. George was after him immediately. After a pause, Norman followed, too.

They descended from the nursery by the back steps and followed Malcolm's lead. The stoat slinked noiselessly along the carpet. George and Norman did their best to be quiet, but it was an old house and every step caused a creak or a squeak in the floorboards. At the end of the hallway, at the entrance to the grand foyer, Malcolm hid himself behind the thick wooden moulding and motioned for them to wait.

The two boys crouched in the shadows while the stoat surveyed the foyer. They watched him dart ahead, leaping nimbly from chair to chest to banister. He scampered halfway up the banister and then paused to listen. After a moment he waved to the boys, pointing to the hallway across the foyer.

Malcolm reached the doorway before them and beckoned them forward with a wave of his bow. They could hear the low murmur of voices now.

"That's either the library or the dining room," George whispered.

"It will be the library, for sure." Norman didn't know why, but it had to be. This house was like a big game of Clue, and knowing the bookweird, it was likely to end with Ernie Wentz in the library with a shotgun.

As they snuck down the hallway, the voices became louder and clearer—two voices, one louder than the other. By the time they'd reached the door they could recognize them.

"I tell you there's no such thing as a time machine. If I had one, I would gladly let you use it." That was Todd, of course. Even with a criminal like Wentz he'd adopted that same grating, superior tone.

"No such thing as a time machine, huh?" the American voice bellowed. "Explain the kid, then. How'd the kid get here?"

"What kid would that be?" Todd asked. He didn't sound even remotely curious.

"The kid with the Rams shirt, wiseguy!" Wentz blustered. "How'd he get here if not by time machine?"

"Well, I imagine he walked or rode his bicycle, if you are talking about one of George Kelmsworth's friends. Their name is Cook. The boy is Gordon."

"Not the red-headed punk with the cricket bat," Wentz growled. "The American kid, the one with the talking weasel."

"Talking weasel, you say?" Fuchs asked skeptically.

"Yes, a talking weasel!" Wentz's voice became gruffer and louder as this continued. "And don't you talk to me like I'm crazy. I know what I saw."

Wisely, Todd chose not to contradict him. "And what makes you think that this boy has use of a time machine?"

"This!" Wentz bellowed. There was a rustle of paper. "This is what makes me think it. This headline here: 'Doughboys Arrive in England. Wilson's Warning to the Kaiser,'" he read slowly. "And here's the date: June 1917."

"Yes," Todd acknowledged, "and like all Englishmen, I'm grateful that your fine country has finally committed to this grand endeavour."

"I'll give you grand endeavour," the criminal fumed. "What do you say to this?"

The boys huddled close to the door. Without seeing, they couldn't know what Wentz was now showing Todd.

"Well, there does seem to be an error in your identification," Todd admitted, breaking the short silence. "The date of birth does appear as 1968. Errors do happen."

There was a loud thud as Wentz struck a table or a desk with something. "It's not a mistake. It's when I was born—the future. It's where the kid comes from, too. What about the kid's sweatshirt—St. Louis Rams? The Rams only just moved from L.A. I dunno know where they were in 1917, but I know damn well they weren't in St. Louis."

Todd bit his tongue, but it didn't stop another burst of anger from Wentz. There was the sound of glass and crashing.

Outside the door, the boys stood frozen. Neither of them wanted to go in there with Wentz raging that way, but surely if they didn't do something, he was going to lose control completely.

"Is there another way in?" Malcolm asked in the lowest of stoat whispers. George motioned to a back passageway.

Malcolm peered down the dark hallway. The boys could see nothing, but Malcolm's sharp stoat eyes took it all in. "Count to sixty, then come in quietly," he ordered. "Don't startle him. I just want his attention on you."

Malcolm disappeared down the corridor that led around to the library's back entrance. George and Norman counted silently in their heads. Norman was still counting when George grasped the door handle firmly and glanced at him for confirmation. Norman had to give it to him—he had guts. They waited just another second, then George gave the knob a good turn and pushed the door open.

There was a sound of scuffling feet. As the door creaked open, they heard a small, girlish shriek. The door opened to reveal Wentz standing on the other side of a large book-covered desk. Wentz had backed up against the bookshelf. He held Todd in front of him. The poacher's thick brown arm snaked across the lawyer's neck. In the other hand he wielded the shotgun menacingly. He'd sawed off the end, to make it easier to carry. He waved it at them now and warned them off.

"Don't come any farther, kids. I don't want to have to hurt anyone." He spoke like a villain from a cheap thriller, because he *was* a villain from a cheap thriller.

Norman stayed rooted to the spot and raised his palms defensively. George scowled but went no farther.

Todd looked terrified as he squirmed in Wentz's grip. His face was as pale as paper and his eyes bugged out like a crazy man's. "Help!" he managed to squawk, before Wentz tightened the grip on his neck. Norman gulped and swallowed as he watched.

"Tell him to take me to the time machine," Wentz commanded, waving the shotgun menacingly.

Neither boy answered. They'd both spotted the stealthy movements of Malcolm at the top of a bookshelf to Wentz's right.

"You know where it is, kid!" Growling, Wentz pointed the shotgun at Norman. "Take me to the machine or the professor here gets it."

Norman's mouth had completely dried up. "I . . ." he croaked. No other sound came from his mouth because he had no idea what to say.

"He can't," George said, more calmly than Norman could ever have imagined. Wentz turned to face the other boy. "The time machine's broken."

"Whaddya mean?" the poacher growled.

"It's broken. Norman's stuck here." He didn't say it meanly or vindictively. He said it quietly, as though he were trying to calm down a screaming kid or an excited dog. "He can't get back." He turned back to Norman, widening his eyes conspiratorially, encouraging him to play along.

Wentz stared at Norman, daring him to repeat it. Norman still couldn't find his voice. He just nodded.

"You're stuck here, too," George continued, his voice still unnaturally calm. "You have to face it."

"No!" the poacher howled. "You're lying!" He lunged across the desk towards the boy, sending books and a glass paperweight crashing to the floor. George jumped back out of reach. The poacher looked ready to shove Todd aside and leap across the obstacle to get at George, but another voice stopped him.

"Hold!" Malcolm commanded.

The stoat's voice wasn't loud, but it had that authority in it that made even Wentz pause. He shrank back, pulled the lawyer close to him again and turned to discover his new attacker. Up on the bookshelf to his right was Malcolm. Partially concealed behind a marble bust of Shakespeare, the stoat was braced on one knee and his bow was drawn. His sharp eye took a bead on Wentz.

"I can take your eye out from here," the stoat king warned. "Do you have any idea how much blood comes out of your eyes?"

Wentz backed towards the bookshelf again, pulling Todd across him as a shield. He put the muzzle of the gun to the lawyer's head.

"I warned you," the poacher blustered. "The professor here's going to get it."

"Go ahead," George replied. "He doesn't mean anything to us."

"What?" Wentz cried incredulously.

"It's true," George repeated more firmly. The corner of his mouth curled mischievously. "He's actually a crook, too. Shoot him. Once you've dealt with him, the police will deal with you."

Wentz's eyes blinked and flicked wildly between George and Norman, trying to see if they were bluffing. "But he's your uncle," he insisted. "I heard you say it."

"I lied," Norman told him. He was surprised by how calm his voice sounded. "I only said that to get into the house. It's like George says. Fuchs—" Norman gulped and corrected himself. "Todd is just a crook like you. Why don't you look after him for us?"

Todd squirmed but could not loosen his captor's grasp. "No, Norman, it's true," the lawyer croaked. "I *am* your uncle." His eyes reached out desperately to Norman. They weren't yellow like a fox's anymore. They were grey-blue, like his own.

Norman shook his head. "He's lying," he whispered, but there was something in the way that Todd had said it.

"Shut up!" Wentz roared. He waved the shotgun around again. "Just take me to the time machine."

"It won't matter," George repeated, gaining confidence. "The machine is broken."

"Well, fix it!" Wentz howled like a spoiled child. "The professor here will just have to fix it."

"He can't," Malcolm chimed in from his perch behind the marble Shakespeare. "He doesn't know a thing about it. George's father built the time machine. Only he can fix it." They were all making this up as they went along.

"Where's your father? Take me to your father," Wentz insisted, getting ever more frantic.

"We can't," George replied firmly.

"He's in jail," Norman added.

There was a long moment of nervous silence as Wentz scrutinized each of their faces, trying to find evidence of their lie, but Norman could tell he believed them.

Todd looked as though he'd given up. He slumped down dejectedly, his head on his chin. His eyes rose slowly to Norman's and he whimpered, "Norman, please help me. I'm your uncle Kit. Meg wouldn't want this."

Norman stared at him for a long moment, then blinked. Suddenly he knew it was true. He glanced around at his companions, but they were focused on the poacher.

George stepped closer to the desk. Wentz could have reached over and grabbed him, but George stood there fearlessly.

"Put the gun down now," he commanded. "Give yourself up before someone gets hurt."

Wentz shook his bald head. Backing into the corner, he waved the gun in front of him. "I can't go to jail," he raged. "Not even here. I can't go back inside. If I can't go home, I'd rather die." He raised the gun in the air, shaking it frantically.

Norman wondered if he was about to shoot himself. To his surprise, he found the idea horrible. After all Wentz had done, he didn't want him to die. He might have been a crook, but he wasn't a killer. He didn't deserve to die.

"Don't!" he heard himself shout. "Don't shoot. There's another way."

They all turned to him expectantly. Only Malcolm kept his aim, the arrow still trained on Wentz. George raised his head questioningly. Todd's eyes seem to plead from beneath Wentz's burly arm. Wentz just looked tired—tired and desperate.

Was there another way? Norman had said it just to buy some time. He hadn't thought it through. He found himself staring at Fuchs or Todd, or . . . his uncle Kit, he supposed. It made so much sense—the mysterious uncle they never saw; the old, unmentioned argument between Norman's mother and her brother; something about the bookweird.

"What, Norman?" George interrupted his reverie. "What other way?"

Norman looked up. As if woken up from a daydream in class, he took a moment to understand the question. Another way, something other than the police, to get Wentz out of here, and Todd, too. Uncle Kit or not, Norman had to get him to leave the world of the Intrepids.

His eyes darted around the room, just as if he'd been caught out in class, looking round for a clue to the answer.

"There's only one way out of this," Wentz groaned, losing his patience if not his mind. He put the gun to Todd's head. "I guess I'll see how much blood comes out of the eye, huh?" he said, glancing at Malcolm's arrow. A crazed look had come over his face. "Or I guess I won't see." He laughed manically.

"Help me!" Todd snivelled pathetically.

Norman's eye fell on the newspaper on the desk in front of them. He read the headline to himself: "Doughboys Arrive in England. Wilson's Warning to the Kaiser."

"The war," he blurted. "You could join the army."

Confusion spread across Wentz's face, resolving into a sort of sadness. "They won't let me join, because of my record."

It was Norman's turn to be confused. "What record?"

"My criminal record," Wentz mumbled, averting his eyes. "They don't take criminals in the U.S. Army. They kicked me out once already."

Norman looked from Wentz to George and back to Wentz. Didn't someone else have an idea? He could tell, just by looking at Wentz—at his slouched shoulders, his crestfallen eyes—that it might have worked. If there was anything that Wentz wanted more than to get out of the book, it was to get into the army.

"No, the boy's right," Todd squeaked desperately. "You can join up. It's 1917. You don't have a record here."

The criminal looked up. "You'd say anything to get out of this. They won't take me." But his eyes brightened like a child's, betraying his hope.

"They'll take anyone who can speak English and fire a gun," Todd affirmed eagerly. "They'll probably make you an officer."

Wentz face took on a wistful, nostalgic look. "My mom would be so proud. My dad was in the marines. My grandpa, too."

They all stood still and silent, unsure what to do next. Wentz had not lowered the gun. His other arm still held Todd firmly.

"You need to leave, too," Norman told Todd sternly. "You have to leave here. Not just Kelmsworth. You have to leave the whole place." He fixed Todd with a stare, making sure he understood that he meant the book. He had to leave the book.

"Of course, of course," Todd assented contritely, but his shifty eyes glinted with something of that old, golden, foxy glimmer.

"You leave George alone," Norman insisted. "You let Mrs. Cook and Mr. Hepplewaithe come back, and you put George's old lawyer, Montague, on his father's case."

"Of course," Todd conceded, his wily confidence returning.

"Or the Undergrowth map goes in the fire back at the Shrubberies," Norman continued, unconvinced by the lawyer's promise. "My mother will be happy to burn it."

Todd's eyes narrowed. He paused for a moment and then nodded in agreement.

Wentz lowered the gun but kept a firm grip on Todd. He looked hopeful. He didn't want to shoot anyone either, but he wasn't sure whether to believe them. Suddenly the doorbell rang. It was the most elaborate doorbell Norman had ever heard. It chimed like a church bell.

Wentz jumped when he heard it. "Who's that?" he asked, raising his gun again.

"That'll be the police," George said coolly. "Shall I tell them to take you to the American base at Norwin Woods?" He paused, waiting for an answer. "Or shall I let them storm in here?"

Wentz finally put the shotgun down on the desk and relaxed his grip on Todd's throat. The imposter lawyer wobbled on unsteady legs and slumped to the floor. He managed to crawl to an armchair in the corner, where he sat with his head between his knees, breathing deeply.

George nodded approvingly at Wentz, keeping his eyes on the intruder until he had picked up the shotgun and handed it to Norman. Norman held it gingerly. He had accidentally fired the last gun he was given to hold. The moment George left to answer the door, Norman put the shotgun down on a side table between a china vase and a bronze statue.

The Intrepid Five

A week later, the Intrepid Three and friends leapt from a crowd-ed London omnibus and marched defiantly up the marble steps of the lawyer's office. Before the imposing brass doors, George halted and turned to review their instructions.

"All right," said George, taking his usual tone of command, "just like last time, I'll go up first. Wait for a few moments, then follow me." He reached his hand to the big brass door.

"Just promise me," Norman entreated, "that when it's over, you'll tell everyone it's ventriloquism. Like we said, we don't want to expose Malcolm."

"For certs, old chap," George assured him. "His secret's safe with us." With that, he pulled open the door and let them all into the lobby.

While George strode up the stairs into the office, Norman and Malcolm waited with the Cooks in the lobby. Pippa bit her lip, her eyes wandering distractedly to the shape squirming inside Norman's borrowed school blazer. Gordon furrowed his brow and listened intently at the door. They could hear only little bits of the conversation—George saying something about a gamekeeper, a crackling old voice lecturing George on the dangers of going into the woods alone.

"Let's do this," Norman declared finally, and he led them up the stairs.

This time the lawyer did not see the Intrepids scurry to their hiding places. This time the lawyer was not the thin, russet-haired Mr. Todd. It was another man altogether, the older, fatter Montague, whom Fuchs had replaced. Norman breathed a sigh of relief when he glimpsed Montague in his black court robes and white powdered wig. Things were getting back to normal in the world of the Intrepids. There was half a chance their plan might work this time.

George stood with his back to them, regaling the lawyer with details of the poor state of the Kelmsworth estate. The lawyer shook his wigged head and tutted as he tried to get a word in.

"My father, if he were alive, would not stand for this!" George bellowed finally. That was the signal.

Malcolm slipped from his hiding place inside Norman's blazer and slinked as stealthily as only a stoat could to a desk just behind George's back.

"What do you mean, if he were alive?" the lawyer asked. "I assure you that he is still alive and well. I have every assurance that he is being treated properly while in custody."

"Liar!" George shouted, leaning over the desk and pointing furiously. "When was the last time you saw him?"

"I saw him last . . . last week," the old lawyer sputtered. "We went over some briefs for his latest appeal."

"He died on Sunday. Murdered in a prison brawl," George spat out. "He blames you, you know. He knows now that you double-crossed him."

"I . . . I don't know what you mean." Montague rose unsteadily to his feet. It was then that he saw Malcolm.

The stoat stood upright on the desk opposite. He was dressed from head to toe like an English lord, in black frock coat and top hat. Pippa had laboured for a week reproducing Lord Kelmsworth's best outfit in miniature.

Montague swayed and pointed a wavering finger at the animal in front of him. "Wh . . . what is that?"

"It's my father," George simply declared.

Norman cast a glance over to Gordon's hiding place. The redhead was only just suppressing his laughter.

"What d–do you mean, it's your f–father?" the lawyer stuttered, confusion in his bleary eyes.

"My father was a Buddhist. Didn't you know that?" George declared coolly, as if it were the most normal thing. "He's been reincarnated."

"As a weasel?" the lawyer cried, his voice cracking.

"As a stoat," Malcolm corrected him, in his poshest accent. "You, sir, are the weasel."

The lawyer's lips quivered, but no words came out.

At that point the big orange cat poked its nose out from behind one of the pillars. It lowered itself into a crouch as if about to pounce.

Malcolm eyed it disdainfully from his podium on the big desk. He drew his sword casually and pointed it at the dumbstruck feline. "Shoo!" he commanded, in a threatening whisper.

The big ginger cat cowered, retreated two steps, then turned and fled with a howl. The lawyer took a few steps backwards, too. He was trembling now and appeared to shrink as Malcolm addressed him.

"Please," Montague begged in the smallest of voices, "make it go away."

"I will not go away. I will have my revenge," Malcolm declared. "You, sir, have betrayed me, and you will suffer for it."

George backed up, allowing Malcolm to leap onto his shoulder. The boy began to walk towards the cowering lawyer. The lawyer pulled his white wig from his head and held it in front of him as if to shield himself.

"No," he whimpered as he shrank away. "Stay back."

But George kept coming towards him until Malcolm's sword was no more than a foot from the quivering lawyer's nose.

"Now, sir, it is time to pay your fee," Malcolm declared ominously.

That was too much for the man. He backed away timorously, taking two slow steps without taking his eyes off the blade. Then, with an agility that no one had expected of him, he turned tail and fled. They heard the shaky tap-tap of his footsteps tripping down the marble stairs and then the slamming of the big brass door.

With the slam of the door, the Cooks erupted in celebration.

"Huzzah!" cried Gordon, finally bursting into laughter. "Did you see his face!" He snickered.

"Well done, Malcolm!" Pippa exclaimed. "You were marvellous."

The stoat removed his top hat and gave Pippa a low bow.

Norman joined in. "Huzzah!" he shouted, listening to it echo off the marble floor and high ceilings, and he flashed back then to his father declaring "Huzzah!" for clotted cream and scones. That had been only days ago, and this was a very different huzzah. "Now, let's get on with the business of ransacking this office, shall we?" he said.

George was already rummaging through Montague's desk, pulling out drawers and riffling through files. He glanced at a few pages quickly, tossing them over his shoulder when he realized they were of no use to him.

It didn't take him very long to find what he was looking for. Norman didn't even question it when George lifted a sheaf of papers into the air and cried, "Aha!"

It was ridiculous that he'd discovered anything so quickly. Legal documents were impossible to read. Norman had seen the contract for the lease of their house back home, and every other word seemed to be *whereas* or *heretofore*. Norman was a pretty smart kid, but he couldn't understand a thing.

There was no way that George should have been able to find what he was looking for and recognize it so quickly, but Norman understood that this was the way things worked in George's world. Just as it was normal for stoats to talk in Undergrowth, it was normal in the Intrepids' London for George to find and read crucial legal documents.

Since the disappearance of Fuchs-Todd, things had gone back

to normal for George and the Intrepids, and normal for them was that all their crazy plans worked, and that George was never wrong.

On the train back to the village of Kestleton, the Intrepids managed to get a compartment to themselves. They pulled the curtain across the window so Malcolm could join the celebration without making the conductor think he was hallucinating. Malcolm was as jubilant as the rest of them, re-enacting the scene at the lawyer's office for their amusement.

"Are you sure that you can't stay at Kelmsworth a little longer?" Pippa asked. She might have meant Norman, too, but her question, as always, was to Malcolm.

"We'd love to, milady, but we have some business of our own to settle back home."

"Not even one night?" Gordon asked. "We could have a proper celebration at the lodge tonight. I'll bring biscuits."

Malcolm gave Norman a questioning glance, but Norman shook his head. "No, we have to carry on to Liverpool tonight," he explained. "The ship sails tomorrow. My father is already there waiting for me."

"Is Malcolm's kingdom very far to the north, then?" George asked. "Farther north than Winnipeg, even?" he said, naming the most northerly outpost of North America he could imagine.

Norman answered before Malcolm could. "Much farther. It's hundreds of miles north of the last train station."

"Cor!" cried Gordon appreciatively. "Do any people ever visit? Human people, I mean?"

"Only Norman so far," Malcolm replied with a tiny grin.

Norman did his best to change the subject. "So, George, what exactly did you find back in London?"

"It's an appeal letter," George explained. "It's dated nearly eight months ago, but it has never been filed." He held the letter up for Norman to see.

Norman scanned the thick text, but it was incomprehensible. "Maybe it's just a rough draft. Maybe it has been filed."

Gordon shot Norman a curious glance. It still shocked the younger Cook when anyone dared to question the wisdom of his idol, George.

"It can't have been filed," George explained calmly, as if tutoring a slow learner. "It mentions some proof, the testimony of an Admiralty official that my father was working for Her Majesty's Secret Service. That's the sort of thing that would have caused the case to be reopened right away."

Norman didn't push it. He only hoped that George had found what he was supposed to find: the papers from the old plot of *Intrepid Amongst the Gypsies.*

"Do you have the letter? The one that will get his case reopened?" Norman asked.

"No, but we'll find it all right," George declared.

Norman smiled. This was the old George Kelmsworth. It might not have been exactly where Fuchs had interrupted the story, but he was sure that it was close.

They said goodbye at Kestleton Station, a little platform surrounded by a dozen brick cottages. A carriage was waiting for George and the Cooks. Norman and Malcolm stood on the train steps and bade their companions farewell.

"Thanks for your help, Norman." George reached out a hand for Norman to shake. "I'm sorry I doubted you to begin with, but you're a real brick."

"You're pretty solid yourself," Norman replied, hoping this was an acceptable compliment.

George turned to address the stoat on Norman's shoulder. "And, Malcolm, you're a wonder. I'd never imagined that an animal could even talk, but you are one of the wisest and bravest creatures of any sort I've ever met."

Malcolm bowed and looked from one child to the other. "An honour fighting at your side, gentlemen . . . and lady."

Norman coughed nervously. "You'll remember . . . ?"

"No worries, old chap. The secret's safe with me. There's no such thing as a talking stoat. It was a ventriloquist's trick." He winked egregiously. "Nobody believes our tales anyway. We're like that mad old poacher chap with his time machine story."

Norman allowed himself a weak smile. What more could he do? When you started to patch up books that you'd broken, you could never be perfect. You just had to do your best.

"Will we see you again?" Pippa asked, her voice thin with hope.

"Oh, I wouldn't doubt it," the stoat answered with a reassuring smile.

"Stranger things have happened," Norman added. It was true. He had never thought that he'd see Malcolm again, but here they were together on a steam train in England. The train whistle sounded twice, as if to underline the strangeness of it all.

They stood at the window and waved till George and the Cooks were nothing but dots on the platform at Kestleton. Alone in the compartment, Norman and Malcolm found themselves strangely quieted. It wasn't like the old days back in Undergrowth, when a victory was a victory. Boy and stoat could only think of everything they had left to do.

Norman rested his head against the train window, listening to the steel wheels clacking along the track. The rhythm began to make him drowsy. His eyes fell shut slowly, but he snapped them open before sleep took over completely.

"Okay," he declared finally, as much to himself as to the stoat sitting across from him, "time to get to work."

The stoat nodded solemnly. While Norman arranged the pens and paper, Malcolm changed out of his English gentleman's costume into his more comfortable fighting clothes.

Norman stared at him in his cloak, his sword belted around his waist, and wondered if he'd made a mistake agreeing to let Malcolm join him.

"You'll stay out of sight, right?" Norman asked again.

Malcolm winked. "Sure as stoats," he replied firmly.

A boy raised by medieval monks might find a talking stoat perfectly believable, but Norman would prefer not to have to find out. He wondered once more if he shouldn't just send Malcolm back. They had his map. That would sort out at least one book.

The stoat eyed him suspiciously, perhaps guessing what he was thinking.

"I'm not letting you go back there alone, Strong Arm," Malcolm insisted. "You'll want someone who knows his way around a siege." He paused, as if waiting for Norman to protest. "You'll want someone with a sharp eye and a quiver full of arrows, too, I'll bet."

Norman couldn't suppress a smile. That was the heart of it. It was easier to face danger with a friend.

Malcolm unfurled a stack of papers from their hiding place inside his quiver. Norman separated the blank sheets from the Undergrowth map and the tattered scroll that was the remains of the king's letter to Sir Hugh. He handed these treasures back to Malcolm to conceal again. From his own blazer pocket he removed George Kelmsworth's copy of *A Secret in the Library*.

"There's a description of Jerome's library in chapter 2. The second paragraph here should do it."

A breeze through the window lifted the pages of the open book, revealing the blurred pages at the end. Reminded of what was at stake, Malcolm and Norman exchanged a determined glance.

The stoat paused for a second. There was something he'd meant to tell Norman about the book, something he had read that night while Norman was away, something about Jerome's father.

Norman interrupted his thoughts. "Let's get at it, then," he said.

Malcolm decided it could wait. They both took up their pens and started the tedious work of Malcolm's scriptorium *ingresso*.

With their heads bent copying, they did not notice the landscape go by. They didn't even glance up as trains whooshed in the other direction, even when they carried carriages full of American infantrymen going off to their debarkation points and on to join their war. Malcolm and Norman were focused on their own debarkation and the war that loomed for them outside a desert fortress in a nearly forgotten book.